RIGHTS OF THE PEOPLE

OR

CIVIL GOVERNMENT

AND

RELIGION

By ALONZO T. JONES

PUBLISHED FOR THE
INTERNATIONAL RELIGIOUS LIBERTY ASSOCIATION,
BY PACIFIC PRESS PUBLISHING CO.,
OAKLAND. CAL.

This book played a formative role in the development of Christian thought and the publisher feels that this book, with its candor and depth, still holds significance for the church today.

*Facsimile Reproduction

*This historical classic has been reproduced in its original form. Frequent variations in the quality of the print are unavoidable due to the condition of the original. Thus the print may look lighter and appear to be missing detail, more in some places than in others.

Copyright © 1998 TEACH Services, Inc.
ISBN 0-945383-90-8

Library of Congress Catalog Card No. 98-85849

Published by

TEACH Services, Inc.
254 Donovan Road
Brushton, New York 12916

PREFACE.

It is hoped that the facts and thoughts presented in this little work will awaken more interest in the study of the Constitution of the United States, and may lead to a better understanding of men's rights and liberties under it, than is commonly shown; and also to a closer study of the relation that should exist between civil government and religion, according to the words of Christ and the American Constitution.

In order that the work may be as helpful as possible to the people generally, the authorities cited have been purposely such as are in the reach of all, rather than the *original* documents and manuscripts, which are accessible to the very, very few at most.   A. T. J.

CONTENTS.

(v)

PART I.

CIVIL GOVERNMENT AND RELIGION.

CIVIL GOVERNMENT AND RELIGION.

CHAPTER I.

CHRISTIANITY AND THE ROMAN EMPIRE.

JESUS CHRIST came into the world to set men free, and to plant in their souls the genuine principle of liberty,—liberty actuated by love,—liberty too honorable to allow itself to be used as an occasion to the flesh, or for a cloak of maliciousness,—liberty led by a conscience enlightened by the Spirit of God,—liberty in which man may be free from all men, yet made so gentle by love that he would willingly become the servant of all, in order to bring them to the enjoyment of this same liberty. This is freedom indeed. This is the freedom which Christ gave to man; for whom the Son makes free, is free indeed. In giving to men this freedom, such an infinite gift could have no other result than that which Christ intended, namely, to bind them in everlasting, unquestioning, unswerving allegiance to him as the royal benefactor of the race. He thus reveals himself to men as the highest good, and brings them to himself as the manifestation of that highest good, and to obedience to his will as the perfection of conduct. Jesus Christ was God manifest in the flesh. Thus God was in Christ reconciling the world to himself, that they might know him, the only true God, and Jesus Christ whom he sent. He gathered to himself disciples, instructed them in his heavenly doctrine, endued them with power from on high, sent them forth into all the world to preach this gospel of freedom to every creature, and to teach them to observe all things whatsoever he had commanded them.

The Roman Empire then filled the world,—"the sublimest incarnation of power, and a monument the mightiest of greatness built by human hands, which has upon this planet been suffered to appear." That empire, proud of its conquests, and exceedingly jealous of its claims, asserted its right to rule in all things, human and divine. As in those times all gods were viewed as national gods, and as Rome had conquered all nations, it was demonstrated by this to the Romans that their gods were superior to all others. And although Rome allowed conquered nations to maintain the worship of their national gods, these, as well as the conquered people, were yet considered only as servants of the Roman State. Every religion, therefore, was held subordinate to the religion of Rome, and though "all forms of religion might come to Rome and take their places in its Pantheon, they must come as the servants of the State." The Roman religion itself was but the servant of the State; and of all the gods of Rome there were none so great as the genius of Rome itself. The chief distinction of the Roman gods was that they belonged to the Roman State. Instead of the State deriving any honor from the Roman gods, the gods derived their principal dignity from the fact that they were the gods of Rome. This being so with Rome's own gods, it was counted by Rome an act of exceeding condescension to recognize legally any foreign god, or the right of any Roman subject to worship any other gods than those of Rome. Neander quotes Cicero as laying down a fundamental maxim of legislation as follows:—

"No man shall have for himself particular gods of his own; no man shall worship by himself any new or foreign gods, unless they are recognized by the public laws."—*Neander's Church History, Vol. I, pp. 86, 87, Torrey's translation, Boston, 1852.*

Thus it is seen that in the Roman view the State took precedence of everything. The State was the highest idea of good. As expressed by Neander:—

"The idea of the State was the highest idea of ethics; and within that was included all actual realization of the highest good; hence the development of all other goods pertaining to humanity was made dependent on this."—*Id., p. 86.*

Man with all that he had was subordinated to the State; he must have no higher aim; he must seek no higher good. Thus every Roman citizen was a subject, and every Roman subject was a slave. Says Mommsen:—

"The more distinguished a Roman became, the less was he a free man. The omnipotence of the law, the despotism of the rule, drove him into a narrow circle of thought and action, and his credit and influence depended on the sad austerity of his life. The whole duty of man, with the humblest and greatest of the Romans, was to keep his house in order, and be the obedient servant of the State."—*Quoted in Ten Great Religions, Chapter VIII, sec. 4.*

It will be seen at once that for any man to profess the principles and the name of Christ, was virtually to set himself against the Roman Empire; for him to recognize God as revealed in Jesus Christ as the highest good, was but treason against the Roman State. It would not be looked upon by Rome as anything else than high treason, because, the Roman State representing to the Roman the highest idea of good, for any man to assert that there was a higher good, and thus make Rome itself subordinate, would not be looked upon in any other light by Roman pride than that such an assertion was a direct blow at the dignity of Rome, and subversive of the Roman State. Consequently the Christians were not only called "atheists," because they denied the gods; but the accusation against them before the tribunals was of the crime of "high treason," because they denied the right of the State to interfere with men's relations to God. The accusation was that they were "irreverent to the Cæsars, and enemies of the Cæsars and of the Roman people."

To the Christian, the word of God asserted with absolute authority: "Fear God, and keep his commandments; for this is the whole duty of man." Eccl. 12: 13. To him, obedience to this word through faith in Christ was eternal life. This to him was the conduct which showed his allegiance to God as the highest good,—a good as much higher than that of the Roman State as the government of God is greater than was the government of Rome, as God is greater than man, as heaven is higher than earth, as eternity is more than time, and as eternal interests are of more value than temporal.

The Romans considered themselves not only the greatest of all nations and the one to whom belonged power over all, but they prided themselves upon being the most religious of all nations. Cicero commended the Romans as the most religious of all nations, because they carried their religion into all the details of life.

"The Roman ceremonial worship was very elaborate and minute, applying to every part of daily life. It consisted in sacrifices, prayers, festivals, and the investigations, by auguries and haruspices, of the will of the gods and the course of future events. The Romans accounted themselves an exceedingly religious people, because their religion was so intimately connected with the affairs of home and State. . . . Thus religion everywhere met the public life of the Roman by its festivals, and laid an equal yoke on his private life by its requisition of sacrifices, prayers, and auguries. All pursuits must be conducted according to a system carefully laid down by the College of Pontiffs. . . . If a man went out to walk, there was a form to be recited; if he mounted his chariot, another."—*Ten Great Religions, Chapter VIII, sec. 3.*

The following extract from Gibbon will give a clear view of the all-pervading character of the Roman religious rites and ceremonies, and it also shows how absolutely the profession of the Christian religion made a separation between the one

who professed it and all things pertaining to the affairs of
Rome:—

"The religion of the nations was not merely a speculative doctrine
professed in the schools or preached in the temples. The innumer-
able deities and rites of polytheism were closely interwoven with
every circumstance of business or pleasure, of public or of private
life; and it seemed impossible to escape the observance of them,
without, at the same time, renouncing the commerce of mankind and
all the offices and amusements of society. . . . The public spectacles were an essential part of the cheerful devotion of the pagans,
and the gods were supposed to accept, as the most grateful offering,
the games that the prince and people celebrated in honor of their
peculiar customs. The Christian, who with pious horror avoided the
abomination of the circus or the theater, found himself encompassed
with infernal snares in every convivial entertainment, as often as his
friends, invoking the hospitable deities, poured out libations to each
others' happiness. When the bride, struggling with well-affected
reluctance, was forced in hymeneal pomp over the threshold of her
new habitation, or when the sad procession of the dead slowly moved
toward the funeral pile, the Christian, on these interesting occasions,
was compelled to desert the persons who were dearest to him, rather
than contract the guilt inherent to those impious ceremonies. Every
art and every trade that was in the least concerned in the framing or
adorning of idols, was polluted by the stain of idolatry.

"The dangerous temptations which on every side lurked in am-
bush to surprise the unguarded believer, assailed him with redoubled
violence on the day of solemn festivals. So artfully were they framed
and disposed throughout the year, that superstition always wore the
appearance of pleasure, and often of virtue. . . . On the days of
general festivity, it was the custom of the ancients to adorn their
doors with lamps and with branches of laurel, and to crown their
heads with garlands of flowers. This innocent and elegant practice
might have been tolerated as a mere civil institution. But it most
unluckily happened that the doors were under the protection of the
household gods, that the laurel was sacred to the lover of Daphne, and
that garlands of flowers, though frequently worn as a symbol either of
joy or mourning, had been dedicated in their first origin to the service
of superstition. The trembling Christians who were persuaded in
this instance to comply with the fashions of their country and the
commands of the magistrates, labored under the most gloomy appre-

hensions from the reproaches of their own conscience, the censures of the church, and the denunciations of divine vengeance."—*Decline and Fall, Chapter XV. par. 15, 16.*

All this clearly shows that to profess the name of Christ a person was compelled to renounce every other relationship in life. He could not attend a wedding or a funeral of his nearest relatives, because every ceremony was performed with reference to the gods. He could not attend the public festival, for the same reason. More than this, he could not escape by not attending the public festival, because on days of public festivity, the doors of the houses, and the lamps about them, and the heads of the dwellers therein, must all be adorned with laurel and garlands of flowers, in honor of the licentious gods and goddesses of Rome. If the Christian took part in these services, he paid honor to the gods as did the other heathen. If he refused to do so, which he must do if he would obey God and honor Christ, he made himself conspicuous before the eyes of all the people, all of whom were intensely jealous of the respect they thought due to the gods; and also in so doing, the Christian disobeyed the Roman law, which commanded these things to be done. He thus became subject to persecution, and that meant death, because the law said: —

"Worship the gods in all respects according to the laws of your country, and compel all others to do the same. But hate and punish those who would introduce anything whatever alien to our customs in this particular "—*Neander, Church History, Vol. I, Section First, Part I, Div. III, par. 2.*

And further:—

"Whoever introduces new religions, the tendency and character of which are unknown, whereby the minds of men may be disturbed, shall, if belonging to the higher rank, be banished; if to the lower, punished with death."—*Id.*

This was the Roman law. Every Christian, merely by the profession of Christianity, severed himself from all the gods of

Rome, and from everything that was done in their honor. And everything *was* done in their honor. The great mass of the first Christians were from the lower ranks of the people. The law said that if any of the lower ranks introduced new religions, they should be punished with death. The Christians, introducing a new religion, and being from the lower ranks, made themselves subject to death whenever they adopted the religion of Christ. This is why Paul and Peter, and multitudes of other Christians, suffered death for the name of Christ. Such was the Roman law, and when Rome put the Christians to death, it was not counted by Rome to be persecution. It would not for an instant be admitted that such was persecution. It was only enforcing the law. The State of Rome was supreme. The State ruled in religious things. Whoever presumed to disobey the law must suffer the penalty; all that Rome did, all that it professed to do, was simply to enforce the law.

If the principle be admitted that the State has the right to legislate in regard to religion, and to enforce religious observances, then no blame can ever be attached to the Roman Empire for putting the Christians to death. Nor can it be admitted that such dealings with the Christians was persecution. The enforcement of right laws can never be persecution, however severely the law may deal with the offender. To hang a murderer is not persecution. To hunt him down, even with bloodhounds, to bring him to justice, is not persecution. We repeat, therefore, that the enforcement of right laws never can be persecution. If, therefore, religion or religious observances be a proper subject of legislation by civil government, then there never has been, and there never can be, any such thing as religious persecution. Because civil governments are ruled by majorities, the religion of the majority must of necessity be the adopted religion; and if civil legislation in religious things be right, the majority may legislate in regard to their own religion.

Such laws made in such a case must be right laws, and the enforcement of them therefore can never be persecution.

But all this, with the authority and all the claims of the Roman Empire, is swept away by the principle of Christ, which everyone then asserted who named the name of Christ,—that civil government can never of right have anything to do with religion or religious observances,—that religion is not a subject of legislation by any civil government,—that religion, religious profession, and religious observances must be left entirely between the individual and his God, to worship as his own conscience shall dictate,—that to God only is to be rendered that which is God's, while to Cæsar is to be rendered only that which is Cæsar's. This is the principle that Christ established, and which, by his disciples, he sent into all the world, and which they asserted wherever they went; in behalf of which they forfeited every earthly consideration, endured untold torments, and for which they freely gave their lives. It was, moreover, because of the establishment of this principle by Jesus Christ, and the assertion of it by his true disciples, that we have to-day the rights and liberties which we enjoy. The following extract from Lecky is worthy to be recorded in letters of gold, and held in sorrowful, but ever grateful, remembrance:—

"Among the authentic records of pagan persecutions, there are histories which display, perhaps more vividly than any other, both the depth of cruelty to which human nature may sink, and the heroism of resistance it may attain. . . . The most horrible recorded instances of torture were usually inflicted, either by the populace, or in their presence in the arena. We read of Christians bound in chairs of red-hot iron, while the stench of their half-consumed flesh rose in a suffocating cloud to heaven; of others who were torn to the very bone by shells or hooks of iron; of holy virgins given over to the lusts of the gladiator, or to the mercies of the pander; of two hundred and twenty-seven converts sent on one occasion to the mines, each with the sinews of one leg severed with a red-hot iron, and with an eye scooped from the socket; of fires so slow that the victims writhed for

CHRIST OR DIANA.

hours in their agonies; of bodies torn limb from limb, or sprinkled with burning lead; of mingled salt and vinegar poured over the flesh that was bleeding from the rack; of tortures prolonged and varied through entire days. For the love of their divine Master, for the cause they believed to be true, men, and even weak girls, endured these things without flinching, when one word would have freed them from their suffering. No opinion we may form of the proceedings of priests in a later age, should impair the reverence with which we bend before the martyr's tomb."—*History of European Morals, end of chapter 3.*

All this was endured by men and women and even weak girls, that people in future ages might be free. All this was endured in support of the principle that with religion, civil government cannot of right have anything to do. All this was endured that men might be free, and that all future ages might know it to be the inalienable right of every soul to worship God according to the dictates of his own conscience.

CHAPTER II.

WHAT IS DUE TO GOD, AND WHAT TO CÆSAR?

"THEN went the Pharisees, and took counsel how they might entangle him in his talk. And they sent out unto him their disciples with the Herodians, saying, Master, we know that thou art true, and teachest the way of God in truth, neither carest thou for any man, for thou regardest not the person of men. Tell us therefore, What thinkest thou? Is it lawful to give tribute unto Cæsar, or not? But Jesus perceived their wickedness, and said, Why tempt ye me, ye hypocrites? Show me the tribute money. And they brought unto him a penny. And he saith unto them, Whose is this image and superscription? They say unto him, Cæsar's. Then saith he unto them, Render therefore unto Cæsar the things which are Cæsar's; and unto God the things that are God's."

In these words Christ has established a clear distinction between Cæsar and God,—between that which is Cæsar's and that which is God's; that is, between the civil and the religious power, and between what we owe to the civil power and what we owe to the religious power. That which is Cæsar's is to be rendered to Cæsar; that which is God's is to be rendered to God alone. With that which is God's, Cæsar can have nothing to do. To say that we are to render to Cæsar that which is God's, or that we are to render to God, by Cæsar, that which is God's, is to pervert the words of Christ, and make them meaningless. Such an interpretation would be but to entangle him in his talk,—the very thing that the Pharisees sought to do.

As the word "Cæsar" refers to civil government, it is apparent at once that the duties which we owe to Cæsar are civil duties; while the duties which we owe to God are wholly moral or religious duties. Webster's definition of *religion* is,—

"The recognition of God as an object of worship, love, and obedience."

Another definition, equally good, is as follows:—

"Man's personal relation of faith and obedience to God."

Yet again, the American definition is:—

"The duty which we owe to our Creator, and the manner of discharging it."

It is evident, therefore, that religion and religious duties pertain solely to God; and as that which is God's is to be rendered to him and not to Cæsar, it follows inevitably that, according to the words of Christ, civil government can never of right have anything to do with religion,—with a man's personal relation of faith and obedience to God.

Another definition which may help in making the distinction appear, is that of *morality*, as follows:—

"*Morality:* The relation of conformity or nonconformity to the true moral standard or rule. . . . The conformity of an act to the divine law."

As morality, therefore, is the conformity of an act to the divine law, it is plain that morality also pertains solely to God, and with that, civil government can have nothing to do. This may appear at first sight to be an extreme position, if not a false one; but it is not. It is the correct position, as we think anyone can see who will give the subject a little careful thought. The first part of the definition already given, says that morality is "the relation of conformity or nonconformity to the true moral standard or rule," and the latter part of the definition shows that this true moral standard is the divine law. Again; moral law is defined as—

"The will of God, as the supreme moral ruler, concerning the character and conduct of all responsible beings; the rule of action as obligatory on the conscience or moral nature." "The moral law is summarily contained in the decalogue, written by the finger of God on two tables of stone, and delivered to Moses on Mount Sinai."

These definitions are evidently according to Scripture. The Scriptures show that the ten commandments are the law of God; that they express the will of God; that they pertain to the conscience, and take cognizance of the thoughts and intents of the heart; and that obedience to these commandments is the duty that man owes to God. Says the Scripture:—

"Fear God, and keep his commandments; for this is the whole duty of man." Eccl. 12: 13.

And the Saviour says:—

"Ye have heard that it was said by them of old time, Thou shalt not kill; and whosoever shall kill shall be in danger of the judgment; but I say unto you, That whosoever is angry with his brother without a cause shall be in danger of the judgment; and whosoever shall say to his brother, Raca ["vain fellow," margin], shall be in danger of the council; but whosoever shall say, Thou fool, shall be in danger of hell fire." Matt. 5: 21, 22.

The apostle John, referring to the same thing, says:—

"Whosoever hateth his brother is a murderer." 1 John 3: 15

Again, the Saviour says:—

"Ye have heard that it was said by them of old time, Thou shalt not commit adultery; but I say unto you, that whosoever looketh on a woman to lust after her hath committed adultery with her already in his heart." Matt. 5: 27, 28.

Other illustrations might be given, but these are sufficient to show that obedience to the moral law is morality; that it pertains to the thoughts and the intents of the heart, and therefore, in the very nature of the case, lies beyond the reach or control of the civil power.   To hate, is murder; to covet, is idolatry; to think impurely of a woman, is adultery;—these are all equally immoral, and violations of the moral law, but no civil government seeks to punish for them.   A man may hate his neighbor all his life; he may covet everything on earth; he may think impurely of every woman that he sees,— he may keep it up all his days; but so long as these things are confined to his thought, the civil power cannot touch him.   It would be difficult to conceive of a more immoral person than such a man would be; yet the State cannot punish him.   It does not attempt to punish him.   This demonstrates again that with morality or immorality the State can have nothing to do.

But let us carry this further.   Only let that man's hatred lead him, either by word or sign, to attempt an injury to his neighbor, and the State will punish him; only let his covetousness lead him to lay hands on what is not his own, in an attempt to steal, and the State will punish him; only let his impure thought lead him to attempt violence to any woman, and the State will punish him.   Yet bear in mind that even then the State does not punish him for his immorality, but for his incivility.   The immorality lies in the heart, and can be measured by God only.   The State punishes no man because he is immoral.   If it did, it would have to punish as a murderer the man who hates another, because, according to the true standard of morality, hatred is murder. Therefore it is clear that in fact the State punishes no man because he is immoral, but because he is uncivil.   It cannot punish immorality; it must punish incivility.

This distinction is shown in the very term by which is designated State or national government; it is called *civil* government.   No person ever thinks of calling it moral government. The government of God is the only moral government. God is the only moral governor.   The law of God is the only moral law.   To God alone pertains the punishment of immorality, which is the transgression of the moral law. Governments of men are civil governments, not moral. Governors of men are civil governors, not moral. The laws of States and nations are civil laws, not moral. To the authorities of civil government pertains the punishment of incivility, that is, the transgression of civil law. It is not theirs to punish immorality. That pertains solely to the Author of the moral law and of the moral sense, who is the sole judge of man's moral relation. All this must be manifest to every one who will think fairly upon the subject, and it is confirmed by the definition of the word "civil," which is as follows:—

"*Civil:* Pertaining to a city or State, or to a citizen in his relations to his fellow-citizens, or to the State."

By all these things it is made clear that we owe to Cæsar (civil government) only that which is civil, and that we owe to God that which is moral or religious. Other definitions show the same thing. For instance, sin as defined by Webster is "any violation of God's will;" and as defined by the Scriptures, "is the transgression of the law." That the law here referred to is the moral law—the ten commandments—is shown by Rom. 7:7:—

"I had not known sin, but by the law; for I had not known lust, except the law had said, Thou shalt not covet."

Thus the Scriptures show that sin is a transgression of the law which says, "Thou shalt not covet," and that is the moral law.

But crime is an offense against the laws of the State. The definition is as follows:—

"Crime is strictly a violation of law either human or divine; but in present usage the term is commonly applied to actions contrary to the laws of the State."

Thus civil statutes define crime, and deal with crime, but

not with sin; while the divine statutes define sin, and deal with sin, but not with crime.

As God is the only moral governor, as his is the only moral government, as his law is the only moral law, and as it per tains to him alone to punish immorality, so likewise *the promotion of morality* pertains to him alone.   Morality is conformity to the law of God; it is obedience to God.   But obedience to God must spring from the heart in sincerity and truth.   This it must do, or it is not obedience; for, as we have proved by the word of God, the law of God takes cognizance of the thoughts and intents of the heart.   But "all have sinned, and come short of the glory of God."   By transgression, all men have made themselves immoral.   "Therefore by the deeds of the law [by obedience] there shall no flesh be justified [accounted righteous, or made moral] in his sight."   Rom. 3: 20.   As all men have, by transgression of the law of God, made themselves immoral, therefore no man can, by obedience to the law, become moral, because it is that very law which declares him to be immoral.   The demands, therefore, of the moral law, must be satisfied before he can ever be accepted as moral by either the law or its Author.   But the demands of the moral law can never be satisfied by an immoral person; and this is just what every person has made himself by transgression.   Therefore it is certain that men can never become moral by the moral law.

From this it is equally certain that if ever men shall be made moral, it must be by the Author and Source of all morality.   And this is just the provision which God has made.   For "now the righteousness [the morality] of God without the law is manifested, being witnessed by the law and the prophets; even the righteousness [the morality] of God which is *by faith of Jesus Christ* unto all and upon all them that believe; for there is no difference; for all have sinned [made themselves immoral], and come short of the glory of God."   Rom. 3: 21–23.   It is by the morality of Christ alone that men can be made moral. And this morality of Christ is the morality of God, which is imputed to us for Christ's sake; and we receive it by faith in Him who is both the author and finisher of faith. Then by the Spirit of God the moral law is written anew in the heart and in the mind, sanctifying the soul unto obedience—unto morality. Thus, and thus alone, can men ever attain to morality; and that morality is the morality of God which is by faith of Jesus Christ; *and there is no other in this world.* Therefore, as morality springs from God, and is planted in the heart by the Spirit of God, through faith in the Son of God, it is demonstrated by proofs of Holy Writ itself, that *to God alone pertains the promotion of morality.*

God, then, being the sole promoter of morality, through what instrumentality does he work to promote morality in the world? What body has he made the conservator of morality in the world? the church or the civil power, which?—The church, and the church alone. It is "the church of the living God." It is "the pillar and ground of the truth." It was to the church that he said, "Go ye into all the world, and preach the gospel to every creature;" "and, lo, I am with you alway, even unto the end of the world." It is by the church, through the preaching of Jesus Christ, that the gospel is "made known to all nations for the obedience of faith." There is no obedience but the obedience of faith; there is no morality but the morality of faith. Therefore it is proved that to the church, and *not* to the State, is committed the conservation of morality in the world. This at once settles the question as to whether the State shall teach morality or religion. The State *cannot* teach morality or religion. It has not the credentials for it. The Spirit of God and the gospel of Christ are both essential to the teaching of morality, and neither of these is committed to the State, but both to the church.

But though this work be committed to the church, even then there is not committed to the church the prerogative either to reward morality or to punish immorality. She beseeches, she entreats, she persuades men to be reconciled to God; she trains them in the principles and the practice of morality. It is hers by moral suasion or spiritual censures to preserve the purity and *discipline* of her membership. But hers it is not either to reward morality or to punish immorality. This pertains to God alone, because, whether it be morality or immorality, it springs from the secret counsels of the heart; and as God alone knows the heart, he alone can measure either the merit or the guilt involved in any question of morals.

By this it is demonstrated that to no man, to no assembly or organization of men, does there belong any right whatever to punish immorality. Whoever attempts it, usurps the prerogative of God.   The Inquisition is the inevitable logic of any assembly of men to punish immorality, because to punish immorality it is necessary in some way to get at the thoughts and intents of the heart. The Papacy, asserting the right to compel men to be moral, and to punish them for immorality, had the cruel courage to carry the evil principle to its logical consequence. In carrying out the principle, it was found to be essential to get at the secrets of men's hearts; and it was found that the diligent application of torture would wring from men, in many cases, a full confession of the most secret counsels of their hearts. Hence the Inquisition was established as the means best adapted to secure the desired end. So long as men grant the proposition that it is within the province of civil government to enforce morality, it is to very little purpose that they condemn the Inquisition; for that tribunal is only the logical result of the proposition.

By all these evidences is established the plain, common-sense principle that to civil government pertains only that which the term itself implies,—that which is civil. The purpose of civil government is civil, and not moral. Its function is to preserve order in society, and to cause all its subjects to rest in assured safety, by guarding them against all incivility. Morality belongs to God; civility to the State. Morality must be rendered to God; civility, to the State. "Render therefore unto Cæsar the things which are Cæsar's; and unto God the things that are God's." [1]

But it may be asked, Does not the civil power enforce the observance of the commandments of God, which say, Thou shalt not steal, Thou shalt not kill, Thou shalt not commit adultery, and, Thou shalt not bear false witness? Does not the civil power punish the violation of these commandments of God? *Answer*—The civil power does not enforce these, nor does it punish the violation of them, *as commandments of God.* The State does forbid murder and theft and perjury, and some States forbid adultery, but not as commandments of God. From time immemorial, governments that knew nothing about God, have forbidden these things. If the civil power attempted to enforce these as the commandments of God, it would have to punish as a murderer the man who hates another; it would have to punish as a perjurer the man who raises a false report; it would have to punish as an adulterer the person who thinks impurely; it would have to punish as a thief the man who wishes to cheat his neighbor; because all these things are violations of the commandments of God. Therefore if the State is to enforce these things as the commandments of God, it will have to punish the thoughts and intents of the heart; but this is not within the province of any earthly power, and it is clear that any earthly power that should attempt it, would thereby simply put itself in the place of God, and usurp his prerogative.

More than this, such an effort would be an attempt to pun-

---

[1] There is an accommodated sense in which the word "morality" is used, in which it is made to refer only to men's relations to their fellow-men; and with reference to this view of morality, it is sometimes said that the civil power is to enforce morality *upon a civil basis.* But morality on a civil basis is only civility, and the enforcement of morality upon a civil basis is the enforcement of civility, and nothing else. Without the Inquisition it is impossible for civil government ever to carry its jurisdiction beyond civil things, or to enforce anything but civility.

ish sin, because transgression of the law of God is sin; but sins will be forgiven upon repentance, and God does not punish the sinner for the violation of his law, when his sins are forgiven. Now if the civil power undertakes to enforce the observance of the law of God, it cannot justly enforce that law upon the transgressor whom God has forgiven. For instance, suppose a man steals twenty dollars from his neighbor, and is arrested, prosecuted, and found guilty. But suppose that between the time that he is found guilty and the time when sentence is to be passed, the man repents, and is forgiven by the Lord. Now he is counted by the Lord as though he never had violated the law of God. The commandment of God does not stand against him for that transgression. And as it is the law of God that the civil law started out to enforce, the civil power also must forgive him, count him innocent, and let him go free. More than this, the statute of God says: "If thy brother trespass against thee, rebuke him; and if he repent, forgive him. And if he trespass against thee seven times in a day, and seven times in a day turn again to thee, saying, I repent; thou shalt forgive him." If civil government is to enforce the law of God, when a man steals, or commits perjury, or any form of violence, and is arrested, if he says, "I repent," he must be forgiven; if he does it again, is again arrested, and again says, "I repent," he must be forgiven; and if he commits it seven times in a day, and seven times in a day says, "I repent," he must be forgiven. It will be seen at once that any such system would be utterly destructive of civil government; and this only demonstrates conclusively that no civil government can ever of right have anything to do with the enforcement of the commandments of God as such, or with making the Bible its code of laws.

God's government can be sustained by the forgiveness of the sinner to the uttermost, because by the sacrifice of Christ he has made provision "to save them to the uttermost that

come unto God by him; seeing he ever liveth to make inter-
cession for them;'' but in civil government, if a man steals, or
commits any other crime, and is apprehended and found guilty,
it has nothing to do with the case if the Lord does forgive him;
he must be punished.

The following remarks of Prof. W. T. Harris, National
Commissioner of Education, are worthy of careful consideration
in this connection:—

"A crime, or breach of justice, is a deed of the individual, which
the State, by its judicial acts, returns on the individual. The State
furnishes a measure for crime, and punishes criminals according to
their deserts. The judicial mind is a measuring mind, a retributive
mind, because trained in the forms of justice, which sees to it that every
man's deeds shall be returned to him, to bless him or to curse him
with pain. Now, a sin is a breach of the law of holiness, a lapse out
of the likeness to the divine form, and as such it utterly refuses to be
measured. It is infinite death to lapse out of the form of the divine.
A sin cannot be atoned for by any finite punishment, but only (as revelation teaches) by a divine act of sacrifice. . . . It would destroy
the State to attempt to treat crimes as sins, and to forgive them in
case of repentance. It would impose on the judiciary the business of
going behind the overt act to the disposition or frame of mind within
the depth of personality. But so long as the deed is not uttered in
the act, it does not belong to society, but only to the individual and to
God. No human institution can go behind the overt act, and attempt
to deal absolutely with the substance of man's spiritual freedom.
. . . Sin and crime must not be confounded, nor must the same
deed be counted as crime and sin by the same authority. Look at it
as crime, and it is capable of measured retribution. The law does not
pursue the murderer beyond the gallows. He has expiated his crime
with his life. But the slightest sin, even if it is no crime at all, as for
example the anger of a man against his brother, an anger which does
not utter itself in the form of violent deeds, but is pent up in the heart,—
such non-criminal sin will banish the soul forever from heaven, unless
it is made naught by sincere repentance.''

The points already presented in this chapter are perhaps
sufficient in this place to illustrate the principle announced in
the word of Christ; and, although that principle is plain, and is

readily accepted by the sober, common-sense thought of every man, yet through the selfish ambition of men the world has been long in learning and accepting the truth of the lesson. The United States is the first and only government in history that is based on the principle established by Christ. In Article VI of the national Constitution, this nation says that "no religious test shall ever be required as a qualification to any office or public trust under the United States." By an amendment making more certain the adoption of the principle, it declares in the first amendment to the Constitution, "Congress shall make no law respecting an establishment of religion, or prohibiting the free exercise thereof." This first amendment was adopted in 1789, by the first Congress that ever met under the Constitution. In 1796 a treaty was made with Tripoli, in which it was delared (Article II) that "the government of the United States of America is not in any sense founded on the Christian religion." This treaty was framed by an ex-Congregationalist clergyman, and was signed by President Washington. It was not out of disrespect to religion or Christianity that these clauses were placed in the Constitution, and that this one was inserted in that treaty. On the contrary, it was entirely on account of their respect for religion, and the Christian religion in particular, as being beyond the province of civil government, pertaining solely to the conscience, and resting entirely between the individual and God. It was because of this that this nation was constitutionally established according to the principle of Christ, demanding of men only that they render to Cæsar that which is Cæsar's, and leaving them entirely free to render to God that which is God's, if they choose, as they choose, and when they choose; or, as expressed by Washington himself, in reply to an address upon the subject of religious legislation:—

"Every man who conducts himself as a good citizen, is accountable alone to God for his religious faith, and should be protected in worshiping God according to the dictates of his own conscience."

We cannot more fitly close this chapter than with the following tribute of George Bancroft to this principle, as embodied in the words of Christ, and in the American Constitution:—

"In the earliest States known to history, government and religion were one and indivisible. Each State had its special deity, and often these protectors, one after another, might be overthrown in battle, never to rise again. The Peloponnesian War grew out of a strife about an oracle. Rome, as it sometimes adopted into citizenship those whom it vanquished, introduced in like manner, and with good logic for that day, the worship of their gods. No one thought of vindicating religion for the conscience of the individual, till a voice in Judea, breaking day for the greatest epoch in the life of humanity, by establishing a pure spiritual and universal religion for all mankind, enjoined to render to Cæsar only that which is Cæsar's. The rule was upheld during the infancy of the gospel for all men. No sooner was this religion adopted by the chief of the Roman Empire than it was shorn of its character of universality, and enthralled by an unholy connection with the unholy State; and so it continued till the new nation, —the least defiled with the barren scoffings of the eighteenth century, the most general believer in Christianity of any people of that age, the chief heir of the Reformation in its purest forms,—when it came to establish a government for the United States, refused to treat faith as a matter to be regulated by a corporate body, or having a headship in a monarch or a State.

"Vindicating the right of individuality even in religion, and in religion above all, the new nation dared to set the example of accepting in its relations to God the principle first divinely ordained of God in Judea. It left the management of temporal things to the temporal power; but the American Constitution, in harmony with the people of the several States, withheld from the Federal Government the power to invade the home of reason, the citadel of conscience, the sanctuary of the soul; and not from indifference, but that the infinite Spirit of eternal truth might move in its freedom and purity and power."— *History of the Formation of the Constitution, last chapter.*

Thus the Constitution of the United States as it is stands as the sole monument of all history, representing the principle which Christ established for earthly government. And under it, in liberty, civil and religious, in enlightenment, and in progress, this nation has deservedly stood as the beacon light of the world, for more than a hundred years.

CHAPTER III.

In support of the doctrine that civil government has the right to act in things pertaining to God, the text of Scripture is quoted which says, "The powers that be are ordained of God." This passage is found in Rom. 13: 1. The first nine verses of the chapter are devoted to this subject, showing that the powers that be are ordained of God, and enjoining upon Christians, upon every soul, in fact, the duty of respectful subjection to civil government. The whole passage reads as follows:—

"Let every soul be subject unto the higher powers. For there is no power but of God; the powers that be are ordained of God. Whosoever therefore resisteth the power, resisteth the ordinance of God; and they that resist shall receive to themselves damnation. For rulers are not a terror to good works, but to the evil. Wilt thou then not be afraid of the power? do that which is good, and thou shalt have praise of the same; for he is the minister of God to thee for good. But if thou do hat which is evil, be afraid; for he beareth not the sword in vain; for he is the minister of God, a revenger to execute wrath upon him that doeth evil. Wherefore ye must needs be subject, not only for wrath, but also for conscience' sake. For for this cause pay ye tribute also; for they are God's ministers, attending continually upon this very thing. Render therefore to all their dues: tribute to whom tribute is due; custom to whom custom; fear to whom fear; honor to whom honor. Owe no man anything, but to love one another; for he that loveth another hath fulfilled the law. For this, Thou shalt not commit adultery, Thou shalt not kill, Thou shalt not steal, Thou shalt not bear false witness, Thou shalt not covet; and if there be any other commandment, it is briefly comprehended in this saying, namely, Thou shalt love thy neighbor as thyself."

It is easy to see that this scripture is but an exposition of the words of Christ, "Render to Cæsar the things that are Cæsar's." In the Saviour's command to render unto Cæsar the things that are Cæsar's, there is plainly a recognition of the rightfulness of civil government, and that civil government has claims upon us which we are in duty bound to recognize; and that there are things which duty requires us to render to the civil government. This scripture in Romans 13 simply states the same thing in other words: "Let every soul be subject unto the higher powers. For there is no power but of God; the powers that be are ordained of God."

Again, the Saviour's words were called out by a question concerning tribute. They said to him, "Is it lawful to give tribute unto Cæsar, or not?" Rom. 13:6 refers to the same thing, saying, "For for this cause pay ye tribute also; for they are God's ministers, attending continually upon this very thing." In answer to the question of the Pharisee about the tribute, Christ said, "Render therefore unto Cæsar the things which are Cæsar's." Rom. 13:7, taking up the same thought, says, "Render therefore to all their dues: tribute to whom tribute is due; custom to whom custom; fear to whom fear; honor to whom honor." These references make positive that which we have stated,—that this portion of Scripture (Rom. 13:1–9) is a divine commentary upon the words of Christ in Matt. 22:17–21.

In the previous chapter we have shown by many proofs that civil government has nothing to do with anything that pertains to God. If the argument in that chapter is sound, then Rom. 13:1–9, being the Lord's commentary upon the words which are the basis of that argument, ought to confirm the position there taken. And this it does.

The passage in Romans refers first to civil government, the higher powers,—not the highest power, but the powers that be. Next it speaks of rulers, as bearing the sword and attending upon matters of tribute. Then it commands to render tribute to whom tribute is due, and says, "Owe no man anything, but to love one another; for he that loveth another hath fulfilled the law." Then he refers to the sixth, seventh, eighth, ninth, and tenth commandments, and says, "If there be any other commandment, it is briefly comprehended in this saying, namely, Thou shalt love thy neighbor as thyself."

There are other commandments of this same law to which Paul refers. Why, then, did he say, "If there be any other commandment, it is briefly comprehended in this saying, Thou shalt love thy neighbor as thyself"? There are the four commandments of the first table of this same law,—the commandments which say, "Thou shalt have no other gods before me;" "Thou shalt not make unto thee any graven image, or any likeness of anything;" "Thou shalt not take the name of the Lord thy God in vain;" "Remember the Sabbath day to keep it holy." Then there is the other commandment in which are briefly comprehended all these,—"Thou shalt love the Lord thy God with all thy heart, and with all thy soul, and with all thy mind, and with all thy strength."

Paul knew full well of these commandments. Why, then, did he say, "If there be any other commandment, it is briefly comprehended in this saying, namely, Thou shalt love thy neighbor as thyself"? *Answer*—Because he was writing concerning the words of the Saviour which relate to our duties to civil government.

Our duties under civil government pertain solely to the government and to our fellow-men, because the powers of civil government pertain solely to men in their relations one to another, and to the government. But the Saviour's words in the same connection entirely separated that which pertains to God from that which pertains to civil government. The things which pertain to God are not to be rendered to civil government—to the powers that be; therefore Paul, although know-

3

ing full well that there were other commandments, said, " If
there be any other commandment, it is briefly comprehended
in this saying, namely, Thou shalt love thy neighbor as thyself;" that is, if there be any other commandment which comes
into the relation between man and civil government, it is
comprehended in this saying, that he shall love his neighbor
as himself, thus showing conclusively that the powers that be,
though ordained of God, are so ordained simply in things pertaining to the relation of man with his fellow-men, and in those
things alone.

As, therefore, the instruction in Rom. 13:1–10 is given to
Christians concerning their duty and respect to the powers that
be; and as this instruction is confined absolutely to man's relationship to his fellow-men; it is evident that when Christians
have paid their taxes, and have shown proper respect to their
fellow-men, then their obligation, their duty, and their respect
to the powers that be, have been fully discharged, and those
powers never can rightly have any further jurisdiction over
their conduct.   This is not to say that the State has jurisdiction of the last six commandments as such.   It is only to say
that the jurisdiction of the State is confined solely to man's
conduct toward man, and never can touch his relationship to
God, even under the second table of the law.

Further, as in this divine record of the duties that men owe
to the powers that be, there is no reference whatever to the
first table of the law, it therefore follows that the powers that
be, although ordained of God, have nothing whatever to do
with the relations which men bear toward God.

As the ten commandments contain the whole duty of man,
and as in the scriptural enumeration of the duties that men owe
to the powers that be, there is no mention of any of the things
contained in the first table of the law, it follows that none of
the duties enjoined in the first table of the law of God, do men
owe to the powers that be; that is to say, again, that the

powers that be, although ordained of God, are not ordained of God in anything pertaining to a single duty enjoined in any one of the first four of the ten commandments. These are duties that men owe to God, and with these the powers that be can of right have nothing to do, because Christ has commanded to render unto God—not to Cæsar, nor by Cæsar—that which is God's.

This is confirmed by other scriptures:—

" In the beginning of the reign of Jehoiakim the son of Josiah king of Judah came this word unto Jeremiah from the Lord, saying, Thus saith the Lord to me: Make thee bonds and yokes, and put them upon thy neck, and send them to the king of Edom, and to the king of Moab, and to the king of the Ammonites, and to the king of Tyrus, and to the king of Zidon, by the hand of the messengers which come to Jerusalem unto Zedekiah king of Judah; and command them to say unto their masters, Thus saith the Lord of hosts, the God of Israel: Thus shall ye say unto your masters: I have made the earth, the man and the beast that are upon the ground, by my great power and by my outstretched arm, and have given it unto whom it seemed meet unto me. And now have I given all these lands into the hand of Nebuchadnezzar the king of Babylon, my servant; and the beasts of the field have I given him also to serve him. And all nations shall serve him, and his son, and his son's son, until the very time of his land come, and then many nations and great kings shall serve themselves of him. And it shall come to pass, that the nation and kingdom which will not serve the same Nebuchadnezzar the king of Babylon, and that will not put their neck under the yoke of the king of Babylon, that nation will I punish, saith the Lord, with the sword, and with the famine, and with the pestilence, until I have consumed them by his hand."

In this scripture it is clearly shown that the power of Nebuchadnezzar, king of Babylon, was ordained of God; nor to Nebuchadnezzar alone, but to his son and his son's son, which is to say that the power of the Babylonian Empire, as an imperial power, was ordained of God. Nebuchadnezzar was plainly called by the Lord, " My servant," and the Lord says, "And now have I given all these lands into the hand of Nebuchadnezzar the king of Babylon." He further says that whatever "nation and kingdom which will not serve the same Nebuchadnezzar the king of Babylon, and that will not put their neck under the yoke of the king of Babylon, that nation will I punish."

Now let us see whether this power was ordained of God in things pertaining to God. In the third chapter of Daniel we have the record that Nebuchadnezzar made a great image of gold, set it up in the plain of Dura, and gathered together the princes, the governors, the captains, the judges, the treasurers, the counselors, the sheriffs, and all the rulers of the provinces, to the dedication of the image; and they stood before the image that had been set up. Then a herald from the king cried aloud:—

"To you it is commanded, O people, nations, and languages, that at what time ye hear the sound of the cornet, flute, harp, sackbut, psaltery, dulcimer, and all kinds of music, ye fall down and worship the golden image that Nebuchadnezzar the king hath set up; and whoso falleth not down and worshipeth shall the same hour be cast into the midst of a burning fiery furnace."

In obedience to this command, all the people bowed down and worshiped before the image, except three Jews,—Shadrach, Meshach, and Abed-nego. This disobedience was reported to Nebuchadnezzar, who commanded them to be brought before him, when he asked them if they had disobeyed his order intentionally. He himself then repeated his command to them.

These men knew that they had been made subject to the king of Babylon by the Lord himself. It had not only been prophesied by Isaiah (chapter 39), but by Jeremiah. At the final siege of Jerusalem by Nebuchadnezzar, the Lord through Jeremiah told the people to submit to the king of Babylon, and that whosoever would do it, it should be well with them; whosoever would not do it, it should be ill with them. Yet these men, knowing all this, made answer to Nebuchadnezzar thus:—

"O Nebuchadnezzar, we are not careful to answer thee in this matter. If it be so, our God whom we serve is able to deliver us from the burning fiery furnace, and he will deliver us out of thine hand, O king. But if not, be it known unto thee, O king, that we will not serve thy gods, nor worship the golden image which thou hast set up."

Then these men were cast into the fiery furnace, heated seven times hotter than it was wont to be heated; but suddenly Nebuchadnezzar rose up in haste and astonishment, and said to his counselors, "Did we not cast three men bound into the midst of the fire?" They answered, "True, O king." But he exclaimed, "Lo, I see four men loose, walking in the midst of the fire, and they have no hurt; and the form of the fourth is like the Son of God." The men were called forth:—

"Then Nebuchadnezzar spake, and said, Blessed be the God of Shadrach, Meshach, and Abed-nego, who hath sent his angel, and delivered his servants that trusted in him, and have changed the king's word, and yielded their bodies, that they might not serve nor worship any god, except their own God."

Here there is demonstrated the following facts: First, God gave power to the kingdom of Babylon; second, he suffered his people to be subjected to that power; third, he defended his people by a wonderful miracle from a certain exercise of that power. Does God contradict or oppose himself?—Far from it. What, then, does this show?—It shows conclusively that this was an undue exercise of the power which God had given. By this it is demonstrated that the power of the kingdom of Babylon, although ordained of God, was not ordained unto any such purpose as that for which it was exercised; and that, though ordained of God, it was not ordained to be authority in things pertaining to God, or in things pertaining to men's consciences. And it was written for the instruction of future ages, and for our admonition upon whom the ends of the world are come.

Another instance: We read above that the power of Babylon was given to Nebuchadnezzar, and his son, and his son's son, and that all nations should serve Babylon until that time, and that then nations and kings should serve themselves of him. Other prophecies show that Babylon was then to be destroyed. Jer. 51:28 says that the kings of the Medes, and all his land, with the captains and rulers, should be prepared against Babylon to destroy it. Isa. 21:2 shows that Persia (Elam) should accompany Media in the destruction of Babylon. Isa. 45:1-4 names Cyrus as the leader of the forces, more than a hundred years before he was born, and one hundred and seventy-four years before the time. And of Cyrus, the prophet said from the Lord, " I have raised him up in righteousness, and I will direct all his ways; he shall build my city, and he shall let go my captives, not for price nor reward, saith the Lord of hosts." Isa. 45:13. But in the conquest of Babylon, Cyrus was only the leader of the forces. The kingdom and rule were given to Darius the Mede; for, said Daniel to Belshazzar, on the night when Babylon fell, " Thy kingdom is divided, and given to the Medes and Persians." Then the record proceeds: " In that night was Belshazzar the king of the Chaldeans slain. And Darius the Median took the kingdom." Of him we read in Dan. 11: 1, the words of the angel Gabriel to the prophet, " I in the first year of Darius the Mede, even I, stood to confirm and to strengthen him."

There can be no shadow of doubt, therefore, that the power of Media and Persia was ordained of God. Darius made Daniel prime minister of the empire. But a number of the presidents and princes, envious of the position given to Daniel, attempted to undermine him. After earnest efforts to find occasion against him in matters pertaining to the kingdom, they were forced to confess that there was neither error nor fault anywhere in his conduct. Then said these men, " We shall not find any occasion against this Daniel, except we find it against him concerning the law of his God." They therefore assembled together to the king, and told him that all the presidents of the kingdom, and the governors, and the princes, and the captains, had consulted together to establish a royal statute, and to make a decree that whoever should ask a petition of any god or man, except the king, for thirty days, should be cast into the den of lions. Darius, not suspecting their object, signed the decree. Daniel knew that the decree had been made, and signed by the king. It was hardly possible for him not to know it, being prime minister. Yet, notwithstanding his knowledge of the affair, he went into his chamber, and, his windows being opened toward Jerusalem, he kneeled upon his knees three times a day, and prayed and gave thanks before God, as he did aforetime. He did not even close the windows. He paid no attention to the decree that had been made, although it forbade his doing as he did, under the penalty of being thrown to the lions. He well understood that, although the power of Media and Persia was ordained of God, it was not ordained to interfere in matters of duty which he owed only to God.

As was to be expected, the men who had secured the passage of the decree found him praying and making supplications before his God. They went at once to the king and asked him if he had not signed a decree that every man who should ask a petition of any god or man within thirty days, except of the king, should be cast into the den of lions. The king replied that this was true, and that, according to the law of the Medes and Persians, it could not be altered. Then they told him that Daniel did not regard the king, nor the decree that he had signed, but made his petition three times a day. The king realized in a moment that he had been entrapped, but there was no remedy. Those who were pushing the matter held before him the law, and said, "Know, O king, that the law of the Medes and Persians is, That no decree or statute which the king establisheth may be changed." Nothing could be done; the decree, being law, must be enforced. Daniel was cast to the lions. In the morning the king came to the den and called to Daniel, and Daniel replied, "O king, live forever; my God hath sent his angel, and hath shut the lions' mouths, that they have not hurt me; forasmuch as before him innocency was found in me; and also before thee, O king, have I done no hurt."

Thus again God has shown that, although the powers that be are ordained of God, they are not ordained to act in things that pertain to men's relation toward God. Christ's words are a positive declaration to that effect, and Rom. 13 : 1–9 is a further exposition of the principle.

Let us look a moment at this question from a common-sense point of view. Of course all we are saying is common sense, but let us have this in addition: When societies are formed, each individual surrenders the personal exercise of certain rights, and, as an equivalent for that surrender, has secured to him the fuller enjoyment of these, and all other rights pertaining to person and property, without the protection of which society cannot exist.

Each person has the natural right to protect his person and property against all invasions, but if this right is to be *personally* exercised in all cases by each person, then in the present condition of human nature every man's hand will be against his neighbor. That is simple anarchy, and in such a condition of affairs society cannot exist. Now suppose a hundred of us are thrown together in a certain place where there is no established order; each one has all the rights of any other one. But if each one is individually to exercise these rights of self-protection, he has the assurance of only that degree of protection which he alone can furnish to himself, which we have seen is exceedingly slight. Therefore all come together, and each surrenders to the whole body that individual right, and in return for this surrender he receives the power of all for his protection. He therefore receives the help of the other ninety-nine to protect himself from the invasion of his rights, and he is thus made many hundred times more secure in his rights of person and property than he is without this surrender.

But what condition of things can ever be conceived of among men that would justify any man in surrendering the personal exercise of his right to believe—which in itself would be the surrender of his right to believe at all? What could he receive as an equivalent? When he has surrendered his right to believe, he has virtually surrendered his right to think. When he surrenders his right to believe, he surrenders everything, and it is impossible for him ever to receive an equivalent; he has surrendered his very soul. Eternal life depends upon believing on the Lord Jesus Christ, and the man who surrenders his right to believe, surrenders eternal life. Says the Scripture, "With the mind I myself serve the law of God." A man who surrenders his right to believe surrenders God. Consequently, no man, no association or organization of men, can ever rightly ask of any man a surrender of his right to believe. Every man has the right, so far as organizations of men are concerned, to believe as he pleases; and that right, so long as he is a Protestant, so long as he is a Christian, yes, so long as he is a man, he never can surrender, and he never will.

Another important question to consider in this connection is, How are the powers that be, ordained of God? Are they directly and miraculously ordained, or are they providentially so? We have seen by the Scripture that the power of Nebuchadnezzar as king of Babylon was ordained of God. Did God send a prophet or a priest to anoint him king, or did he send a heavenly messenger, as he did to Moses and Gideon? —Neither. Nebuchadnezzar was king because he was the son of his father, who had been king. How did his father become king?—In 625 B. C. Babylonia was but a province of the empire of Assyria; Media was another. Both revolted, and at the same time. The king of Assyria gave Nabopolassar command of a large force, and sent him to Babylonia to quell the revolt, while he himself led other forces into Media, to put down the insurrection there. Nabopolassar did his work so well in Babylonia that the king of Assyria rewarded him with the command of that province, with the title of king of Babylon. Thus we see that Nabopolassar received his power from the king of Assyria. The king of Assyria received his from his father, Asshur-bani-pal; Asshur-bani-pal received his from his father, Esar-haddon; Esar-haddon received his from his father, Sennacherib; Sennacherib received his from his father, Sargon; and Sargon received his from the troops in the field, that is, from the people. Thus we see that the power of the kingdom of Babylon, and of Nebuchadnezzar the king, or of his son, or of his son's son, was simply providential, and came merely from the people.

Take, for example, Victoria, queen of Great Britain. How did she receive her power?—Simply by the fact that she was the first in the line of succession when William the Fourth died. Through one line she traces her royal lineage to William the Conqueror. But who was William the Conqueror?—He was a Norman chief who led his forces into England in 1066, and established his power there. How did he become a chief of the Normans?—The Normans made him so, and in that line it is clear that the power of Queen Victoria sprang only from the people.

Following the other line: The house that now rules Britain, represented in Victoria, is the house of Hanover. Hanover is a province of Germany. How came the house of Hanover to reign in England?—When Queen Anne died, the next in the line of succession was George of Hanover, who became king of England, under the title of George the First. How did he receive his princely dignity?—Through his lineage, from Henry

the Lion, son of Henry the Proud, who received the duchy of
Saxony from Frederick Barbarossa, in 1156.   Henry the Lion,
son of Henry the Proud, was a prince of the house of Guelph,
of Swabia.   The father of the house of Guelph was a prince of
the Alemanni, who invaded the Roman Empire and established
their power in what is now Southern Germany, and were the
origin of what is now the German nation and empire.   But who
made this man a prince?—The savage tribes of Germany.   So
in this line also the royal dignity of Queen Victoria sprang
from the people.

And besides all this, the imperial power of Queen Victoria
as she now reigns is circumscribed—limited—by the people.
It has been related, and has appeared in print, that on one
occasion, Gladstone, while prime minister and head of the
House of Commons, took a certain paper to the queen to be
signed.   She did not exactly approve of it, and said she would
not sign it.   Gladstone spoke of the merit of the act, but the
queen still declared she would not sign it.   Gladstone replied,
"Your Majesty *must* sign it."   "*Must* sign!" exclaimed the
queen; "*must* sign!   Do you know who I am?   I am the queen
of England."   Gladstone calmly replied, "Yes, Your Majesty,
but I am the PEOPLE of England;" and she had to sign it.
The people of England can command *the queen* of England;
the power of the people of England is above that of the queen
of England.   She, as queen, is simply the representative of
their power.   And if the people of England should choose to
dispense with their expensive luxury of royalty, and turn their
form of government into that of a republic, it would be but
the legitimate exercise of their right; and the government thus
formed, the power thus established, would be ordained of God
as much as that which now is, or as any could be.

Personal sovereigns in themselves are not those referred to
in the words, "The powers that be are ordained of God."   It
is *the governmental power*, of which the sovereign is the repre-

sentative, and that sovereign receives his power from the people. Outside of the theocracy of Israel, there never has been a ruler on earth whose authority was not, primarily or ultimately, expressly or permissively, derived from the people. It is not particular sovereigns whose power is ordained of God, nor any particular form of government. *It is the genius of government itself.* The absence of government is anarchy. Anarchy is only governmental confusion. But says the Scripture, "God is not the author of confusion." God is the God of order. He has ordained order, and he has put within man himself that idea of government, of self-protection, which is the first law of nature, and which organizes itself into forms of one kind or another, wherever men dwell on the face of the earth. And it is for men themselves to say what shall be the form of government under which they shall dwell. One people has one form; another has another. This genius of civil order springs from God; its exercise within its legitimate sphere is ordained of God; and the Declaration of Independence simply asserted the eternal truth of God when it said, "Governments derive their just powers from the consent of the governed." It matters not whether they be exercised in one form of government or in another, the governmental power and order thus exercised are ordained of God. If the people choose to change their form of government, it is still the same power; it is to be respected still, because it is still ordained of God in its legitimate exercise,—in things pertaining to men and their relation to their fellow-men; but no power, whether exercised through one form or another, is ordained of God to act in things pertaining to God; nor has it anything whatever to do with man's relations toward God.

Except in the nation of Israel, it is not, and never has been, personal sovereigns in themselves that have been referred to in the statement that "the powers that be are ordained of God." It is not the persons that be in power, but *the powers that be in the person,* that are ordained of God. The inquiry of Rom. 13: 3 is not, Wilt thou then not be afraid of the person? but it is, "Wilt thou then not be afraid of the *power?*" It is not the person, therefore, but the power that is represented in the person, that is under consideration here. *And that person derives his power from the people,* as is clearly proved by the scriptural examples and references given. "To the people we come sooner or later; it is upon their wisdom and self-restraint that the most cunningly devised scheme of government will in the last resort depend."—*Bryce, American Commonwealth, chapter 24, last sentence.*

PART II.

THE RIGHTS OF THE PEOPLE.

THE RIGHTS OF THE PEOPLE.

CHAPTER I.

On the reverse side of the great seal of the United States there is a Latin inscription—*Novus Ordo Seclorum*—meaning "A New Order of Things." This new order of things was designed and accomplished in the American Revolution, which was the expression of two distinct ideas: First, that government is of the people; and, second, that government is of right entirely separate from religion.

These two ideas are but the result of the one grand fundamental principle, the chief corner stone of American institutions, which is THE RIGHTS OF THE PEOPLE.

This is briefly comprehended, and nobly expressed, in the following words of the Declaration of Independence:—

"We hold these truths to be self-evident: that all men are created equal; that they are endowed by their Creator with certain unalienable rights; that among these are life, liberty, and the pursuit of happiness. That to secure these rights governments are instituted among men, deriving their just powers from the consent of the governed; that when any form of government becomes destructive of these ends, it is the right of the people to alter or to abolish it, and to institute a new government, laying its foundation on such principles and organizing its powers in such form, as to them shall seem most likely to effect their safety and happiness."

Thus in two sentences was annihilated the despotic doctrine, which had become venerable, if not absolutely hallowed, by the precedents of a thousand years—the doctrine of the divine

4

right of rulers; and in the place of the old *falsehood*, and despotic *theory*, of the sovereignty of the government and the subjection of the people, there was declared, to all nations and for all time, the self-evident *truth* and divine *principle* of *the subjection of the government* and THE SOVEREIGNTY OF THE PEOPLE.

In declaring the equal and inalienable right of all men to life, liberty, and the pursuit of happiness, and that governments derived their just powers from the consent of the governed, there is not only declared the sovereignty of the people, but also the entire capability of the people. The declaration, in itself, presupposes that men are men indeed, and that as such they are fully capable of deciding for themselves as to what is best for their happiness, and how they shall pursue it, without the government's being set up as a parent or guardian to deal with them as with children.

In declaring that governments are instituted by the governed, for certain ends, and that when any government becomes destructive of these ends, it is *the right of the people* to *alter* or *to abolish* it, and to institute a new government, in such form as *to them* shall seem most likely to effect their safety and happiness, it is likewise declared that, instead of the people's needing to be cared for by the government, the government *must be cared for by the people.*

In declaring the objects of government to be to secure to the people the rights which they already possess in full measure and inalienable degree, and to effect their safety and happiness in the enjoyment of those rights; and in declaring the right of the people, in the event named, to alter or abolish the government which they have, and institute a new one on such principles and in such form as to them seems best; there is likewise declared not only the complete subordination but also the absolute *impersonality* of government. It is therein declared that the government is but a device, a piece of political machinery, framed and set up by the people, by which they would make themselves secure in the enjoyment of the inalienable rights which they already possess as men, and which they have by virtue of being men in society and not by virtue of government—the right which was theirs before government was, which is *their own* in the essential meaning of the term, and "which they do not hold by any sub-infeudation, but by direct homage and allegiance to the Owner and Lord of all" (Stanley Matthews[1]), their Creator, who has endowed them with those rights. And in thus declaring the impersonality of government, there is wholly uprooted every vestige of any character of *paternity* in the government.

In declaring the equality of all men in the the possession of these inalienable rights, there is likewise declared the strongest possible safeguard of the people. For, this being the declaration of the people, each one of the people stands thereby pledged to the support of the principle thus declared. Therefore, each individual is pledged, in the exercise of his own inalienable right to life, liberty, and the pursuit of happiness, so to act as not to interfere with any other person in the free and perfect exercise of *his* inalienable right to life, liberty, and the pursuit of happiness. Any person who so acts as to restrict or interfere with the free exercise of any other person's right to life, or liberty, or the pursuit of happiness, denies the principle, to the maintenance of which he is pledged, and does in effect subvert the government. For, rights being equal, if one may so act, every other one may do so; and thus no man's right is recognized, government is gone, and only anarchy remains.

Therefore, by every interest, personal as well as general, private as well as public, every individual among the people is pledged in the enjoyment of his right to life, or liberty, or the pursuit of happiness, so to conduct himself as not to interfere

---

[1] In argument in Cincinnati case, Minor *et al.*, on "Bible in the Public Schools," p. 241.

in the least degree with the equal right of every other one to the free and full exercise of his enjoyment of life, liberty, and the pursuit of happiness. "For the rights of man, as man, must be understood in a sense that can admit of no single exception; for to allege an exception is the same thing as to deny the principle. We reject, therefore, with scorn, any profession of respect to the principle which, in fact, comes to us clogged and contradicted by a petition for an exception. . . . To profess the principle and then to plead for an exception, let the plea be what it may, is to deny the principle, and it is to utter a treason against humanity. The rights of man must everywhere all the world over be recognized and respected."
—*Isaac Taylor.*[2]

The Declaration of Independence, therefore, announces the perfect principle of civil government. If the principle thus announced were perfectly conformed to by all, then the government would be a perfect civil government. It is but the principle of self-government—government of the people, by the people, and for the people. And to the extent to which this principle is exemplified among the people, to the extent to which the individual governs himself, just to that extent and no further will prevail the true idea of the Declaration, and the republic which it created.

Such is the first grand idea of the American Revolution. And it is the scriptural idea, the idea of Jesus Christ and of God. Let this be demonstrated.

The Declaration holds that all men are endowed by their Creator with certain inalienable rights. Now the Creator of all men is the God and Father of our Lord Jesus Christ, and "is he the God of the Jews only? is he not also of the Gentiles? Yes, of the Gentiles also." And as he "hath made of one blood all nations of men for to dwell on all the face of the earth" (Acts 17:26), "there is no respect of persons with God" (Rom. 2:11).

---

[2] Quoted by Stanley Matthews, *Id.*, p. 242.

Nor is this the doctrine of the later Scripture only; it is the doctrine of all the Book. The most ancient writings in the Book have these words: "If I did despise the cause of my manservant or of my maidservant, when they contended with me; what then shall I do when God riseth up? and when he visiteth, what shall I answer him? Did not he that made me in the womb make him?" Job 31:13-15. And, "The Lord your God is God of gods, and Lord of lords, a great God, a mighty, and a terrible, which regardeth not persons, nor taketh reward; he doth execute the judgment of the fatherless and widow, and loveth the stranger, in giving him food and raiment. Love ye therefore the stranger." Deut. 10:17-19. "The stranger that dwelleth with you shall be unto you as one born among you, and thou shalt love him as thyself." Lev. 19:34.

All men are indeed created equal, and are endowed by their Creator with certain inalienable rights.

And this is the American doctrine,—the doctrine of the Declaration of Independence. In the discussions which brought forth the Declaration and developed the Revolution, the doctrine found expression in the following forceful and eloquent words:—

"Government is founded not on force, as was the theory of Hobbes; nor on compact, as was the theory of Locke and of the revolution of 1688; nor on property, as was asserted by Harrington. It springs from the necessities of our nature, and has an everlasting foundation in the unchangeable will of God. Man came into the world and into society at the same instant. There must exist in every earthly society a supreme sovereign, from whose final decision there can be no appeal but directly to heaven. *This supreme power is originally and ultimately in the people;* and the people *never did in fact freely, nor can rightfully* make unlimited renunciation of this divine right. Kingcraft and priestcraft are a trick to gull the vulgar. The happiness of mankind demands that this grand and ancient alliance should be broken off forever.

"The omniscient and omnipotent Monarch of the universe has,

by the grand charter given to the human race, placed the end of government in the good of the whole. The form of government is left to the individuals of each society; its whole superstructure and administration should be conformed to the law of universal reason. There can be no prescription old enough to supersede the law of nature and the grant of God Almighty, who has given all men a right to be free. If every prince since Nimrod had been a tyrant, it would not prove a right to tyrannize. The administrators of legislative and executive authority, when they verge toward tyranny, are to be resisted; if they prove incorrigible, are to be deposed.

"The first principle and great end of government being to provide for the best good of all the people, this can be done only by a supreme legislative and executive, ultimately in the people, or whole community, where God has placed it; but the difficulties attending a universal congress gave rise to a right of representation. Such a transfer of the power of the whole to a few was necessary; but to bring the powers of all into the hands of one or some few, and to make them hereditary, is the interested work of the weak and the wicked. Nothing but life and liberty are actually hereditable. The grand political problem is to invent the best combination of the powers of legislation and execution. They must exist in the State, just as in the revolution of the planets; one power would fix them to a center, and another carry them off indefinitely; but the first and simple principle is EQUALITY and THE POWER OF THE WHOLE. . . .

"The British colonists do not hold their liberties or their lands by so slippery a tenure as the will of the prince. Colonists are men, the common children of the same Creator with their brethren of Great Britain. The colonists are men; the colonists are therefore freeborn; for, by the law of nature, all men are freeborn, white or black. No good reason can be given for enslaving those of any color. Is it right to enslave a man because his color is black, or his hair short and curled like wool, instead of Christian hair? Can any logical inference in favor of slavery be drawn from a flat nose or a long or short face? The riches of the West Indies, or the luxury of the metropolis, should not have weight to break the balance of truth and justice. Liberty is the gift of God, and cannot be annihilated.

"Nor do the political and civil rights of the British Colonies rest on a charter from the crown. Old Magna Charta was not the beginning of all things, nor did it rise on the borders of chaos out of the unformed mass. A time may come when Parliament shall declare every American charter void; but the natural, inherent, and inseparable rights of the colonists, as men and as citizens, can never be abolished. . . .

The world is at the eve of the highest scene of earthly power and grandeur that has ever yet been displayed to the view of mankind. Who will win the prize, is with God. But human nature must and will be rescued from the general slavery that has so long triumphed over the species."—*James Otis.*[3]

Thus spoke an American "for his country and for the race," bringing to "the conscious intelligence of the people the elemental principles of free government and human rights." Outside of the theocracy of Israel, there never has been a ruler or an executive on earth whose authority was not, primarily or ultimately, expressly or permissively, derived from the people.

The conclusion of the whole matter, the end of all that can be said, is that, where the Declaration of Independence says that governments derive their just powers from the consent of the governed, it asserts THE ETERNAL TRUTH OF GOD.

In a previous chapter we have shown that the Constitution of the United States is the only form of government that has ever been on earth which is in harmony with the principle announced by Christ, demanding of men only that which is Cæsar's and refusing to enter in any way into the field of man's relationship to God. This Constitution originated in the principles of the Declaration of Independence, and here we have found that the Declaration of Independence, on this point, simply asserts the truth of God. The American people do not half appreciate the value of the Constitution under which they live. They do not honor in any fair degree the noble men who pledged their lives, their fortunes, and their sacred honor, that these principles might be the heritage of posterity. All honor to these noble men! All integrity to the principles of the Declaration of Independence! All allegiance to the Constitution as it was made, which gives to Cæsar all his due, and leaves men free to render to God all that he, in his holy word, requires of them!

So much for the principle.

---

[3] Quoted in Bancroft's "History of the United States," Vol. III, chapter 7, par. 21-41.

CHAPTER II.

HOW THE UNITED STATES BECAME A NATION.

WHEN the fathers of '76 had declared that "these Colonies are, and of right ought to be, free and independent States," Britain did not agree with the proposition, and consequently it had to be proved. In the war from 1776–1783, the proposition was so fully demonstrated that Britain and all other nations admitted its entire truthfulness.

No sooner was this question settled, however, than dangers, unrealized until now, threatened the very existence, not only of *the union* of the thirteen States, but of the separate States themselves. When the question had been settled that these Colonies were and of right ought to be free and independent States, then free and independent States was precisely what they were. There were thirteen of them, and each one of the thirteen was as entirely free and independent of all the others, as were the whole thirteen free and independent of Great Britain. Each of the thirteen States was as free and independent of any or all of the others, as though it stood alone on this continent.

True, articles of confederation had been entered into under which a Congress acted, but the Congress had no real power. It could recommend to the States measures to be carried into effect, but the States could and did do just as they pleased as to paying any attention to the recommendations. If the measure suited them, they would act upon it; but if not, they would not. And if it suited part of them and did not suit the rest, even if it met the approval of all but one, only the ones that chose would comply with the recommendation, and as to the others, or the other one, there was no power on earth that could require them or it to act with the States that chose to comply. Washington described the situation by saying, "We are one nation to-day, and thirteen to-morrow." This is the exact truth. Practically they were thirteen independent nations, just as those of Europe are.

It was soon found that they could not long exist with such a fast and loose order of things as that. By their enemies prophecies were frequent of "the downfall of the United States," and, indeed, the signs were so abundant and ominous that their friends were compelled to fear that this would certainly result. As soon as peace with Britain had been settled, Washington, Jefferson, Madison, and other prominent ones, began to agitate for a federal government, a national power. Washington "had hardly reached home from the war" before he, in a letter to the governor of Virginia, January 18, 1784, stated the situation and the great need of the country in the following forcible words:—

"The prospect before us is fair. I believe all things will come right at last, but the disinclination of the States to yield competent powers to Congress for the federal government will, if there is not a change in the system, be our downfall as a nation. This is as clear to me as A, B, C. We have arrived at peace and independency to very little purpose if we cannot conquer our own prejudices. The powers of Europe begin to see this, and our newly acquired friends, the British, are already and professedly acting upon this ground, and wisely, too, if we are determined to persevere in our folly. They know that individual opposition to their measures is futile, and boast that we are not sufficiently united as a nation to give a general one. Is not the indignity of this declaration, in the very act of peace-making and conciliation, sufficient to stimulate us to vest adequate powers in the sovereign of these United States?

"An extension of federal powers would make us one of the most wealthy, happy, respectable, and powerful nations that ever inhab-

ited the terrestrial globe. Without them [federal powers] we shall soon be everything which is the direct reverse. I predict the worst consequences from a half-starved, limping government, always moving upon crutches and tottering at every step."—*History of the Constitution of the United States, Bancroft, Vol. I, p. 153.*[1]

Nearly the end of the same year, December 14, 1784, "the French minister at Versailles" wrote as follows:—

"The American confederation has a strong tendency to dissolution. It is well that on this point we have neither obligations to fulfill nor any interest to cherish."—*Id., p. 167.*

In November, 1785, during a discussion in the General Assembly of Virginia over the question of an extension of power to a federal government, Washington was asked for suggestions, to which, November 30, he replied:—

"The proposition is self-evident. We are either a united people or we are not so. If the former, let us in all matters of national concern act as a nation which has a national character to support." "If the States individually attempt to regulate commerce, an abortion or a many-headed monster will be the issue. If we consider ourselves, or wish to be considered by others, a united people, why not adopt the measures which are characteristic of it, and support the honor and dignity of one? If we are afraid to trust one another under qualified powers, there is an end of the union."—*Id., p. 251.*

At the suggestion of the Legislature of Maryland to the General Assembly of Virginia, in December, 1785, a resolution was passed by that body January 21, 1786, "proposing that commissioners from all the States should be invited to meet and regulate the restrictions on commerce for the whole."— *Id., p. 253.* Madison was the first named of the commis-

---

[1] The quotations from Bancroft herein throughout are taken *directly* from his "History of the Formation of the Constitution of the United States." The same quotations, however, precisely as here given, can be found in Vol. VI of his latest revision of his "History of the United States," so that anyone who has access to his "History of *the United States*," needs not his "History *of the Formation of the Constitution* of the United States." This history of the Constitution is practically only a reprint of the last volume of his "History of the United States," with the addition of a vast number of letters of the men of the times.

sioners of Virginia; Annapolis, Md., was named as the place, and "the first Monday in September," 1786, the time, of the meeting. In accepting the invitation New Jersey empowered her commissioners "to consider how far a uniform system in their commercial regulations and OTHER IMPORTANT MATTERS might be necessary to the common interest and permanent harmony of the several States," and these "other important matters" turned out to be definite instructions "to be content with nothing less than *a new federal government.*"—*Id., pp. 257, 268.*

In February, 1786, the Congress of the confederation, after having discussed for two days the many and increasing difficulties which it was compelled to meet, referred the subject to a committee. After deliberating five days the committee, February 15, made their report. After stating the chief difficulties the report concluded as follows:—

"After the most solemn deliberation, and under the fullest conviction that the public embarrassments are such as above represented, and that they are daily increasing, the committee are of opinion that it has become the duty of Congress to declare most explicitly that *the crisis has arrived when the people of the United States,* by whose will and for whose benefit the federal government was instituted, *must decide* whether they will support their rank as a nation by maintaining the public faith at home and abroad, or whether, for want of a timely exertion in establishing a general revenue, and thereby giving strength to the confederacy, they will hazard not only the existence of the Union, but of those great and invaluable privileges for which they have so arduously and so honorably contended."—*Id., 255.*

Yet, after this strong and pointed report, the Congress failed to take any decisive steps toward the relief and safety of the country. "The discussion brought Congress no nearer to the recommendation of a general convention. Its self-love refused to surrender its functions, least of all on the ground of its own incapacity to discharge them."—*Id., p. 259.* The effect of this report, however, was such that "far and wide a general convention was become the subject of thought, and 'a plan for it was forming, though it was as yet immature.' "—*Id., p. 256.*

Commissioners were not present at the Annapolis Convention from *all* the States, but such as were present unanimously adopted a report to Congress asking that body to use its endeavors to secure a meeting of commissioners from all the States, "to meet at Philadelphia on the second Monday of May [1787] to consider the situation of the United States," etc.—*Id., p. 268.* This recommendation was not adopted by Congress,[2] so that in itself that was the end of this particular effort. Meanwhile the difficulties and dangers of the country had multiplied, and the impotency of Congress, as it then existed, to deal with them was becoming more and more apparent.

In this crisis Madison, who had been all along a tireless worker for the new federal government, for a national power which should be really such, stepped boldly forward and appealed to "the people of America" to take the necessary steps without the lead of Congress. He carried in the General Assembly of Virginia, November, 1786, the unanimous indorsement of the recommendation of the Annapolis convention, with the following preamble, written by himself:—

---

[2] Mr. Bryce ("American Commonwealth," chapter 3, par. 4, edition 1895) says that Congress "approved" this report "and recommended the States to send delegates," etc. This seems, however, certainly to be a mistake. Bancroft says that "a grand committee of the seventh Congress *reported*, in February [1787], by a bare majority of one," approving the report of the Annapolis convention, and strongly recommending "to the different Legislatures *to send* forward delegates," etc., "but that they never ventured to ask for a vote upon their report."—*History of the Constitution, Vol. I, p. 273.* I have not access myself to the original documents, so as positively to decide this contradiction between these two eminent authors; but, as Mr. Bancroft's account is so full and circumstantial, I have no hesitation in accepting it in preference to Mr. Bryce's statement. I must believe that Mr. Bryce has, from some cause, overlooked this failure of Congress to approve the Annapolis report, and confounded the recommendation that Congress did finally make with this one that it did not make.

"The commissioners who assembled at Annapolis, on the four-teenth day of September last, for the purpose of devising and report-ing the means of enabling Congress to provide effectually for the commercial interests of the United States, have represented the neces-sity of *extending the revision of the federal system to all its defects*, and have recommended that deputies for that purpose be appointed by the several Legislatures, to meet in convention in the city of Phila-delphia on the second day of May next—*a provision preferable to a discussion of the subject in Congress*, where it might be too much interrupted by ordinary business, and where it would, besides, be deprived of the counsels of individuals who are restrained from a seat in that assembly.

"The general assembly of this commonwealth [Virginia], taking into view the situation of the confederacy, as well as reflecting on the alarming representations made from time to time by the United States in Congress *particularly in their act of the fifteenth day of February last*, can no longer doubt that a crisis is arrived at which *the people of America* are to decide the solemn question whether they will, by wise and magnanimous efforts, reap the fruits of independence and of union; or whether, by giving way to unmanly jealousies and prjeudices, or to partial and transitory interests, they will renounce the blessings prepared for them by the Revolution.

"The same noble and extended policy, and the same fraternal and affectionate sentiments which originally *determined the citizens of this commonwealth to unite with their brethren of the other States in estab-lishing a federal government*, cannot but be felt with equal force now as motives to lay aside every inferior consideration, and to concur in such further concessions and provisions as may be necessary to secure the objects for which that government was instituted, and to render the United States as happy in peace as they have been glorious in war."—*Id., pp. 271, 272.*

It was as late as the middle of November, 1786, when this was passed by the Virginia Assembly. As soon as New Jersey received the news, she endorsed the action, November 23; in December, Pennsylvania joined these two; in January, North Carolina, and in February, 1787, Delaware joined the former three. Congress, seeing how the tide was moving, thought it best to move also; and accordingly thought to maintain its dignity by totally ignoring all that had been done and gravely recommending precisely such a convention as was going to meet, and also recommending it to meet in the same place and on the identical day. One after another of the remaining States fell into line, except Rhode Island, which never did. And so only twelve States had any part in the work of the convention that created the national government under which we live.

As soon as it became apparent that the convention would certainly assemble, Madison began to prepare an outline of a constitution for the expected new government, "and, in advance of the federal convention, he had sketched for his own use and that of his friends, and ultimately of the convention, a thoroughly comprehensive constitutional government for the Union."—*Id.*, *p. 278.*

The delegates were slow in arriving, and it was the 29th of May, 1787, before the convention was fully organized for business. The regular business of the convention was begun by Randolph, the governor of Virginia, in these words:—

"To prevent the fulfillment of the prophecies of the downfall of the United States, it is our duty to inquire into the defects of the confederation and the requisite properties of the government now to be framed, the danger of the situation, and the remedy."—*Id.*, *Vol. II*, *p. 10.*

After a few further remarks he proposed for a working basis for a constitution, the outline that had been drawn by Madison, and to which, with some amendments and alterations, the whole Virginia delegation had agreed.

The convention went steadily on with its work, and on September 17, 1787, with the unanimous consent of the representatives of the eleven States present, there was completed and signed *the Constitution of the United States* as it stands, from the " Preamble " down to " Amendments."

Not all who signed it, however, were satisfied with it. Nevertheless, those who were not entirely favorable to it, signed it because it was the only course in which there lay any hope. Though dissatisfied with it, they accepted it in order to escape a much worse fate than anything under it could possibly be.

Charles Pinckney, of South Carolina, said:—

"I, too, object to the power of a majority of Congress over commerce, but apprehending the danger of a general confusion, and an ultimate decision by the sword, I shall give the plan my support." —*Id., p. 218.*

Gouverneur Morris, of Pennsylvania, remarked:—

"I, too, had objections; but, considering the present plan the best that can be obtained, I shall take it with all its faults. The moment it goes forth, the great question will be, Shall there be a national government, or a general anarchy?"—*Id., p. 220.*

Alexander Hamilton signed with the following explanation:—

"No man's ideas are more remote from the plan than my own are known to be; but is it possible to deliberate between anarchy and convulsion on the one side, and the chance of good to be expected from the plan on the other?"—*Id.*

And after the proposed constitution had been sent forth to the people, for their consideration, Washington sought further to disarm opposition by a letter in which he used the following words:—

"My decided opinion is that there is no alternative between the adoption of the proceedings of the convention and anarchy. . . . The Constitution or disunion is before us to choose from."—*Id., pp. 279, 280.*

So well was this situation understood outside of the country, as well as by these leading men in the country, that Great Britain was really considering whether she should not administer upon the estate, in the event of the convention failing to

come to any agreement upon a plan of government. " The
ministry of England harbored the thought of a constitutional
monarchy, with a son of George III. as king; and they were
not without alarm lest gratitude to France should place on an
American throne a prince of the House of Bourbon."—*Id.*,
Vol. I, p. 277.

Thus, and for these reasons, was the government of the
United States created; and thus the United States became *a
nation.*

CHAPTER III.

WHAT IS THE NATION?

THE United States—the nation indeed —is not composed of the States. The original thirteen States did not compose the nation, nor do the forty-four now compose it. The United States, the nation, is that power, that system, that organization, above all the States and distinct from them, which was created to perform, in behalf of the States and the people, what neither the people, nor any of the States, nor yet all the States together, could do for themselves.

In the facts and the statements presented in the preceding chapter, it is clear enough that "the United States" before the establishment of the Constitution were not a nation. There was no national power; there was no national action; there was no national character; there was no national spirit. This was seen and expressed by the friends as well as the foes of the country.

True, when the thirteen independent States were firmly agreed upon any measure so that they could all act unreservedly together—as in the war for their independence—then they were powerful, and *so far* in that particular measure displayed somewhat of the characteristics of a nation. But after such united effort had secured their independence, there was literally not a single question upon which there was unanimity of opinion and consequent action, such as could display any of the characteristics of a nation.

This is why there were so many "prophecies of the downfall of the United States;" this is why it was that they were "one nation to-day, and thirteen to-morrow;" and this is why

(68)

it was certainly true that there was no alternative between anarchy and the formation of a national government. James Wilson, of Pennsylvania, a member of the convention which framed the Constitution for the making of the nation, in pleading for the approval of the Constitution by the Pennsylvania convention called for that purpose, stated the case thus:—

"By adopting this Constitution *we shall become a nation;* we are *not now one.*"—*Elliott's Debates, Vol. II, p. 526, quoted by Bryce, Am. Com., chapter 3, par. 8, note.*

They must by choice become a nation, or else without their choice they would become nothing. And as by the adoption of the Constitution they would " become a nation;" as with the Constitution there would be a nation, while without it there would be none; it is perfectly clear that THE NATION IS THAT ORDER OF GOVERNMENT, *that system, that organization, that power*, WHICH IS DEFINED IN THE CONSTITUTION OF THE UNITED STATES.

It is also clear that, in truth and in fact, the nation is the United States, and the United States is the nation. The nation is not composed of the States. The *thirteen States* did not become a nation. The *people* of the thirteen States *created a nation*. After the nation had been created, the thirteen States still remained intact as States. The nation is a thing in and of itself, created to perform what could not be performed without it. The nation is a government, and a governmental system, as distinct from the thirteen, or the forty-four, States, as any one of these States is distinct from the others. As respects the States and the nation, they are not *one* government, nor are they *two* governments. When the people of the thirteen States in 1787–1789 had created the national government, there was *not* then *only one* government in this country, there were more than one. There were then more than *thirteen* governments—*there were* FOURTEEN. There was the United States, and besides this there were still the thirteen

States; there was the national government, and besides this there were thirteen State governments, making fourteen in all. Now, May, 1895, there is the national government, and besides this there are the forty-four State governments, making forty-five governments in the country.   There is the United States, and besides this there are the forty-four States.   But the United States, the nation, is ever and always a government in and of itself, distinct from all State governments.   This distinction is neatly made by John Fiske in the following pointed sentences:—

"From 1776 to 1789 the United States *were* a confederation.   After 1789, *it* was a federal nation."—*Fiske's Civil Government, p. 234.*

The distinction here drawn between *the* United States *were*, and *it was*, tells the whole story.

The United States is not as this:—

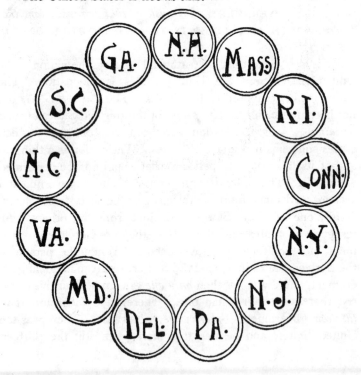

That is as they were before 1789, while they were a confederacy and not a nation. Nor is the United States a governmental band drawn through the existing States to hold them together, as though it were this:—

The United States is as neither of these.   It is as this:—

A much finer conception, and perhaps a much better illustration, is contained in the following view, presented by Bryce:[1]—

"The central or national government and the State governments
may be compared to a large building and a set of smaller buildings
standing on the same ground, yet distinct from each other.   It is a
combination sometimes seen where a great church has been erected
over more ancient houses of worship.   First the soil is covered by a
number of small shrines and chapels, built at different times and in
different styles of architecture, each complete in itself.   Then over
them and including all in its spacious fabric there is reared a new pile,

[1] My rude and perhaps even crude illustration had been conceived and marked
out before I found this illustration of Mr. Bryce's.   I have therefore let it stand, though
his is much the better one.

with its own loftier roof, its own walls, . . . its own internal plan. The identity of the earlier buildings has, however, not been obliterated; and if the later and larger structure were to disappear, a little repair would enable them to keep out wind and weather, and be again what they once were, distinct and separate edifices. So the American States are now all inside the Union, and have become subordinate to it. Yet the Union is more than the aggregate of States, and the States are more than parts of the Union.''— *The American Commonwealth, chapter 3, par. 7, edition of February, 1895.*

The United States—the nation—is a government distinct from all the States, outside of them, and above them, which was created to do for the States and for the people what neither the States nor the people could do for themselves, nor yet for one another. It was not anything within their boundaries that troubled any of the thirteen States; it was altogether those of their interests which reached *beyond* their boundaries that caused the perplexity. For just as soon as any State attempted to follow up any of its interests which reached beyond its own boundaries, it entered the jurisdiction of another power equally independent with itself; and not only was this other an independent power, but with respect to that particular thing it might be a hostile power as well. Consequently, for the best interests of all, it was essential that there should be formed a government separate and distinct from all, which, in behalf of all, should have jurisdiction of all interests which should extend beyond the boundaries of any State.

This, in brief, defines the line that separates between the States and the United States, and between the jurisdiction of the State governments and that of the national government. Wilson, of Pennsylvania, who helped to make the nation, in explaining to the Pennsylvania convention the provisions of the Constitution, clearly defined this line as follows:—

"The convention found themselves embarrassed with another difficulty of peculiar delicacy and importance. I mean that of drawing a proper line between the national government and the governments of the several States. Whatever object of government is confined in its operation and effects within the bounds of a particular State, should be considered as belonging to the government of that State. Whatever object of government extends in its operation or effects beyond the bounds of a particular State, should be considered as belonging to the government of the United States."—*Bancroft's History of the Formation of the Constitution, pp. 244, 245.*

Such was the intention of the framers of the original Constitution. Yet, as it was not distinctly expressed in the Constitution, an amendment respecting the point was required. Consequently, the tenth of the ten amendments that were passed in regular course through the first Congress that ever met under the Constitution, declares as follows:—

"The powers not delegated to the United States by the Constitution, nor prohibited by it to the States, are reserved to the States respectively, or to the people."

Thus in all matters not delegated to the United States, nor prohibited by the Constitution to the States, each State may do fully and freely just as it pleases within its own boundaries; while in any matters so delegated or prohibited it has nothing whatever to do, but the nation in these things has power to do fully and freely as it chooses. The nation has nothing whatever to do with any matter the operation and effects of which lie within the boundaries of any State; and no State has anything whatever to do with any matter the operation or effects of which reach beyond its boundaries. State boundaries are no more a mark of the limits of State jurisdiction, than they are a barrier to the exercise of the national power. Thus stands the line *in principle* between the States and the United States; and it is described *in words* in the tenth amendment—that the powers not delegated to the United States by the Constitution, nor prohibited by it to the States, are reserved to the States or to the people—and these powers are to be exercised exclusively by the States or by the people, *never by the United States—*

never by the nation. Abraham Lincoln stated this point thus:—

"Each community, or a State, has a right to do exactly as it pleases with all the concerns within that State that interfere with the right of no other State; and the general government, upon principle, has no right to interfere with anything other than that general class of things that does concern the whole."—*Chicago Speech, July 10, 1858, Political Speeches and Debates, p. 83.*

And Bancroft states this fact as follows:—

"*The United States of America,* . . . *within its own sphere, is supreme* and self-supporting. For this end it has its own Legislature to make enactments; its own functionaries to execute them; its own courts; its own treasury; and it alone may have an army and a navy. All sufficient powers are so plainly given that there is no need of striving for more by straining the words in which they are granted, beyond their plain and natural import.

"Aside from the sphere of the federal government, *each State is in all things supreme,* not by grace, but of right. The United States may not interfere with any ordinance or law that begins and ends within a State. *This supremacy of the States in the powers which have not been granted,* is as essentially a part of the system as the supremacy of the general government in its sphere. . . .

"The powers of government are not divided between them; they are *distributed;* so that there need be no collision in their exercise."— *History of the Constitution, Vol. II, p. 332.*

Thus "the acceptance of the Constitution of 1789 made the American people *a nation.*"—*Bryce, Am. Com., first sentence of chapter 4.* And that thing, that governmental organization, which was created by the people, which is defined and regulated in the Constitution of 1789—THAT IS THE NATION.

CHAPTER IV.

WHO MADE THE NATION?

WE have seen how that, after long and anxious waiting, and after repeated efforts to get the States or the Congress to call a general convention, it was only when an appeal was made to the "people of America" that the movement for the creation of a national government was crowned with success. It was only when the "people of America" began to move that either Congress or the States could be brought to realize that they *must* move.

Providentially and logically, rather than intentionally, it was not in the proper order of things that the new movement should be carried out either by the States as such or by the Congress. It was the doctrine of the Declaration that rights belong to *the people*, and that governments "derive their just powers *from the consent of the governed.*" It was therefore only the clear logic of the Declaration that the movement for the establishment of a new form of government should receive its original impulse from *the people* of America, rather than from *the governments* of America.

This word, "the people of these United States," "the people of America," which was rung out by the Committee of Congress, February 15, and by Madison, in November, 1786, was the spring of all that followed in the making of the nation. It was the keynote to which the pæan of the liberty and the rights of the people *in government* was to be sung to all the world, and for all time.

At every step of the way in the making of the nation the idea was never lost sight of that it was "*the people* of these United States," "*the people* of America," and not *the States* who were doing it. This was made to appear in the published call of the convention, in the provision that when the Constitution should have been framed by the convention and agreed to by Congress, it was to be established and made of force, *not* by the Legislatures of the States, that is, not by the States as such, but *by conventions in the States, chosen by* THE PEOPLE. For Madison, who was the open and positive leader in the movement, "held it as a fixed principle that the new system should be ratified by *the people* of the several States, so that it might be clearly paramount to their individual legislative authority."—*Bancroft, History of Constitution, Vol. I, p. 278.*

How certainly this principle was recognized, and how strictly it was followed in the convention, is shown by a remarkable fact. And it is this: In the first draft of the Constitution, as arranged and printed, after "more than two months'" deliberation, and distributed to the members, the preamble ran as follows:—

"We, the people of *the States* [and then followed in detail the names of all the thirteen] do ordain, declare, and establish the following Constitution *for the government of ourselves and our posterity.*"——*Id., Vol. II, pp. 119, 120.*

But when the Constitution was completed, and was ready to be sent forth by the convention, the preamble stood thus:—

"We, the people of the *United States, in order to form a more perfect union,* establish justice, insure domestic tranquillity, provide for the common defense, promote the general welfare, and secure the blessings of liberty to ourselves and our posterity, do ordain and establish this Constitution *for the United States* of America."

Where the first draft said, "We, the people of the States," the final preamble was made to say, "We, the people of the United States:" clearly showing that the question had been discussed and decided that it was not the people of *the States* as such, but the people of the *United States* by whom this thing was done.

Again, where the first draft said, "We, the people of the States, do ordain and establish this Constitution for *the government of ourselves*"—the people of the States—the final preamble was made to say, "We, the people of the United States, do ordain and establish this Constitution for *the United States of America*."

It is true that the delegates in the convention voted *by States*, in accordance with the forms of the governments as they then existed; but in any or all their action "they did not pretend to be 'the people,' and could not institute a general government in its name. The instrument which they framed was like the report of a bill beginning with the words 'be it enacted,' though the binding enactment awaits the will of the Legislature; or like a deed drawn up by an attorney for several parties awaiting its execution by the principals themselves. Only by its acceptance could the words, 'We, the people of the United States,' become words of truth and power."—*Id.*, *p. 208*. And when afterwards in the Pennsylvania convention for the ratification of the Constitution, it was charged by one of the members that the "federal convention had exceeded the powers given them by their respective Legislatures," James Wilson answered in the following emphatic words:—

"The federal convention *did not proceed at all* upon the powers given them *by the States, but upon original principles;* and, having framed a Constitution which they thought would promote the happiness of their country, they have submitted it to their [the people's] consideration, who may either adopt or reject it as they please."— *Id.*, *p. 246*.

In the convention that framed the Constitution there was even "a disinclination to ask the approbation of Congress" upon the result of their labors, though this was not acted upon.

Nevertheless the Constitution was not to be put to the risk of defeat by being submitted to Congress for a vote of approval or disapproval; but was to be submitted to the people only, for that purpose. This was made clear by the convention in its adoption, September 10, 1787, of the following "directory resolution" —

"This Constitution shall be laid before the United States in Congress assembled; and it is the opinion of this convention that it should be afterwards submitted to a convention chosen in each State, under the recommendation of its Legislature, in order to receive the ratification of such convention."—*Id.*, *pp. 205, 206.*

Later the "Committee on Style" reported, September 13, resolutions "for the ratification of the Constitution through Congress, by *conventions of the people* of the several States;" and in this report was embodied the above "directory resolution."

The object of having the Constitution pass through Congress and the Legislatures of the respective States, yet without allowing them to act in approval or disapproval upon it, was to give them the opportunity of *proposing amendments* if they should choose to do so.

The Constitution was laid before Congress September 20, 1787, and on the 28th of the same month that body unanimously resolved "that the said report, with the resolutions and letter accompanying the same, be transmitted to the several Legislatures *in order* to be submitted to a convention of delegates chosen in each State *by the people thereof* in conformity to the resolves of the convention."—*Id.*, *p. 230.*

In the Pennsylvania convention for the ratification of the Constitution, James Wilson, who from beginning to end was a master spirit in the framing of that masterly instrument, again defined its principles, November 24, 1787, in the following sublime passage:—

" To control the power and conduct of the Legislature by an over-ruling Constitution limiting and superintending the operations of the legislative authority, was an improvement in the science and practice of government reserved to the United States. Oft have I marked with silent pleasure and admiration the force and prevalence through the United States of the principle that *the supreme power resides in the people, and that* THEY NEVER PART WITH IT. There can be no disorder in the community but may here receive a radical cure. Error in the Legislature may be corrected by the Constitution; error in the Constitution, *by the people.* The streams of power run in different directions, but they all originally flow from *one abundant fountain. In this Constitution* ALL AUTHORITY IS DERIVED FROM THE PEOPLE." —*Id., p. 245.*

And finally, after the people of the United States through their conventions had passed upon the Constitution as origi-nally framed and submitted, they ratified it, but yet with the addition of ten amendments, two of which, in the very words of that supreme law itself, define the rights of the people. The ninth amendment declares that—

" The enumeration in the Constitution of *certain rights* shall not be construed to deny or disparage others *retained by the people.*"

And the tenth amendment declares that—

" The powers *not delegated* to the United States by the Constitution, nor prohibited by it to the States, *are reserved* to the States respec-tively *or to the people.*"

Thus was the nation made; these are they who made it; and thus the government of the United States of America became, and *is,* "a GOVERNMENT OF THE PEOPLE, BY THE PEOPLE, AND FOR THE PEOPLE."

NOTE.

Nothing in this chapter is to be construed to convey the idea that in the action of "the people of the United States" the States are ignored. Not at all. The people of the United States, acting as such, do not act as a whole, but in divisions according to their respective

States. The government of the United States, though distinct and separate from that of the States, is yet *not* a democracy in which the people act in a mass; but it is as truly a republic in which the people act through representatives, as is the government of the States. In all things in which the people act as the people of the United States, they do so through representatives chosen by themselves from within their respective States. Even the President, who, more than any other, is the representative of *all the people*, is not directly chosen—voted for—by the people. No; the people in their respective States vote for *electors* chosen from among themselves in their respective States, and these electors elect the President. In all things the form of government, whether State or national, is republican; *that is*, the form in which the people govern and act is *through representatives* chosen by themselves.

CHAPTER V.

RELIGIOUS RIGHT IN THE UNITED STATES.

"ALL men are created equal, and are endowed by their Creator with certain unalienable rights." The first and greatest of all the rights of men is religious right. Religion is the duty which men owe to their Creator, and the manner of discharging it. The first of all duties is to the Creator, because to him we owe our existence. Therefore the first of all commandments, and the first that there can possibly be, is this: "Hear, O Israel: The Lord thy God is one Lord; and thou shalt love the Lord thy God with all thy heart, and with all thy soul, and with all thy mind, and with all thy strength; this is the first commandment." Mark 12 : 29, 30.

This commandment existed as soon as there was an intelligent creature in the universe; and it will continue to exist as long as there shall continue one intelligent creature in the universe. Nor can a universe *full* of intelligent creatures modify in any sense the bearing that this commandment has upon any single one, any more than if that single one were the *only* creature in the universe. For as soon as an intelligent creature exists, he owes his existence to the Creator. And in owing to him his existence, he owes to him the first consideration in all the accompaniments and all the possibilities of existence. Such is the origin, such the nature, and such the measure, of religious right.

Did, then, the fathers who laid the foundation of this nation in the rights of the people—did they allow to this right the place and deference among the rights of the people which, according to its inherent importance, is justly its due? That is, Did they leave it sacred and untouched solely between man and his Creator?

The logic of the Declaration demanded that they should; for the Declaration says that governments derive "their just powers *from the consent of the governed.*" Governments, then, deriving their just powers from the consent of the governed, can never of right exercise any power not delegated by the governed. But religion pertains solely to man's relation to God, and to the duty which he owes to him as his Creator, and therefore in the nature of things it can never be delegated.

It is utterly impossible for any person ever, in any degree, to delegate or transfer to another any relationship or duty, or the exercise of any relationship or duty, which he owes to his Creator. To attempt to do so would be only to deny God and renounce religion, and even then the thing would not be done; for, whatever he might do, his relationship and duty to God would still abide as fully and as firmly as ever.

As governments derive their just powers from the governed; as governments cannot justly exercise any power not delegated; and as it is impossible for any person in any way to delegate any power in things religious; it follows conclusively that the Declaration of Independence logically excludes religion in every sense and in every way from the jurisdiction and from the notice of every form of government that has resulted from that Declaration.

This is scriptural, too. For to the definition that religion is "the recognition of God as an object of worship, love, and obedience," the Scripture responds: "It is written, as I live, saith the Lord, every knee shall bow to me, and every tongue shall confess to God. So then every one of us shall give account of himself to God." Rom. 14 : 11, 12.

6

To the statement that religion is "man's personal relation of faith and obedience to God," the Scripture responds, "Hast thou faith? have it *to thyself* before God." Rom. 14 : 22.

And to the word that religion is "the duty which we owe to our Creator, and the manner of discharging it," the Scripture still responds. "For we must all appear before the judgment seat of Christ; that everyone may receive the things done in his body, according to that he hath done, whether it be good or bad." 2 Cor. 5 : 10.

No government can ever account to God for any individual. No man nor any set of men can ever have faith for another. No government will ever stand before the judgment seat of Christ to answer even for itself, much less for the people or for any individual. Therefore, no government can ever of right assume any responsibility in any way in any matter of religion.

Such is the logic of the Declaration, as well as it is the truth of Holy Writ. But did the fathers who made the nation recognize this and act accordingly?—They did. And the history of this subject runs parallel, step by step, with the history of the subject of the fixing of the civil rights of the people in the supreme law—this history occurred in the same time precisely as did that; it occurred in the same place precisely as did that; it was made by the same identical men who made that history; and the recognition and declaration of this right were made a fixture in the same identical place by the same identical means as was that of the other. This being so makes it impossible to be escaped by anybody who has any respect for the work of those noble master-builders, or for the rights of the people.

Let us trace the history of this right of the people through the time which we have traversed in tracing the history of the rights of the people in the abstract.

Like the other series of events, this too began in Virginia. While Virginia was yet a Colony and subject to Great Britain, and while the Church of England was the established church of the Colony, the colonial House of Burgesses, June 12, 1776, adopted a Declaration of Rights, composed of sixteen sections, every one of which, in substance, afterward found a place in the Declaration of Independence and the Constitution.   The sixteenth section, in part, reads thus:—

"That *religion*, or *the duty which we owe to our Creator, and the manner of discharging it*, can be directed only by reason and conviction, not by force or violence, and therefore all men are equally entitled to the free exercise of religion, according to the dictates of conscience."

July 4 following, the Declaration of Independence was made, wherein, as we have already seen, this principle is embodied in the statement that "governments derive their just powers from the consent of the governed."   This is precisely the view that was taken of it, and the use that was made of the principle as it appeared in the Declaration of Independence, as soon as that Declaration was published to the world.   For no sooner was the Declaration published abroad than the Presbytery of Hanover, in Virginia, openly took its stand with the new and independent nation, and, with the Baptists and Quakers, addressed to the General Assembly of Virginia a memorial reading as follows:—

"*To the Honorable, the General Assembly of Virginia:* The memorial of the Presbytery of Hanover humbly represents: That your memorialists are governed by the same sentiments which have inspired the United States of America, and are determined that nothing in our power and influence shall be wanting to give success to their common cause.   We would also represent that dissenters from the Church of England in this country have ever been desirous to conduct themselves as peaceful members of the civil government, for which reason they have hitherto submitted to various ecclesiastical burdens and restrictions that are inconsistent with equal liberty.   But now, when the many and grievous oppressions of our mother country have laid this continent under the necessity of casting off the yoke of tyranny, and of forming independent governments upon equitable and liberal foundations, we flatter ourselves that we shall be freed from all the incumbrances which a spirit of domination, prejudice, or bigotry has interwoven with most other political systems. This we are the more strongly encouraged to expect by the Declaration of Rights, so universally applauded for that dignity, firmness, and precision with which it delineates and asserts the privileges of society, and the prerogatives of human nature, and which we embrace as the Magna Charta of our commonwealth, that can never be violated without endangering the grand superstructure it was designed to sustain. Therefore we rely upon this Declaration, as well as the justice of our honorable Legislature, to secure us the free exercise of religion according to the dictates of our own consciences; and we should fall short in our duty to ourselves, and the many and numerous congregations under our care, were we, upon this occasion, to neglect laying before you a statement of the religious grievances under which we have hitherto labored, that they may no longer be continued in our present form of government.

"It is well known that in the frontier counties, which are justly supposed to contain a fifth part of the inhabitants of Virginia, the dissenters have borne the heavy burdens of purchasing glebes, building churches, and supporting the established clergy, where there are very few Episcopalians, either to assist in bearing the expense, or to reap the advantage; and that throughout other parts of the country there are also many thousands of zealous friends and defenders of our State who, besides the invidious and disadvantageous restrictions to which they have been subjected, annually pay large taxes to support an establishment from which their consciences and principles oblige them to dissent; all of which are confessedly so many violations of their natural rights, and, in their consequences, a restraint upon freedom of inquiry and private judgment.

"In this enlightened age, and in a land where all of every denomination are united in the most strenuous efforts to be free, we hope and expect that our representatives will cheerfully concur in removing every species of religious as well as civil bondage. Certain it is that every argument for civil liberty gains additional strength when applied to liberty in the concerns of religion; and there is no argument in favor of establishing the Christian religion but may be pleaded with equal propriety for establishing the tenets of Mohammed by those who believe the Alcoran; or, if this be not true, *it is at least impossible for the magistrate to adjudge the right of preference among the various sects that profess the Christian faith* WITHOUT ERECTING A CLAIM TO INFALLIBILTY, WHICH WOULD LEAD US BACK TO THE CHURCH OF ROME.

"We beg leave farther to represent that religious establishments are highly injurious to the temporal interests of any community. Without insisting upon the ambition and the arbitrary practices of those who are favored by the government, of the intriguing, seditious spirit which is commonly excited by this as well as by every other kind of oppression, such establishments greatly retard population, and consequently the progress of arts, sciences, and manufactures. Witness the rapid growth and improvement of the northern provinces compared with this. No one can deny that the more early settlements and the many superior advantages of our country would have invited multitudes of artificers, mechanics, and other useful members of society to fix their habitation among us, who have either remained in their place of nativity or preferred worse civil governments and a more barren soil, where they might enjoy the rights of conscience more fully than they had a prospect of doing in this; from which we infer that Virginia might have been now the capital of America, and a match for the British arms, without depending on others for the necessaries of war, had it not been prevented by her religious establishment.

"Neither can it be made to appear that the gospel needs any such civil aid. We rather conceive that when our blessed Saviour declares his kingdom is not of this world, he renounces all dependence upon State power, and as his weapons are spiritual, and were only designed to have influence on the judgment and heart of man, we are persuaded that if mankind were left in quiet possession of their inalienable religious privileges, Christianity, as in the days of the apostles, would continue to prevail and flourish in the greatest purity by its own native excellence, and under the all-disposing providence of God.

"We would also humbly represent that the only proper objects of civil government are the happiness and protection of men in the present state of existence, the security of the life, liberty, and property of the citizens, and to restrain the vicious and encourage the virtuous by wholesome laws, equally extending to every individual; but that the duty which we owe to our Creator, and the manner of discharging it, can only be directed by reason and conviction, and is nowhere cognizable but at the tribunal of the universal Judge.

"Therefore we ask no ecclesiastical establishments for ourselves; neither can we approve of them when granted to others. This, indeed, would be giving exclusive or separate emoluments or privileges to one set of men without any special public services, to the common reproach and injury of every other denomination. And for the reason recited, we are induced earnestly to entreat that all laws now in force in this commonwealth which countenance religious domination may be speedily repealed; that all of every religious sect may be protected in the full exercise of their several modes of worship; exempted from all taxes for the support of any church whatsoever, farther than what may be agreeable to their own private choice or voluntary obligation. This being done, all partial and invidious distinction will be abolished, to the great honor and interest of the State, and every one be left to stand or fall according to his merit, which can never be the case so long as any one denomination is established in preference to the others.

"That the great Sovereign of the universe may inspire you with unanimity, wisdom, and resolution, and bring you to a just determination on all the important concerns before you, is the fervent prayer of your memorialists."—*Baird's Religion in America, Book III, chap. 3, par. 9-16.*

The Episcopalian being the established church of Virginia, and having been so ever since the planting of the Colony, it was of course only to be expected that the Episcopalians would send up counter-memorials, pleading for a continuance of the system of established religion. But this was not all—the Methodists joined with the Episcopalians in this plan. Two members of the Assembly, Messrs. Pendleton and Nicolas, championed the establishment, and Jefferson espoused the cause of liberty and right. After nearly two months of what Jefferson pronounced the severest contest in which he was ever engaged, the cause of freedom prevailed, and December 6, 1776, the Assembly passed a law repealing all the colonial laws and penalties prejudicial to dissenters, releasing them from any further compulsory contributions to the Episcopal Church, and discontinuing the State support of the Episcopal clergy after January 1, 1777.

A motion was then made to levy a general tax for the support of "teachers of the Christian religion," but it was postponed till a future Assembly.   To the next Assembly petitions were sent by the Episcopalians and the Methodists, pleading for the general assessment.   But the Presbytery of Hanover, still strongly supported by the Baptists and the Quakers, was again on hand with a memorial, in which it referred to the points previously presented, and then proceeded as follows:—

"We would also humbly represent that the only proper objects of civil government are the happiness and protection of men in the present state of existence, the security of the life, liberty, and property of the citizens, and to restrain the vicious and to encourage the virtuous by wholesome laws, equally extending to every individual; but that the duty which we owe to our Creator, and the manner of discharging it, can only be directed by reason and conviction, and is nowhere cognizable but at the tribunal of the universal Judge.

"To illustrate and confirm these assertions, we beg leave to observe that to judge for ourselves, and to engage in the exercise of religion agreeably to the dictates of our own consciences, is an unalienable right, which, upon *the principles on which the gospel was first propagated and the Reformation from popery carried on*, can never be transferred to another.   Neither does the church of Christ stand in need of a general assessment for its support; and most certain we are that it would be of no advantage but an injury to the society to which we belong; and as every good Christian believes that Christ has ordained a complete system of laws for the government of his kingdom, so we are persuaded that by his providence he will support it to its final consummation.   In the fixed belief of this principle, that the kingdom of Christ and the concerns of religion are beyond the limits of civil control, we should act a dishonest, inconsistent part were we to receive any emoluments from human establishments for the support of the gospel.

"These things being considered, we hope that we shall be excused for remonstrating against a general assessment for any religious purpose.   As the maxims have long been approved, that every servant is to obey his master, and that the hireling is accountable for his conduct to him from whom he receives his wages, in like manner, if the Legislature has any rightful authority over the ministers of the gospel in the exercise of their sacred office, and if it is their duty to levy a maintenance for them as such, then it will follow that they may revive the old establishment in its former extent, or ordain a new one for any sect they may think proper; they are invested with a power not only to determine, but it is incumbent on them to declare, who shall preach, what they shall preach, to whom, when, and in what places they shall preach; or to impose any regulations and restrictions upon religious societies that they may judge expedient. These consequences are so plain as not to be denied, and they are so *entirely subversive of religious liberty* that if they should take place in Virginia we should be reduced to the melancholy necessity of saying with the apostles in like cases, 'Judge ye whether it is best to obey God or men,' and also of acting as they acted.

"Therefore, as it is contrary to our principles and interest, and, as we think, subversive of religious liberty, we do again most earnestly entreat that our Legislature would never extend any assessment for religious purposes to us or to the congregations under our care."—*Id., par. 21–23.*

In 1779, by this memorial, and, more, "by the strenuous efforts of the Baptists," the bill was defeated, after it had been ordered to the third reading.

At this same time in 1779 Jefferson prepared with his own hand and proposed for adoption "as a part of the Revised Code" of Virginia, "An Act for Establishing Religious Freedom," which ran as follows:—

"Well aware that Almighty God hath created the mind free; that all attempts to influence it by temporal punishments or burdens, or by civil incapacitations, tend only to beget habits of hypocrisy and meanness, and are a departure from the plan of the holy Author of our religion, who, being Lord both of body and mind, yet chose not to propagate it by coercions on either, as was in his almighty power to do; that the impious presumption of legislators and rulers, civil as well as ecclesiastical, who, being themselves but fallible and uninspired men, have assumed dominion over the faith of others, setting up their own opinions and modes of thinking as the only true and infallible, and as such endeavoring to impose them on others, hath established and maintained false religions over the greatest part of the world, and through all time; that to compel a man to furnish contributions of

money for the propagation of opinions which he disbelieves, is sinful and tyrannical; that even the forcing him to support this or that teacher of his own religious persuasion, is depriving him of the comfortable liberty of giving his contributions to the particular pastor whose morals he would make his pattern, and whose powers he feels most persuasive to righteousness, and is withdrawing from the ministry those temporal rewards which, proceeding from an approbation of their personal conduct, are an additional incitement to earnest and unremitting labors for the instruction of mankind; that our civil rights have no dependence on our religious opinions, more than our opinions in physics or geometry; that, therefore, the proscribing any citizen as unworthy the public confidence, by laying upon him an incapacity of being called to the offices of trust and emolument, unless he profess or renounce this or that religious opinion, is depriving him injuriously of those privileges and advantages to which, in common with his fellow-citizens, he has a natural right; that it tends to corrupt the principles of that very religion it is meant to encourage, by bribing with a monopoly of worldly honors and emoluments those who will externally profess and conform to it; that, though indeed these are criminal who do not withstand such temptation, yet neither are those innocent who lay the bait in their way; that to suffer the civil magistrate to intrude his powers into the field of opinion, and to restrain the profession or propagation of principles, on the supposition of their ill tendency, is a dangerous fallacy, which at once destroys all religious liberty, because, he being of course judge of that tendency, will make his opinions the rule of judgment, and approve or condemn the sentiments of others only as they shall square with, or differ from, his own; that it is time enough for the rightful purposes of civil government for its officers to interfere when principles break out into overt actions against peace and good order; and, finally, that truth is great, and will prevail if left to herself; that she is the proper and sufficient antagonist to error, and has nothing to fear from the conflict, unless by human interposition disarmed of her natural weapons, free argument and debate, errors ceasing to be dangerous when it is permitted freely to contradict them.

"*Be it therefore enacted by the General Assembly*, that no man shall be compelled to frequent or support any religious worship, place, or ministry whatsoever, nor shall be enforced, restrained, molested, or burthened in his body or goods, nor shall otherwise suffer on account of his religious opinions or belief; but that all men shall be free to profess, and by argument to maintain, their opinions in matters of religion, and that the same shall in nowise diminish, enlarge, or affect their civil capacities.

"And though we well know that this Assembly, elected by the people for the ordinary purposes of legislation only, have no power to restrain the acts of succeeding assemblies, constituted with powers equal to our own, and that therefore to declare this act irrevocable, would be of no effect in law, yet we are free to declare, and do declare, that the rights hereby asserted are of the natural rights of mankind, and that if any act shall be hereafter passed to repeal the present or to narrow its operation, such act will be an infringement of natural right."—*Id., par. 27, note.*

This proposed law was submitted to the whole people of Virginia for their "deliberate reflection" before the vote should be taken in the General Assembly for its enactment into law as a part of the revised code.

From this time forward the war for independence became the all-absorbing question, and this movement for the establishment of "the Christian religion," was compelled to stand in abeyance until the war had ended. At the first opportunity, however, after peace had come again to the country, the subject was again forced upon the General Assembly of Virginia, in the fall of 1784, by the petitioners, under the lead of "The Protestant Episcopal Church," for the establishment of "a provision for teachers of the Christian religion." "Their petitions, favored by Patrick Henry; Harrison, then governor; Pendleton, the chancellor; Richard Henry Lee, and many others of the foremost men, alleged a decay of public morals; and the remedy asked for was a general assessment."—*Bancroft, History of Constitution, Vol. I, p. 213.*

At this point the Presbyterian *clergy* swerved and "accepted the measure, provided it should respect every human belief, even 'of the Mussulman and the Gentoo.' "—*Id.* The Presbyterian *people*, however, held fast to the principle. And the Baptists, as ever *in those days*, "alike ministers and people," held steadfastly to the principle and "rejected any alliance with the State."—*Id.*

Early in the session Patrick Henry introduced a resolution to allow the presentation of a bill in accordance with the wishes of the petitioners. Personally Jefferson was out of the country, being minister to France; but his bill for "Establishing Religious Freedom," which had been submitted to the people in 1779, was still before them; and, though personally absent, he took a lively interest in the contest, and his pen was busy. His place in the General Assembly was most worthily filled by Madison, as the leader in the cause of religious right. Madison declared against the bill, that—

"The assessment bill exceeds the functions of civil authority. The question has been stated as if it were, Is religion necessary? The true question is, Are establishments necessary to religion? And the answer is, They corrupt religion. The difficulty of providing for the support of religion is the result of the war, to be remedied by voluntary association for religious purposes. In the event of a statute for the support of the Christian religion, are the courts of law to decide what is Christianity? and as a consequence, to decide what is orthodoxy and what is heresy? The enforced support of the Christian religion dishonors Christianity."—*Id., p. 214.*

"Yet, in spite of all opposition, leave to bring in the bill was granted by forty-seven votes against thirty-two."—*Id.* Accordingly there was introduced "A Bill Establishing a Provision for Teachers of the Christian Religion;" which provided a general assessment on all taxable property for the purpose named; that each person as he paid his tax should say to what particular denomination he desired it to be conveyed; and that in all cases wherein persons declined to name any religious society, all such tax received from these was to be turned to the support of schools in the counties of said persons respectively.

The bill was successfully carried to the third reading, and was there checked only by a motion to postpone the subject to the next General Assembly, meantime to print the bill and distribute it among the people for their consideration, that their will in the matter might be signified to the next Assembly, which then could act accordingly. "Thus the people of Virginia had before them for their choice the bill of the revised code for 'Establishing Religious Freedom,' and the plan of desponding churchmen for supporting religion by a general assessment."

"All the State, from the sea to the mountains and beyond them, was alive with the discussion. Madison, in a remonstrance addressed to the Legislature, embodied *all that could be said* against the compulsory maintenance of Christianity, and in behalf of religious freedom as a natural right, the glory of Christianity itself, the surest method of supporting religion, and the only way to produce harmony among its several sects."—*Id., p. 215.*

This noble remonstrance, which "embodied all that could be said" upon the subject, should be ingrained in the minds of the American people to-day; because all that it said then needs to be said now, even with a double emphasis. This masterly document, which on the subject of religious right holds the same high place as does the Declaration of Independence on the subject of rights in general, is here given in full, and runs as follows:—

"We, the subscribers, citizens of the said commonwealth, having taken into serious consideration a bill printed by order of the last session of General Assembly, entitled 'A Bill Establishing a Provision for Teachers of the Christian Religion,' and conceiving that the same, if finally armed with the sanctions of a law, will be a dangerous abuse of power, are bound as faithful members of a free State to remonstrate against it, and to declare the reasons by which we are determined. We remonstrate against the said bill:—

"1. Because we hold it for a fundamental and undeniable truth 'that religion, or the duty which we owe to our Creator, and the manner of discharging it, can be directed only by reason and conviction, not by force or violence.' The religion, then, of every man must be left to the conviction and conscience of every man; and it is the right of every man to exercise it as these may dictate. This right is in its

James Madison

nature an unalienable right. It is unalienable, because the opinions of men, depending only on the evidence contemplated in their own minds, cannot follow the dictates of other men. It is unalienable, also, because what is here a right towards men is a duty towards the Creator. It is the duty of every man to render to the Creator such homage, and such only, as he believes to be acceptable to him. This duty is precedent, both in order of time and in degree of obligation, to the claims of civil society. Before any man can be considered as a member of civil society, he must be considered as a subject of the Governor of the universe; and if a member of civil society who enters into any subordinate association, must always do it with a reservation of his duty to the general authority, much more must every man who becomes a member of any particular civil society do it with a saving of his allegiance to the universal Sovereign. We maintain, therefore, that in matters of religion no man's right is abridged by the institution of civil society, and that religion is wholly exempt from its cognizance. True it is, that no other rule exists by which any question which may divide a society can be ultimately determined than the will of the majority; but it is also true that the majority may trespass upon the rights of the minority.

"2. Because, if religion is exempt from the authority of the society at large, still less can it be subject to that of the legislative body. The latter are but the creatures and vicegerents of the former. Their jurisdiction is both derivative and limited. It is limited with regard to the coördinate departments; more necessarily is it limited with regard to the constituents. The preservation of a free government requires not merely that the metes and bounds which separate each department of power be invariably maintained, but more especially that neither of them be suffered to overleap the great barrier which defends the rights of the people. The rulers who are guilty of such an encroachment exceed the commission from which they derive their authority, and are tyrants. The people who submit to it are governed by laws made neither by themselves nor by any authority derived from them, and are slaves.

"3. Because it is proper to take alarm at the first experiment upon our liberties. We hold this prudent jealousy to be the first duty of citizens, and one of the noblest characteristics of the late Revolution. The freemen of America did not wait till usurped power had strengthened itself by exercise, and entangled the question in precedents. They saw all the consequences in the principle, and they avoided the consequences by denying the principle. We revere this lesson too much soon to forget it. Who does not see that the same authority which can establish Christianity, in exclusion of all other religions, may establish, with the same ease, any particular sect of Christians, in exclusion of all other sects? that the same authority which can force a citizen to contribute threepence only, of his property, for the support of any one establishment, may force him to conform to any other establishment in all cases whatsover?

"4. Because the bill violates that equality which ought to be the basis of every law, and which is more indispensable in proportion as the validity or expediency of any law is more liable to be impeached. 'If all men are by nature equally free and independent,' all men are to be considered as entering into society on equal conditions, as relinquishing no more, and, therefore, retaining no less, one than the other, of their natural rights. Above all, are they to be considered as retaining an 'equal title to the free exercise of religion according to the dictates of conscience.' Whilst we assert for ourselves a freedom to embrace, to profess, and to observe the religion which we believe to be of divine origin, we cannot deny an equal freedom to them whose minds have not yet yielded to the evidence which has convinced us. If this freedom be abused, it is an offense against God, not against man. To God, therefore, not to man, must an account of it be rendered. As the bill violates equality by subjecting some to peculiar burdens, so it violates the same principle by granting to others peculiar exemptions. Are the Quakers and Menonists the only sects who think a compulsive support of their religions unnecessary and unwarrantable? Can their piety alone be intrusted with the care of public worship? Ought their religions to be endowed above all others with extraordinary privileges by which proselytes may be enticed from all others? We think too favorably of the justice and good sense of these denominations to believe that they either covet preëminences over their fellow-citizens, or that they will be seduced by them from the common opposition to the measure.

"5. Because the bill implies either that the civil magistrate is a competent judge of religious truths, or that he may employ religion as an engine of civil policy. The first is an arrogant pretension, falsified by the contradictory opinions of rulers in all ages and throughout the world; the second, an unhallowed perversion of the means of salvation.

"6. Because the establishment proposed by the bill is not requisite for the support of the Christian religion. To say that it is, is a contradiction to the Christian religion itself, for every page of it disavows a dependence on the powers of this world. It is a contradiction to fact; for it is known that this religion both existed and flourished, not only without the support of human laws, but in spite of every opposition from them, and not only during the period of miraculous aid, but long after it had been left to its own evidence and the ordinary care of Providence. Nay, it is a contradiction in terms; for a religion not invented by human policy must have preëxisted and been supported before it was established by human policy. It is, moreover, to weaken in those who profess this religion a pious confidence in its innate excellence and the patronage of its Author, and to foster in those who still reject it a suspicion that its friends are too conscious of its fallacies to trust it to its own merits.

"7. Because experience witnesseth that ecclesiastical establishments, instead of maintaining the purity and efficacy of religion, have had a contrary operation. During almost fifteen centuries has the legal establishment of Christianity been on trial. What have been its fruits? More or less, in all places, pride and indolence in the clergy; ignorance and servility in the laity; in both, superstition, bigotry, and persecution. Inquire of the teachers of Christianity for the ages in which it appeared in its greatest luster; those of every sect point to the ages prior to its incorporation with civil polity. Propose a restoration of this primitive state, in which its teachers depend on the voluntary regard of their flocks—many of them predict its downfall. On which side ought their testimony to have greatest weight—when for, or when against, their interest?

"8. Because the establishment in question is not necessary for the support of civil government. If it be urged as necessary for the support of civil government only as it is a means of supporting religion, and it be not necessary for the latter purpose, it cannot be necessary for the former. If religion be not within the cognizance of civil government, how can its legal establishment be necessary to civil government? What influence, in fact, have ecclesiastical establishments had on civil society? In some instances they have been seen to erect a spiritual tyranny on the ruins of civil authority; in many instances they have been seen upholding the thrones of political tyranny; in no instance have they been seen the guardians of the liberties of the people. Rulers who wished to subvert the public liberty may have found in established clergy convenient auxiliaries. A just government, instituted to secure and perpetuate it, needs them not. Such a government will be best supported by protecting every citizen in the enjoyment of his religion with the same equal hand which protects his person and his property, by neither invading the equal rights of any sect, nor suffering any sect to invade those of another.

"9. Because the proposed establishment is a departure from that generous policy which, offering an asylum to the persecuted and oppressed of every nation and religion, promised a luster to our country, and an accession to the number of its citizens. What a melancholy mark is this bill, of sudden degeneracy! Instead of holding forth an asylum to the persecuted, it is itself a signal of persecution. It degrades from the equal rank of citizens all those whose opinions in religion do not bend to those of the legislative authority. Distant as it may be in its present form from the Inquisition, it differs from it only in degree. The one is the first step, the other is the last in the career of intolerance. The magnanimous sufferer of this cruel scourge in foreign regions, must view the bill as a beacon on our coast warning him to seek some other haven, where liberty and philanthrophy, in their due extent, may offer a more certain repose from his troubles.

"10. Because it will have a like tendency to banish our citizens. The allurements presented by other situations are every day thinning their number. To superadd a fresh motive to emigration by revoking the liberty which they now enjoy, would be the same species of folly which has dishonored and depopulated flourishing kingdoms.

"11. Because it will destroy that moderation and harmony which the forbearance of our laws to intermeddle with religion has produced among its several sects. Torrents of blood have been spilt in the Old World in consequence of vain attempts of the secular arm to extinguish religious discord by proscribing all differences in religious opinion. Time has at length revealed the true remedy. Every relaxation of narrow and rigorous policy, wherever it has been tried, has been found to assuage the disease. The American theater has exhibited proofs that equal and complete liberty, if it does not wholly eradicate it, sufficiently destroys its malignant influence on the health and prosperity of the State. If, with the salutary effects of this system under our own eyes, we begin to contract the bounds of religious freedom, we know no name which will too severely reproach our folly. At least let warning be taken at the first fruits of the threatened innovation. The very appearance of the bill has transformed 'that Christian forbearance, love, and charity,' which of late mutually prevailed, into animosities and jealousies which may not be appeased. What mischiefs may not be dreaded, should this enemy to the public quiet be armed with the force of law?

"12. Because the policy of the bill is adverse to the diffusion of the light of Christianity. The first wish of those who enjoy this precious gift ought to be that it may be imparted to the whole race of mankind. Compare the number of those who have as yet received it with the number still remaining under the dominion of false religions, and how small is the former? Does the policy of the bill tend to lessen the disproportion?—No; it at once discourages those who are strangers to the light of revelation from coming into the region of it, and countenances by example the nations who continue in darkness in shutting out those who might convey it to them. Instead of leveling, as far as possible, every obstacle to the victorious progress of truth, the bill, with an ignoble and unchristian timidity, would circumscribe it with a wall of defense against the encroachments of error.

"13. Because attempts to enforce, by legal sanctions, acts obnoxious to so great a proportion of citizens, tend to enervate the laws in general, and to slacken the bands of society. If it be difficult to execute any law which is not generally deemed necessary or salutary, what must be the case where it is deemed invalid and dangerous? And what may be the effect of so striking an example of impotency in the government, on its general authority?

" 14. Because a measure of such singular magnitude and delicacy ought not to be imposed without the clearest evidence that it is called for by a majority of citizens; and no satisfactory method is yet proposed by which the voice of the majority in this case may be determined, or its influence secured. ' The people of the respective counties are,' indeed, 'requested to signify their opinion respecting the adoption of the bill, to the next session of the Assembly.' But the representation must be made equal before the voice either of the representatives or of the counties will be that of the people. Our hope is that neither of the former will, after due consideration, espouse the dangerous principle of the bill. Should the event disappoint us, it will still leave us in full confidence that a fair appeal to the latter will reverse the sentence against our liberties.

" 15. Because, finally, ' The equal right of every citizen to the free exercise of his religion, according to the dictates of conscience,' is held by the same tenure with all our other rights. If we recur to its origin, it is equally the gift of nature; if we weigh its importance, it cannot be less dear to us; if we consult the declaration of those rights 'which pertain to the good people of Virginia as the basis and foundation of government,' it is enumerated with equal solemnity, or rather with studied emphasis. Either, then, we must say that the will of the Legislature is the only measure of their authority, and that in the plenitude of that authority they may sweep away all our fundamental rights, or that they are bound to leave this particular right untouched and sacred. Either we must say that they may control the freedom of the press, may abolish the trial by jury, may swallow up the executive and judiciary powers of the State; nay, that they may despoil us of our very rights of suffrage, and erect themselves into an independent and hereditary assembly, or we must say that they have no authority to enact into a law the bill under consideration.

"We, the subscribers, say that the General Assembly of this commonwealth have no such authority. And in order that no effort may be omitted on our part against so dangerous an usurpation, we oppose to it this remonstrance, earnestly praying, as we are in duty bound, that the Supreme Lawgiver of the universe, by illuminating those to whom it is addressed, may, on the one hand, turn their councils from every act which would affront his holy prerogative or violate the trust committed to them, and, on the other, guide them into every measure which may be worthy of his blessing, redound to their own praise, and establish more firmly the liberties, the prosperity, and the happiness of the commonwealth."—*Blakely's American State Papers*, *pp. 27–38; Two Republics, pp. 687–692.*

Washington being asked his opinion on the question as it stood in the contest, answered that "no man's sentiments were more opposed to any kind of restraint upon religious principles" than were his, and further said:—

"As the matter now stands, I wish an assessment had never been agitated; and, as it has gone so far, that the bill could die an easy death."—*Bancroft, Hist. Const., Vol. I, p. 215.*[1]

---

[1] The following passage from Wakeley's "Anecdotes of the Wesleys," is also worth recalling in this connection:—

"Martin Rodda was an English preacher in America during the war, and by incautiously meddling with politics exposed himself to the displeasure of those in power. At a certain time he was brought before General Washington, who asked who he was. Rodda told him he was one of John Wesley's preachers. 'Mr. Wesley,' rejoined his excellency, 'I respect; but Mr. Wesley, I presume, never sent you to America to interfere with political matters, but to preach the gospel to the people. Now go and mind your own proper work, and leave politics alone.'"—*Anecdote, Washington and Wesley, p. 119.*

The foregoing remonstrance was so thoroughly discussed and so well understood, and the will of the people on the subject was made so plain and emphatic, that "when the Legislature of Virginia assembled, *no person was willing to bring forward the Assessment Bill; and it was never heard of more.* Out of a hundred and seventeen articles of the revised code which were then reported, *Madison selected for immediate action* the one which related to religious freedom [on pages 90–93]. The people of Virginia had held it under deliberation for six years. In December, 1785, it passed the House by a vote of *nearly four to one.* Attempts in the Senate for amendment produced only insignificant changes in the preamble, and on *the 16th of January, 1786,* Virginia placed among its statutes *the very words of the original draft by Jefferson,* WITH THE HOPE THAT THEY WOULD ENDURE FOREVER: 'No man shall be compelled to frequent or support any religious worship, place, or ministry whatsoever, nor shall suffer on account of his religious opinions or belief; opinion in matters of religion shall in nowise diminish, enlarge, or affect civil capacities. The rights hereby asserted are of the natural rights of mankind.' "—*Id., 216.*

Of this blessed result Madison happily exclaimed:—

"Thus in Virginia was extinguished forever the ambitious hope of making laws for the human mind."—*Id.*

The effect of this notable contest in Virginia could not possibly be confined to that State; nor was such a thing desired by those who conducted it. It was understood and intended by those who then and there made this contest for religious right, that their labors should extend to all mankind this blessing and this natural right. The benefit of it was immediately felt throughout the country; and "in every other American State oppressive statutes concerning religion fell into disuse, and were gradually repealed."—*Id.* This statute of Virginia is the model upon which the clause respecting religious right has been founded in the constitutions of all the States in the Union to this day.   In every instance this statute has been embodied in its substance, and often in its very words, in the State constitutions.

Nor was this all.   It had also "been foreseen that 'the happy consequences of this grand experiment . . . would not be limited to America.'   The statute of Virginia, translated into French and into Italian, was widely circulated through Europe.   A part of the work of 'the noble army of martyrs' was done."—*Id. 217.*

Yet the work of those who accomplished this grand victory was not then fully done, even in their direct efforts relating to their and our own country.

As we have seen, this victory was completed January 16, 1786.   Just a month before this, December, 1785, the proposition made by Maryland to Virginia to call together commissioners from all the States to consider and "regulate restrictions on commerce for the whole" was laid before the very Legislature which passed the "Bill Establishing Religious Freedom in Virginia."   This proposition of Maryland, as we have seen (chapter 2) created the opening, which was instantly seized by Madison, through which to push to successful issue the desire for the creation of the nation by the forming of the Constitution of the United States.   And in pushing to successful issue the desire for the creation of a national power, there was carried along, also, and finally fixed in the Constitution of the United States, the same principle of religious right that had been so triumphantly fixed in the code of Virginia.

The sole reference to religion in the Constitution as formed by the convention, and submitted to the people, is in the declaration that—

"No religious test shall ever be required as a qualification to any office or public trust under the United States."

The national government being one of delegated powers only, no mention whatever of religion, nor any reference to the subject, in the Constitution, would have totally excluded that subject from the cognizance of the government. And this sole mention that was made of it, was a clear and positive evidence that the makers of the Constitution intended to exclude the subject of religion from the notice of the national power. So the people understood it when the Constitution was submitted to them for their approval. And the assurance of "the perfect liberty of conscience, prevented religious differences from interfering with zeal for a closer union."—*Bancroft, Hist. Const., Vol. II, p. 239.*

As we have seen, the contest for religious right in Virginia in 1785–86, had awakened a deep interest in the subject in the other States, and when the principle of this natural right had triumphed in Virginia, the effect of it was felt in every other State. And when the Constitution came before them with a clear recognition of the same principle, this was a feature immensely in its favor throughout the country.

After five States had ratified the Constitution, "the country from the St. Croix to the St Mary's now fixed its attention on Massachusetts, whose adverse decision would inevitably involve the defeat of the Constitution."—*Id., p. 258.* Massachusetts ratified the Constitution, and *in the doing of it* she considered this very question of religious right.

One member of the convention objected against the proposed Constitution that "there is no provision that men in power should have any religion; a Papist or an infidel is as eligible as Christians."

He was answered by three members, that "no conceivable advantage to the whole will result from a test."

Another objected that "it would be happy for the United States if our public men were to be of those who have a good standing in the church."

To this it was answered that "human tribunals for the consciences of men are impious encroachments upon the prerogatives of God. A religious test, as a qualification for office, would have been a great blemish."

Again it was objected that the absence of a religious test would "open the door to popery and the Inquisition."

And to this it was answered: " In reason and the Holy Scriptures, religion is ever a matter between God and individuals; and therefore no man or men can impose any religious test without invading the essential prerogative of the Lord Jesus Christ. Ministers first assumed this power under the Christian name; and then Constantine approved of the practice when he adopted the profession of Christianity as an engine of State policy. And let the history of all nations be searched from that day to this, and it will appear that the imposing of religious tests has been the greatest engine of tyranny in the world." —*Id., pp. 263, 271, and Blakely's American State Papers, p. 46; Two Republics, pp. 695–6.*

As the action of Massachusetts, by its example, made sure the adoption of the Constitution; and as this particular point of religious right was specially discussed in that convention; and was decided in favor of the Constitution as it stood with reference to that subject; it is certain from this fact alone, if there were no other, that it was the intent of the Constitution and the makers thereof totally to exclude religion in every way from the notice of the general government.

Yet this is not all. In the Virginia Convention objection was made that the Constitution did not fully enough secure religious right, to which Madison, "the Father of the Constitution," answered:—

"There is not a shadow of right in the general government to intermeddle with religion. Its least interference with it would be a most flagrant usurpation. I can appeal to my uniform conduct on this subject, that I have warmly supported religious freedom."—*Blakely's American State Papers, p. 44; Two Republics, p. 695.*

Nor yet was this all.   By the people of the United States this was not deemed sufficient.   Knowing the inevitable tendency of men in power to fall in love with power, and to give *themselves* credit for inherent possession of it, and so to assert power that in nowise belongs to them—knowing this, the people of the United States were not satisfied with the silence of the national charter, nor yet with this clear evidence of intention to exclude religion from the notice of the national power; they demanded positive provisions which should, in so many words, prohibit the government of the United States from touching religion.   They required that there should be added to the Constitution, articles of the nature of a Bill of Rights; and that religious right should in this be specifically declared. A letter of Jefferson's dated Paris, February 2, 1788, tells the whole story as to this point; it is therefore here presented:—

"DEAR SIR: I am glad to learn by letters which come down to the 20th of December, that the new Constitution will undoubtedly be received by a sufficiency of the States to set it a-going.   Were I in America, I would advocate it warmly till nine should have adopted, and then as warmly take the other side to convince the remaining four that they ought not to come into it till the declaration of rights is annexed to it; by this means we should secure all the good of it, and procure as respectable an opposition as would induce the accepting States to offer a bill of rights; this would be the happiest turn the thing could take.   I fear much the effects of the perpetual reëligibility of the President, but it is not thought of in America, and have, therefore, no prospect of a change of that article; but I own it astonishes me to find such a change wrought in the opinions of our countrymen since I left them, as that three-fourths of them should be contented to live under a system which leaves to their governors the power of taking from them the *trial by jury* in civil cases, FREEDOM OF RELIGION, *freedom of the press*, freedom of commerce, the habeas corpus laws, and of yoking them with a standing army.   That is a degeneracy in the principles of liberty to which I had given four centuries instead of four years, but I hope it will all come about."—*Bancroft, Hist. Con., Vol. II, pp. 459, 460.*

To see how fully this letter stated the case, it is necessary only to read the first ten amendments to the Constitution. These ten amendments were the bill of rights which the people required to be added to the Constitution as it was originally framed.   The first Congress under the Constitution met March 4, 1789, and in September of the same year, these ten amendments were adopted.   And in the very first of these provisions stands the declaration of the freedom of religious right under the United States Government.   Thus it reads:—

"Congress shall make no law respecting an establishment of religion or prohibiting the free exercise thereof."

Thus the people of the United States, in their own capacity as such, made the supreme law of the land positively and explicitly to declare the total exclusion of religion from any consideration whatever on the part of the national government.

Nor was the matter permitted to stand even thus on that question; for in 1797 the treaty with Tripoli was made and signed by President Washington, and approved by the Senate of the United States, in which it is declared that—

"The government of the United States is not in any sense founded upon the Christian religion."

This being a material part of a treaty "made under the authority of the United States," it thus became a material part of "the supreme law of the land."—*Article VI of the Constitution, par. 2.*

Such is the history, such the establishment, and such *the perfect supremacy* of religious right in the United States. Thus, for the people of the United States and for the world, "religion was become avowedly *the attribute of man* and *not* of a *corporation.*"—*Bancroft, Hist. Con., Vol. II, p. 325.*

CHAPTER VI.

RELIGIOUS RIGHT INVADED.

ALTHOUGH religious right was so carefully, so explicitly, and so completely, excluded from the cognizance of the national government by the people when that government was made, yet it is a fact that the national government, in all its branches, has directly and explicitly assumed cognizance of religion, instead of allowing religion to remain as the fathers and the Constitution left it—"avowedly the attribute of man, and not of a corporation." The government of the United States has once more made it avowedly the attribute of *a corporation* and *not of man.* Instead of maintaining the "new order of things" to which by its great seal the nation stands pledged, the government of the United States has gone back to the old order of things which it was the purpose of our governmental fathers to escape. In other words, and in short, there has been wrought a counter-revolution.

This counter-revolution was accomplished in A. D. 1892. It began, and *in principle* was consummated, in the Supreme Court of the United States in a decision rendered February 29, 1892.

The said decision came forth in this way:[1] In 1887 Congress enacted a law forbidding any alien to come to this country under contract to perform labor or service of any kind. The reason of that law was that large contractors and corporations

---

[1] See the decision in full at end of this book, Appendix C.

in the United States would send agents to Europe to employ the lowest of the people whom they could get to come over and work. They would pay their expenses to this country, and, because of this, require them to work at so much the smaller wages after they arrived. This was depreciating the price that Americans should receive for their labor, and therefore Congress enacted a law as follows:—

"*Be it enacted by the Senate and House of Representatives of the United States of America in Congress assembled,* That from and after the passage of this act it shall be unlawful for any person, company, partnership, or corporation, in any manner whatsoever to prepay the transportation, or in any way assist or encourage the importation or migration of any alien or aliens, any foreigner or foreigners, into the United States, its Territories, or the District of Columbia, under contract or agreement, parol or special, expressed or implied, made previous to the importation or migration of such alien or aliens, foreigner or foreigners, to perform labor or service of any kind in the United States, its Territories, or the District of Columbia."

Trinity Church corporation, in New York City, employed a preacher in England to come over here and preach for them. They contracted with him before he came. He was an alien, and came under contract to perform service for that church. The United States District Attorney entered suit against the church for violating this law. The United States Circuit Court decided that the church was guilty, and rendered judgment accordingly. An appeal was taken to the Supreme Court of the United States, upon writ of error.

The Supreme Court reversed the decision, *first* upon the correct and well-established principle that "the intent of the lawmaker is the law." The court quoted directly from the reports of the Senate Committee and the House Committee who had the bill in charge when it was put through Congress; and these both said in express terms that the term "laborer," or "labor or service," used in the statute, was intended to mean only *manual* labor or service, and not *professional* service of any kind. For instance, the Senate Committee said:—

"The committee report the bill back without amendment, although there are certain features thereof which might well be changed or modified, in the hope that the bill may not fail of passage during the present session. Especially would the committee have otherwise recommended amendments, substituting for the expression 'labor and service,' whenever it occurs in the body of the bill, the words 'manual labor' or 'manual service,' as sufficiently broad to accomplish the purposes of the bill, and that such amendments would remove objections which a sharp and perhaps unfriendly criticism may urge to the proposed legislation. The committee, however, believing that the bill in its present form will be construed as including only those whose labor or service is manual in character, and being very desirous that the bill become a law before the adjournment, have reported the bill without change."—*6059 Congressional Record, 48th Congress.*

Such being the plainly declared intent of the law, by those who made it, and at the time of the making of it, there was nothing left for the Supreme Court to do but to give effect to the law as it was intended, by reversing the decision of the court below. And in all reason, when the court had thus made plain the intent of the law, this was all that was necessary to the decision of the case.

But instead of stopping with this that was all-sufficient, the court took up a line of reasoning(?) by which it would reach the same point from another direction, and then, as the result of each and of both, decided what the true intent of the law was, and reversed the decision of the lower court accordingly. And never were the aptness and wisdom of that piece of advice which Abraham Lincoln once gave to a friend, "Never say what you *need* not, lest you be obliged to prove what you *cannot*," more completely illustrated than in this unnecessary line of argument which was pursued by the Supreme Court of the United States in this decision of February 29, 1892.

The court unanimously declared that "this is a religious people," "a religious nation," and even "a *Christian* nation," and that such is "the voice of the entire people." In support of these declarations the court offered considerable argument, which will be noticed presently. But the first thing to be noted is that, whether the court supported the declarations with considerable argument or with none at all, *it had no shadow of right to make any such declarations.*

By the whole history of the making of the Constitution, by its spirit, and by its very letter, the government of the United States, and, therefore, the Supreme Court as a coördinate branch of the government, is precluded from declaring or arguing in favor of the Christian religion, or any religion whatever. Let it not be forgotten that James Madison, in persuading the Virginia convention to ratify the Constitution, gave the assurance that "there is not a shadow of right in the general government to intermeddle with religion. Its least interference with it would be a most flagrant usurpation."[2] Whereas it is certain that in the declarations set forth, in the argument conducted, in the citations made, and in the conclusion reached, in this decision, the Supreme Court did "intermeddle with religion," and in so doing did that which it had "not a shadow of right" to do.

The first words of the court in this line are as follows:—

" But beyond all these matters no purpose of action against religion can be imputed to any legislation, State or national, because this is a religious people. This is historically true. From the discovery of this continent to the present hour there is a single voice making this affirmation."

Every citizen of the United States knows that it is *not* true, either historically or otherwise, that this is a religious people. Not even a majority of the people are religious. There is not

---

[2] Page 106 of this book.

a single city in the United States in which the people are
religious—no, not a single town or village.

That is to say, this was so up to the time of the rendering
of this decision, February 29, 1892. Since that of course the
people are religious, because the Supreme Court says so. To
be sure, some of our neighbors, and many other people whom
we meet, do not know that they are religious people, as they
have never chosen to be so, and do not profess it at all; but
all that makes no difference. The Supreme Court of the
United States has, by unanimous decision, declared that they
are religious people, and it must be so whether they know it
or not.

Nor is this all. The court not only declares that this is a
'*religious* nation," but that it is a "*Christian* nation." The
people, therefore, are not only religious but they are Christians—yes, Jews, infidels, and all. For is not the Supreme
Court the highest judicial authority in the United States? and
what this court declares to be the law, is not that the law? and
when this court lays it down as the supreme law—as the meaning of the Constitution—that the people are religious, and are
Christians, then does not that settle the question?—Not at all.
The very absurdity of the suggestion only demonstrates that
the court can have nothing at all to do with any such matters,
and shows how completely the court transcended its powers
and went out of the right way. No; men are not made religious by law, nor by judicial decision, nor by historical precedents.

The statement that "from the discovery of this continent
to the present hour there is a single voice," making the affirmation that this nation is a religious people, is equally wide of
the mark, for at the time of the making of this national government there was a new, fresh voice heard contradicting the
long, dismal monotone of the ages, and declaring for this new
nation that it "is not *in any sense* founded upon the Christian

religion," and that it can never of right have anything to do
with religion—that it has "not a shadow of right to intermeddle with religion," and that "its least interference with it
would be a most flagrant usurpation." And this voice it was
which gave rise to the "new order of things" for this country
and for the world. Let the reader think for only a moment
of the history presented in the preceding chapter, and then
explain, if he can, how the court could make such a statement
as this which we have quoted and commented upon—remem-
bering at the same time, too, that "every case is discussed by
the whole body [of the court] twice over—once to ascertain
the opinion of the majority, which is then directed to be set
forth in a written judgment; then again, when that written
judgment, which one of the judges has prepared, is submitted
for criticism and adoption as the judgment of the court."—
Bryce, American Commonwealth, chap. 22, par. 4.

THE ARGUMENT FROM EUROPEAN NATIONS.

After this deliverance the court proceeds to cite historical
evidences to prove the proposition that this is a "religious
people" and a "Christian nation." The first is as follows:—

"The commission to Christopher Columbus, prior to his sail westward, is from 'Ferdinand and Isabella, by the grace of God, king and
queen of Castile,' etc., and recites that 'it is hoped that by God's
assistance some of the continents and islands in the ocean will be
discovered,' etc."

What religion did Ferdinand and Isabella have in mind
when they issued that document? What religion did they
profess? And what religion did they *possess*, too?—The
Catholic religion, to be sure. And not only that, it was the
Catholic religion with the Inquisition in full swing; for it was
Ferdinand and Isabella who established the Inquisition in Spain
under the generalship of Torquemada, and who, because Spain
was a "Christian nation," sentenced to confiscation of all goods

and to banishment every Jew who would not turn Catholic. And by virtue of such religious activity as this Ferdinand and Isabella fairly earned as an everlasting reward, and by·way of preëminence, the title of ''THE CATHOLICS.'' And this is the first piece of ''historical'' authority by which the Supreme Court of the United States adjudges American citizens ''to be a religious people,'' and by which that court decides that this is a ''Christian nation.''

Now that is quoted to prove that this is a ''religious people'' and a ''Christian nation,'' and it is declared that this language of Ferdinand and Isabella, and the language of the Constitution of the United States, ''have one meaning.''

Then, in view of that quotation and this decision, should it be wondered at if the Catholic Church should claim that this is so indeed, and should demand favors from the government as such? Everybody knows that the Catholic Church already is not slow to take part in political questions, to interfere with the govern-· ment, and to have the government recognize the Catholic Church and give it every year from the public treasury nearly $400,000 of the money of all the people. The people know that this is already the case. And now when this Catholic document is cited by the Supreme Court to prove this a Christian nation; and when that court declares that this document and the Constitution have one meaning, should it be thought strange if the Catholic Church should claim that that is correct, and act upon it.

However, it is not denominational or sectarian Christianity that the court proposes to recognize as the national religion here, but, as was attempted in Virginia, simply ''Christianity, general Christianty.'' Accordingly, British documents are next quoted which designate the ''true Christian faith'' as professed in the Church of England in colonial times. And here is the quotation:—

---

[3] This sentence was inflicted, too, *after* the commission to Christopher Columbus under which he discovered this ''Christian nation.''

8

"The first colonial grant, that made to Sir Walter Raleigh in 1584, was from ' Elizabeth, by the grace of God; of England, Fraunce, and Ireland, queene, Defender of the Faith,' etc.; and the grant authorized him to enact statutes for the government of the proposed Colony; *Provided*, That ' they be not against the true Christian faith now professed in the Church of England.' . . . Language of a similar import may be found in the subsequent charters, . . . and the same is true of the various charters granted to other colonies. In language more or less emphatic, is the establishment of the Christian religion declared to be one of the purposes of the grant." [4]

It is true that the "establishment of the Christian religion was one of the purposes" of all these grants. But are the American people still bound by the purposes and intentions of Queen Elizabeth and her British successors? Does Britain still rule America, that the intent and purposes of British sovereigns shall be held binding upon the American people?—Nay, nay. After all these documents were issued there was the American Revolution and the Declaration of Independence, by which it was both declared and demonstrated that these Colonies are and of right ought to be free and independent States—free and independent of British rule, and the intents and purposes of British sovereigns in all things, religious as well as civil. And then after that the national Constitution was formed, expressly repudiating "establishments of the Christian religion."

It is true that the "establishment of the Christian religion was one of the purposes" of these grants. But shall the Constitution of the United States count for nothing, when it positively prohibits any religious test, and any establishment of religion of any kind? Shall the supreme law of this nation count for nothing in its solemn declaration that " the government of the

---

[4] It may very properly be noted here, in passing, that this and the previous quotation just as certainly prove the divine right of rulers in this country, as they prove that this is "a religious people" or "a Chrisian nation." And this is the logic of the discussion, too; for it is plainly declared that these documents and the Constitution have all one languge and "one meaning."

United States is not in any sense founded on the Christian religion"? Has the Supreme Court of the United States the right to supplant the supreme law of this land with the intents and purposes of the sovereigns of England? Is the Supreme Court of the United States the interpreter of the supreme law of the United States? or is it the interpreter of the intents and purposes of the sovereigns of England, France, and Ireland, "Defenders of the Faith"?

It is true that "the establishment of the Christian religion was one of the purposes" of these grants, and that purpose was accomplished in the Colonies settled under those grants. But, though all this be true, what possible bearing can that rightly have on any question under the Constitution and laws of the national government? The national system was not intended to be a continuation of the colonial system; on the contrary, it was intended to be distinct from both the colonial and State systems. And the chief, the very fundamental, distinction that the national system was intended to have from both the others, was in its complete separation from every idea of an establishment of religion.

And though it be true that all the Colonies except Rhode Island had establishments of "the Christian religion" in pursuance of the purpose of these British grants; and though all the States except Rhode Island and Virginia had these same establishments of "the Christian religion" when the national system was organized; yet this had no bearing whatever upon the national system except to make all the more emphatic its total separation from them all, and from every conception of an establishment of "the Christian religion."

Let us reduce to a short argument this reasoning of the court. The proposition to be proved is, "This is a Christian nation." The principal statement is, "The establishment of the Christian religion was one of the purposes" of the British grants here. We have then these two statements of the court.

But this is not enough; we must know how the conclusion is derived from the principal statement.

So far the argument stands merely thus:—

(*a*) "The establishment of the Christian religion was one of the purposes of the British grants in America."

(*b*) Consequently, "this is a Christian nation."

But this will never do; there is a destructive hiatus between the antecedent and the consequent. This blank must be filled, or else there is a total absence of reasoning, and the conclusion is nothing. With what, then, shall this blank be filled? It could be filled thus:—

(*a*) "The establishment of the Christian religion was one of the purposes of the British grants in America."

(*b*) America is subject to British sovereignty.

(*c*) Consequently, "this is a Christian nation."

This would complete the formula, would give the conclusion something to rest upon, and would connect it with the chief statement. But the difficulty with it is that it is not true. It is not only contrary to the history and the experience of the nations concerned, but it is contrary to the argument of the court itself; for the court, in its argument, does recognize and name the Declaration of Independence and the national Constitution. This thought, then, is not allowable in the argument.

What thought, then, will fit the place and make the argument complete? There is one, and only one, possible thought that can fit the place and make the connection between the court's principal statement and its conclusion. That thought is given by the court itself as the turning point, and is indeed the pivot—the very crucial test—of the whole argument presented by the court. Here is the argument complete:—

(*a*) "The establishment of the Christian religion is declared to be one of the purposes of the [British] grants [in America]."

(*b*) This declaration and the national Constitution have one language and "one meaning." [5]

(*c*) Consequently, "this is a Christian nation."

This and this alone is the course of reasoning by which the court reaches its conclusion that "this ·is a Christian nation." This is the thought, and, indeed, those are the words, of the court. The thing is accomplished solely by making the language of the Constitution bear "one meaning" with these quoted declarations, whose purpose was plainly "the establishment of the Christian religion."

But some may say, This formula encounters the same difficulty as did the other one, viz., it is not true, and is contrary to all the history and experience of the nation in the times of the making of the Constitution. It is true, as the preceding chapters of this book plainly show, that the connecting statement between the premise and the conclusion in this latter formula is, *in itself*, as false as is that one in the former. It is true that the Constitution was never intended to bear any such meaning as is here given to it in harmony with the declarations quoted. It was both intended and declared to bear a meaning directly the opposite of that which these declarations bear. And if any other person, persons, or tribunal, on earth (except all the people) had said that such is the meaning of the Constitution, it would have amounted to nothing. Such a statement made by the Supreme Court, however, does amount to something. And—

HERE IS THE DECISIVE POINT.

The Supreme Court of the United States is constitutionally authorized to interpret and declare the meaning of the Consti-

---

[5] Immediately after quoting the First Amendment to the Constitution, along with all these others, the court's words are these:—

"There is no dissonance in these declarations.(! !) There is a universal language pervading them all, having one meaning.(! ! !) They affirm and reaffim that this is a religious nation."

tution.   Whatever the Supreme Court says the meaning of the
Constitution is, that is legally its meaning so long as said decision stands.   The meaning which the court gives to the Constitution may be utterly false, as in the Dred Scott decision
and in this one, but that matters nothing; the false meaning
stands as firmly as though it were true, until the decision is
reversed either by the Supreme Court itself, or by *the higher
court*—the people—as was done in the matter of the Dred
Scott decision, of which this decision now under consideration
is a complete parallel.

Such, then, is indisputably the meaning which the Supreme
Court of the United States has given to the Constitution of the
United States—a meaning the purpose of which is "the establishment of the Christian religion." This is a meaning which,
by every particle of evidence derivable from the makers and
the making of the Constitution, is demonstrated to be directly
the reverse of that which it was intended to bear and which it
did bear while the makers of it lived.   Therefore, as certainly
as logic is logic and truth is truth, it is demonstrated that in
this decision the Supreme Court of the United States has subverted the Constitution of the United States in its essential
meaning as regards the Christian religion or the establishment thereof.

Nor was the court content with a little.   These declarations
of Ferdinand and Isabella, Elizabeth, James I., *et al.*, were not
sufficient to satisfy the zeal of the court in behalf of "Christianity, general Christianity," as the established and national
religion here; but it must needs heap upon these *fifteen* more,
from different sources, to the same purpose.   Having extracted
the real substance of the court's argument throughout, in the
foregoing analysis, it will not be necessary for us to apply the
set formula to each citation in all the long list.   This the reader
can readily enough do in his own mind.   We shall, however,
present all of the court's quotations and its application of them,
with such further remarks as may be pertinent.

FROM COLONIAL CHARTERS.

Next following the citations from Ferdinand and Isabella, Elizabeth, and the others of Britain, the court sets forth documents of the New England Puritans which also plainly declare that "the establishment of the Christian religion was one of the purposes" of their settlement in the land. Here is the language of the court and of the Puritans:—

"The celebrated compact made by the Pilgrims in the *Mayflower*, 1620, recites: 'Having undertaken for the glory of God and advancement of the Christian faith, and the honor of our king and country, a voyage to plant the first Colony in the northern parts of Virginia; Do by these Presents, solemnly and mutually, in the presence of God and one another, covenant and combine ourselves together into a civil Body Politick, for our better ordering and preservation and furtherance of the ends aforesaid.'

"The fundamental orders of Connecticut, under which a provisional government was instituted in 1638–1639, commence with this declaration:—

"'Forasmuch as it hath pleased the Almighty God by the wise dispensation of his diuyne pruidence so to order and dispose of things that we, the inhabitants and residents of Windsor, Hartford, and Wethersfield are now cohabiting and dwelling in and upon the River Conectecotte and the lands thereunto adioyneing; and well knowing where a people are gathered together the word of God requires that to mayntayne the peace and vnion of such a people there should be an orderly and decent government established according to God, to order and dispose of the affayres of the people at all seasons as occasion shall require; doe therefore assotiate and conioyne ourselves to be as one publike State or Comonwelth; and doe, for ourselves and our successors and such as shall be adioyned to vs att any tyme hereafter, enter into combination and confederation togather, to mayntayne and presearue the liberty and purity of the gospell of our Lord Jesus wch we now prfesse, as also the disciplyne of the churches, wch according to the truth of the said gospell is now practised amongst us.'"

It is worthy of remark in this connection, that by this "historical" citation, the Supreme Court just as certainly justifies the employment of the "civil body politick" for the maintenance of the "disciplyne of the churches," as by this and the previous ones it establishes the Christian religion as the religion of this nation.   For it was just as much and as directly the intention of those people to maintain the discipline of the churches, as it was to "preserve the liberty and purity of the gospel then practiced" among them.   Indeed, it was only by maintaining the discipline of the churches that they expected to preserve "the liberty and purity of the gospell" as there and then practiced.   All their history shows that they never thought, nor made any pretensions, of doing it in any other way. And, in fact, order number four of these very "fundamental orders" required that the governor of that "publike State or Comonwelth" should "be always a member of some approved congregation," and should take an oath that he would "further the execution of justice according to the rule of God's word; so help me God in the name of the Lord Jesus Christ."

We know, and it can be abundantly shown, that the maintenance of the discipline of the churches by the power of "the civil Body Politick" is precisely what the churches of the United States are aiming at, and is what they design to accomplish through the enforcement of national Sunday laws.   This is what is done always in the enforcement of Sunday laws, whether State or national.   And all this purpose, the Supreme Court fully sanctions and justifies in its (mis)interpretation of the national Constitution, when it declares that the language of these "fundamental orders of Connecticut" and the language of the national Constitution is "one language," "having one meaning."

The court proceeds:—

"In the charter of privileges granted by William Penn to the province of Pennsylvania, in 1701, it is recited: 'Because no People can be truly happy, though under the greatest Enjoyment of Civil Liberties, if abridged of the Freedom of their Consciences, as to their Religious

Profession and Worship; And Almighty God being the only Lord of Conscience, Father of Lights and Spirits; and the Author as well as Object of all divine Knowledge, Faith, and Worship, who only doth enlighten the Minds, and persuade and convince the Understandings of People, I do hereby grant and declare,' etc.''

Yes, and the same document provided that in order to ''be capable to serve the government in any capacity'' a person must ''also profess to believe in Jesus Christ, the Saviour of the world.'' And according to the same document, in order to be assured that ''he should in no ways be molested,'' etc., a person living in that province was required to ''confess and acknowledge the only Almighty and Eternal God to be Creator, Upholder, and Ruler of the world.''

FROM THE DECLARATION OF INDEPENDENCE.

Still citing proof that this is a Christian nation, the court continues in the following queer-fashion:—

''Coming nearer to the present time, the Declaration of Independence recognizes the presence of the Divine in human affairs in these words: 'We hold these truths to be self-evident, that all men are created equal, that they are endowed by their Creator with certain unalienable Rights, that among these are Life, Liberty, and the pursuit of Happiness.' 'We, therefore, the Representatives of the United States of America, in General Congress Assembled, appealing to the Supreme Judge of the world for the rectitude of our intentions, do, in the Name and by Authority of the good People of these Colonies, solemnly publish and declare,' etc. 'And for the support of this Declaration, with a firm reliance on Divine Providence, we mutually pledge to each other our Lives, our Fortunes, and our sacred Honor.' ''

It is undoubtedly true that the Declaration of Independence does recognize the presence of the divine in human affairs. But it is a hazardous piece of logic to conclude from this that ''this is a Christian nation.'' For what nation has there ever been on earth that did not recognize the presence of the divine in human affairs? But it would be rather risky to conclude from this that all nations have been and are "Christian nations."

But, it may be said, the Declaration recognizes the "Creator," and "the Supreme Judge of the world," as well as "Divine Providence." Yes, that is true, too. And so do the Turks, the Arabs, the Hindoos, and others; but that would hardly justify the Supreme Court or anybody else in concluding and officially declaring that Turkey, Arabia, and Hindoostan, are Christian nations.

But it may still be said that those who made this Declaration used these expressions with none other than the God of Christianity in mind. This may or may not be true, according to the way of thinking of the respective individuals who signed or espoused the Declaration.[6] But whatever these expressions may have meant to those who used them at the time, it is certain that they did not mean what the Supreme Court has here made them mean. Of this we have the most positive evidence.

Thomas Jefferson was the author of the Declaration of Independence, and from that day and forward he exerted all his powers to *dis*establish "the true Christian faith professed in the Church of England," which, according to the purpose of Elizabeth and her successors, had been established in Virginia for more than a hundred and fifty years. When this was accomplished, and an attempt was made to establish "Christianity, general Christianity," under the title of "the Christian religion," Jefferson again enlisted all his powers to defeat the attempt, and it was defeated. And to the day of his death, the one thing in all his career upon which he looked with the most satisfaction was this disestablishment of "the Christian reli-

---

[6] Thomas Paine, though not a signer of the Declaration, had no small part in bringing it about, and it is certain that he did most heartily support it. And it is evident. enough that he did not use these terms with reference to Christianity, nor with the intention to establish a "Christian nation" here. Ethan Allen, the Green Mountain hero was another, and there were thousands of others.

gion" in Virginia. And now, lo! this document of which Jefferson was the author is quoted by the Supreme Court of the United States, and classed with documents "one of the purposes" of which was "the establishment of the Christian religion;" and, as having "one meaning" with these, is used to prove a proposition with reference to this nation which Jefferson spent all his powers and the best part of his life in combating. What would Jefferson himself say to this use of his language were he here to read this decision? [7]

Except in the matter of the Dred Scott decision, a more perverse use of the language of the Declaration of Independence certainly never was made than is thus made in this "Christian nation" decision, February 29, 1892.

FROM THE STATES.

Next the court says:—

"If we examine the constitutions of the various States, we find in them a constant recognition of religious obligations. Every constitution of every one of the forty-four States contains language which either directly or by clear implication recognizes a profound reverence for religion and an assumption that its influence in all human affairs is essential to the well-being of the community."

This is all true enough in itself; but even though it be true respecting all the States, that can have no bearing whatever in any matter respecting the nation or the national jurisdiction or the consideration of any national question. The Constitution declares that—

"The powers not delegated to the United States by the Constitution, nor prohibited by it to the States, are reserved to the States respectively, or to the people."

When the nation was made, eleven of the States had established religions, the most of them had slavery, and these institutions were reserved to the control of the States themselves.

---

[7] Pages 90, 92 of this book.

This is one reason why the tenth amendment was made to read as it does. These matters belonged, and were left, to the jurisdiction of the States, and with them the national government could have nothing at all to do. And so it continued until the adoption of the fourteenth amendment, by which the control as to both slavery and established religions was prohibited to the States by the national Constitution. So that, admitting the assumption of the court that the States still have control of religion as at the beginning, the court's conclusion does not follow; because then the true argument is this: No power in, over, or concerning religion has been delegated to the United States—the nation—by the Constitution, nor has such power been prohibited by it to the States. All power and jurisdiction, therefore, in all questions and all matters of whatever kind concerning religion, are reserved and belong exclusively to the States or to the people.

But since the fourteenth amendment, this assumption even is entirely baseless. See further on this point in chapter 13.

More than this: As all power respecting religion has *actually been prohibited to the United States by the Constitution*, even though all the forty-four States had one and the same religion, and that specifically and by law established, this would mean absolutely nothing, and could never rightly be made to mean anything, to the United States, *i. e.*, to the nation. The Supreme Court of *the nation* has no right to cite religious characteristics of the *States*, and then from these draw conclusions and make official declarations that the *nation* is "religious" or "Christian" or anything else in the way of religion. This is why Madison said that "there is not a shadow of right in the general government to intermeddle with religion." And this is why he also declared that the "least interference" of the general government with religion "would be a most flagrant usurpation." This because in so doing it would be intruding into a field, and entering upon the consideration of that which is not only reserved but positively prohibited, both to the nation and to the States.[8]

As no power in matters of religion has been delegated to the nation, but, on the contrary, all such power has been positively prohibited to the nation, and also to the States, so the Supreme Court of the nation was trebly precluded from drawing from the example of the States anything on the subject of religion, and was also trebly precluded from ever making any such declaration as that "this is a Christian nation." Since the fourteenth amendment the matter of religion as respects both States and nation belongs exclusively to the people.

It is worth while, however, to give the citations which the court makes from the State constitutions, that the use which the court makes of the national Constitution in connection therewith may be clearly seen. So here they are exactly as the court sets them forth:—

"This recognition may be in the preamble, such as is found in the Constitution of Illinois, 1870: 'We, the people of the State of Illinois, *grateful to Almighty God* for the civil, political, and religious liberty which he hath so long permitted us to enjoy, and *looking to him for a blessing* upon our endeavors to secure and transmit the same unimpaired to succeeding generations,' etc.

"It may be only in the familiar requisition that all officers shall take an oath closing with the declaration '*so help me God.*' It may be in clauses like that of the constitution of Indiana, 1816, Article XI, section 4: 'The manner of administering an oath or affirmation shall be such as is most consistent with the conscience of the deponent, and shall be esteemed the most solemn *appeal to God.*' Or in provisions such as are found in Articles XXXVI and XXXVII of the Declaration of Rights of the Constitution of Maryland, 1867: 'That as it is *the duty of every man to worship God* in such manner as he thinks most acceptable to him, all persons are equally entitled to protection in their religious liberty; wherefore, no person ought, by any law, to be molested in his person or estate on account of his religious persuasion or profession, or for his religious practice, *unless, under the color of religion,* he shall dis-

---

[8] Look again at chapter 3, "What Is the Nation?"

turb the good *order, peace, or safety of the State*, or shall infringe *the laws of morality*, or injure others in their natural, *civil, or religious rights;* nor ought any person to be compelled to frequent or maintain or contribute, unless on contract, to maintain any place of worship, or any ministry; nor shall any person, otherwise competent, be deemed incompetent as a witness, or juror, on account of his religious belief: *Provided*, He *believes in the existence of God,* and that, *under his dispensation*, such person will be held morally accountable for his acts, and be rewarded or punished therefor, either in this world or the world to come. That no religious test ought ever to be required as a qualification for any office of profit or trust in this State, *other than a declaration of belief in the existence of God;* nor shall the Legislature prescribe *any other oath* of office than the oath prescribed by this Constitution.' Or like that in Articles II and III, of Part Ist, of the Constitution of *Massachusetts*, 1780: 'It is the right as well as *the duty* of all men in society publicly and at stated seasons, *to worship the Supreme Being, the Great Creator and Preserver of the universe.* . . . *As the happiness of a people* and the good *order* and *preservation of civil government* essentially depend upon *piety, religion,* and *morality*, and as these cannot be generally diffused through a community *but by the institution of the public worship of God* and *of public instructions in piety, religion*, and *morality;* Therefore, to promote their happiness and to secure the good order and preservation of their government, the people of this commonwealth have a right to *invest their Legislature with power to authorize and require*, and *the Legislature shall,* from time to time, *authorize and require*, the several *towns, parishes, precincts*, and other *bodies-politic* or religious societies to *make suitable provisions*, at their own expense, *for the institution of the public worship of God* and *for the support and maintenance of public Protestant* teachers of piety, religion, and morality in all cases where such provision shall not be made voluntarily.' Or, as in sections 5 and 14 of Article VII of the Constitution of Mississippi, 1832: '*No person who denies the being of a God*, or a future state of rewards and punishments, *shall hold any office in the civil department of this State.* . . . Religion, morality, and knowledge being necessary to good government, the preservation of liberty, and the happiness of mankind, schools, and the means of education, shall forever be encouraged in this State.' Or by Article XXII of the Constitution of Delaware, 1776, which required all officers, besides an oath of allegiance, to make and subscribe the following declaration: 'I, A. B., *do profess faith in God the Father, and in Jesus Christ his only Son, and in the Holy Ghost, one God, blessed forever more;* and I do acknowledge *the Holy Scriptures of the Old and New Testament to be given by divine inspiration.*' "

And the doctrine that is held all through the decision, that these things and the Constitution speak the same language and have one meaning, is just at this point emphasized in the following words:—

"*Even the Constitution of the United States,* which is supposed to have little touch upon the private life of the individual, *contains* in the first amendment *a declaration common to the constitutions of all the States,* as follows: 'Congress shall make no law respecting an establishment of religion, or prohibiting the free exercise thereof.' And also provides that the executive shall have ten days (Sundays excepted), within which to determine whether he will approve or veto a bill. [Here is a sly indication that the enforcement of Sunday observance is constitutional.]

"*There is no dissonance in these declarations.* There is a *universal language* pervading *them all, having one meaning;* they affirm and reaffirm that this is a religious nation. These are not individual sayings, declarations of private persons; they are *organic utterances; they speak the voice of the entire people.*"

According to this interpretation, then, when the Constitution of the United States declares that "no religious test *shall* ever be required as a qualification to any office or public trust under the United States," it *means* that "no religious test *ought* ever to be required . . . *other than a belief in the existence of God,*" and of "a future state of rewards and punishments," and a profession of "faith in God the Father, and in Jesus Christ his only Son, and in the Holy Ghost, one God, blessed forevermore; and I do acknowledge the Holy Scriptures of the Old and New Testament to be given by divine inspiration." (!!) For this is what the Constitutions of Maryland, Mississippi, and Delaware plainly mean; and these and the Constitution of the United States are pervaded by a " universal language," "having one meaning." (!!!)

And when the Constitution of the United States declares that "Congress shall make no law respecting an establishment of religion," it *means* that the Congress "shall, from time to time, authorize and require the several towns, parishes, precincts, and other bodies politic, or religious societies, to make suitable provisions, at their own expense, for the institution of the public worship of God, and for the support and maintenance of public Protestant teachers of piety, religion, and morality, in all cases where such provisions shall not be made voluntarily."!! For plainly that is what the Constitution of Massachusetts means, and behold that and the Constitution of the United States are pervaded by "a universal language" "having one meaning." (!!!)

How the court could present such a string of quotations, every one of which distinctly contemplated an establishment of religion and the prohibition of the free exercise thereof, and then quote this clause of the national Constitution, which in every feature and every intent absolutely prohibits any establishment of religion, and any interference with the free exercise thereof—how the court could do all this and then declare that "there is no dissonance" in the declarations, that they all have the same language and "one meaning," is a most astonishing thing. If such a thing had been done by any of the "common run" of American citizens, it could have been considered as nothing less than wildly absurd; but coming as it does from such a source as the Supreme Court of the whole nation, it is as far worse as could be possible. To say that it is absurd is not enough, it is simply preposterous. And yet, preposterous as it is, it is expected to, and, so far as the great mass of the people are concerned, it undoubtedly will, carry with it all the weight of supreme national law.

All this is bad enough, and preposterous enough, in itself; but there is another consideration that even magnifies it, that is, the leaving out, the complete ignoring, of all of the history and all the essential facts which are pertinent to the question. Why should the court leave out Jefferson, Madison, and Washington from the place where they only and wholly belong, and drag Ferdinand, Isabella, and Elizabeth into the place where they do not and cannot by any shadow of right belong? Why should Jefferson, Madison, and Washington not only be allowed no place by the court, but be compelled by the court to give place to Ferdinand, Isabella, and Elizabeth?

Why should the purposes of Jefferson, Madison, and Washington, and the other fathers who made this nation, be completely ignored, and the purposes of Ferdinand, Isabella, Elizabeth, and the Puritans be taken up and exalted to their place? Why should all the history of the making of the national Constitution be ignored as completely as though there were no such history, and all this other stuff be taken up and discussed and approved as though this were the only historical evidence there is on the subject?

Why should the national Constitution be interpreted and construed according to the purposes of Ferdinand, Isabella, Elizabeth and her successors, the Puritans, and the constitutions of the States, instead of the purposes of Jefferson, Madison, Washington, and the other fathers who made it? Why should the real meaning which our fathers gave to the Constitution be supplanted with a meaning that is as foreign to it as the sovereigns of Spain and England are foreign to the nation itself to-day? Why should the only history that is pertinent to the question be wholly ignored, and that which in every element is absolutely impertinent be exalted and honored in its stead?[9]

The language in which Abraham Lincoln characterized the position of Chief Justice Taney in the Dred Scott decision, and

---

[9] The reader will readily perceive that not a vestige of the history which is given in the preceding chapters of this work, which is simply the history of the Constitution—not a vestige of it is noticed by the court.

9

of Stephen A. Douglas in the defense of it, is the language that is most fitting to the position of the Supreme Court in this "Christian nation" decision; for here the two decisions are perfectly parallel.   Lincoln's words are as follows:—

"I ask, How extraordinary a thing it is that a man who has occupied a seat on the floor of the Senate [or on the bench of the Supreme Court—A. T. J.] of the United States . . . pretending to give a truthful and accurate history of the slavery question [or of the question of religion and the nation—A. T. J.] in this country, should so entirely ignore the whole of that portion of our history—the most important of all! Is it not a most extraordinary spectacle that a man should stand up and ask for any confidence in his statements who sets out as he does with portions of history, calling upon the people to believe that it is a true and fair representation, when the leading part, the controlling feature, of the whole history is carefully suppressed?

"And now he asks the community to believe that the men of the Revolution were in favor of his 'great principle,' when we have the naked history that they themselves dealt with this very subject matter of his principle, and utterly repudiated his principle—acting upon a precisely contrary ground.   It is as impudent and absurd as if a prosecuting attorney should stand up before a jury, and ask them to convict A as the murderer of B while B was standing alive before them."

But the court does not stop even here.   Having established "the Christian religion" for "the entire people," and settled all the appurtenances thereto as within the meaning of the Constitution, the court cites and sanctions the declaration of the Supreme Court of Pennsylvania that "Christianity, general Christianity, is, and always has been, part of the common law," and then proceeds to sanction also the doctrine that it is blasphemy to speak or act in contempt "of the religion professed by almost the whole community."   This is done by citing the pagan decision of "Chancellor Kent, the great commentator on American law, speaking as chief justice of the Supreme Court of New York," which "assumes that we are a Christian people."   Here is the language of the court on that strain:—

"While because of the general recognition of this truth the question has seldom been presented to the courts, yet we find that in Updegraph *versus* The Commonwealth (11 Serg. and Rawle, 394, 400) it was decided that 'Chiistianity, general Christianity, is, and always has been, *a part of the common law of Pennsylvania;* . . . not Christianity with an established church, and tithes, and spiritual courts, but Christianity with liberty of conscience to all men.' And in The People *versus* Ruggles (8 Johns. 290, 294, 295), *Chancellor Kent,* the great commentator on American law, speaking as chief justice of the Supreme Court of New York, said: 'The people of this State, in common with the people of this country, profess *the general doctrines of Christianity,* as the rule of their faith and practice; and to scandalize the Author of these doctrines is not only, in a religious point of view, extremely impious, but, even in respect to the obligations due to society, is a gross violation of decency and good order. . . . The free, equal, and undisturbed enjoyment of religious opinion, whatever it may be, and free and decent discussions on any religious subject, is granted and secured; *but to revile with malicious and blasphemous contempt, the religion professed by almost the whole community, is an abuse of that right.* Nor are we bound, by any expressions in the Constitution, as some have strangely supposed, either not to punish at all, or to punish indiscriminately, the like attacks upon the religion of *Mahomet* or of the Grand *Lama;* and for *this plain reason,* that *the case assumes that we are a Christian people,* and the morality of the country is deeply ingrafted upon Christianity, and not upon the doctrines or worship of those impostors.' And in the famous case of Vidal *versus* Girard's Executors (2 How. 127, 128), this court, while sustaining the will of Mr. Girard, with its provision for the creation of a college into which no minister should be permitted to enter, observed, ' It is also said, and truly, that the *Christian religion* is a *part* of the common law of *Pennsylvania.'* "

But even though it be decided, and declared, and admitted, that "Christianity, general Christianity, is and always has been" not only a part but the whole of the common law, and the statute law also, *of Pennsylvania,* and that it is "blasphemy" in New York to speak or act in contempt of the established religion, that never can rightly be made to mean anything to *the nation.* And even though all this were a fact within the legitimate consideration of the Supreme Courts of

Pennsylvania, New York, and all the other State Supreme Courts in the land, it never could by any kind of right be a fact within the legitimate consideration of the Supreme Court of the nation in the construction of any national law or the decision of any national question. [10]

There remains but one thing more to cover the whole ground of the old order of things, but one thing more to complete the perfect likeness of the whole papal system, and that is the direct and positive sanction of Sunday laws. Nor is this one thing lacking. As before observed, it is indirectly indicated in the quotation from the national Constitution. But the court does not stop with that; it makes Sunday laws one of the proofs that "this is a Christian nation." The words are as follows:—

"If we pass beyond these matters to a view of American life as expressed by its laws, its business, its customs, and its society, we find everywhere a clear recognition of the same truth. Among other matters, note the following: The form of oath usually prevailing, concluding with an appeal to the Almighty; the custom of opening sessions of all deliberative bodies, and most conventions, with prayer; the prefatory words of all wills, 'In the name of God, Amen;' *the laws respecting the observance of the Sabbath* with the general cessation of all secular business, and the closing of courts, Legislatures, and other similar public assemblies on that day. . . . *These*, and many other matters which might be noticed, *add a volume* of unofficial declarations to the mass *of organic utterances* that THIS IS A CHRISTIAN NATION."

Here we may properly present in summary form again this whole discussion as presented by the Court. So stated it stands thus:—

(*a*) "The establishment of the Christian religion," "Christianity, general Christianity," "is one of the purposes of all these" documents.

(*b*) "Even the Constitution of the United States . . .

---

[10] Think again on chapter 3.

contains in the first amendment a declaration common to'' all these; for '' there is *a universal language* pervading *them all, having one meaning;* they affirm and reaffirm that this is a religious nation. . . . They are organic utterances; they speak the voice of the entire people.''

(*c*) Conclusion: '' This is a Christian nation.''

And therefore the decision concludes as follows:—

'' The construction [''of this statute''] invoked cannot be accepted as correct. It is a case where there was presented a definite evil, in view of which the Legislature used general terms with the purpose of reaching all phases of that evil, and thereafter, unexpectedly, it is developed that the general language thus employed is broad enough to reach cases and acts which the whole history and life of the country affirm could not have been intentionally legislated against. It is the duty of the courts, under those circumstances, to say that, however broad the language of the statute may be, the act, although within the letter, is not within the intention of the Legislature, and therefore cannot be within the statute.

'' The judgment will be reversed, and the case remanded for further proceedings in accordance with this opinion.''

'' In accordance with this opinion'' then, let us recapitulate, and see what has been done by it. ''The Christian religion,'' that is, ''Christianity, general Christianity,'' is legally recognized and declared to be the established religion of this nation, and that consequently ''this *is* a Christian nation.'' With this also, ''in language more or less emphatic,'' there is justified as the ''meaning of the Constitution of the United States, (1) the maintenance of the discipline of the churches by the civil power; (2) the requirement of the religious oath; (3) the requirement of the religious test oath as a qualification for office; (4) public taxation for the support of religion and religious teachers; (5) the requirement of a belief in the Trinity and the inspiration of ''the Holy Scriptures of the Old and New Testaments;'' (6) the guilt of blasphemy upon everyone who speaks or acts in contempt of the established religion; and (7) laws for the observance of Sunday, with the general cessation of all "*secular* business."

All this is declared by unanimous decision of the Supreme Court of the United States to be the meaning of the Constitution of the United States. And what the Supreme Court says the meaning of the Constitution is, that *is* its meaning and *that is the law* until the decision is reversed. Therefore, again, we say, and it is not too much to say, as certainly as logic is logic, and truth is truth, it is demonstrated that in this decision the Supreme Court of the United States has subverted the Constitution of the United States in its essential meaning as regards the Christian religion or the establishment thereof.

Now what more was ever required by the Papacy, and all phases of the old order of things, than is thus brought within the meaning of the national Constitution by this decision? What more was ever required by the Papacy itself than that "the Christian religion" should be the national religion; that the discipline of the church should be maintained by the civil power; that the religious test oath should be applied to all; that the public should be taxed for the support of religion and religious worship; that there should be required a belief in the doctrine of the Trinity, and the inspiration of the "Holy Scriptures of the Old and New Testament;" that the guilt of "blasphemy" should be visited upon everyone who should speak or act "in contempt of the religion professed by almost the whole community;" and that everybody should be required by law to observe Sunday? Indeed, what more than this could be required or even desired by the most absolute religious despotism that could be imagined?

Therefore, it is pertinent here to inquire, Does this decision maintain the "new order of things" to which this nation stands pledged by the great seal of the United States?—No, no; twenty times no. On the contrary, it sanctions, and restores, and fastens upon this nation, the old order of things which our revolutionary fathers hoped that we should forever escape, through their sublime efforts, which culminated in the creation of this nation and the formation of the national Constitution— *as it reads*, and as *they* meant it.

What more could be done to create the very image of the Papacy in this nation, in *the principle* of the thing, than is done in this decision? In *principle* we say; not in its positive workings, of course, because the decision in itself on this point does not bear the force of a statute that can be made at once obligatory upon all by the executive power of the nation. But it does sanction and justify beforehand any and every encroachment that the religious power may make upon the civil, and every piece of legislation that Congress might enact on the subject of religion or religious observances; so that by it the national door is opened wide for the religious element to enter and take possession in whatever way it chooses or can make effective. And there stands at the door, ready and determined to enter and take possession, the strongest religio-political combination that could be formed in the land.

Therefore we say that, although *life* is not by this given to this image that it should of itself speak and act (Rev. 13: 15), yet so far as the *making* of the evil thing, and the establishment of *the principle* of it are concerned, it is certainly done. The tree does not yet stand with its branches widespread, bearing its pernicious fruit, but *the tree is planted*. And as certainly as the branches and the fruit are all in the natural stock that is planted, and it is only a question of time when they will appear, so certainly the widespreading branches and the pernicious fruit of the full-grown tree of religious despotism are in the evil stock of Church and State, of "the establishment of the Christian religion," that has been planted by the Supreme Court in and for this nation; and it is only a question of time when these fruits will inevitably appear.

This decision was followed in the same year, 1892, by an

act of Congress declaring Sunday to be the Sabbath of the fourth commandment, instead of the seventh day, as named in the commandment, and requiring its observance at the World's Columbian Exposition.   Congress did this specifically as a religious thing.   And, although other things defeated the actual closing of the gates, defeated the *enforcement* of the law, yet that in nowise weakens the fact that this law respecting religion was enacted by Congress.

And the president, Benjamin Harrison, approved this law respecting religion.   This he did under the mistaken notion that he was pledged to maintain the *government* of the United States, rather than the *Constitution* of the United States.[11]

Thus in the year A. D. 1892 the government of the United States, by specific official acts of the three departments—the Judiciary, the Legislative, and the Executive—of which that government is composed, was turned from the "new order of things" to which it was committed by our revolutionary fathers, and to which it stands pledged by the great seal of the government itself, and was thrown into the evil tide of the old order of things.   And thus this enlightened nation, the example and glory of the world, was caused to assume the place and the prerogatives of the governments of the Middle Ages in embody-

---

[11] This is a fact.   In a personal interview with the author of this book, the reason (?) and the only reason which he gave for approving this legislation. was that it was "part of the general appropriation bill for the running expenses of the government; that to disapprove this he would have to disapprove the whole bill; and if that were done, all the machinery of the government would have to stop, and the whole government itself be brought to a standstill."   This, too, while admitting that if this Sunday legislation had come before him separated from other legislation, so that it might be considered upon its merits alone, the result might be different.   This was nothing else than to argue that he was responsible for the maintenance of the government.   But this was altogether a mistake.   The maintenance of the government devolves altogether upon Congress.   And if the President were to veto a general appropriation bill because of an unconstitutional piece of legislation which had been tacked to it; and if the whole government should in consequence be brought indeed to a standstill; he would be no more responsible for it than would any private citizen.   President Harrison's assumption, therefore, was altogether a mistaken one, and this plea wholly irrelevant.

ing in law the dogmas and definitions of the theologians, and executing the arbitrary and despotic will of the church.

As the acts of Congress and the executive must in any case rest for their validity upon their constitutionality; as their constitutionality or otherwise must, so far as the action of the government is concerned, rest upon a decision of the Supreme Court; and as the court in this Christian nation decision has already practically decided beforehand every such question; this makes this decision the pivot of the whole question of an established national religion, as against the perfect freedom of religious right as the meaning of the Constitution and the right of mankind.

For this reason we confine ourselves to the discussion of the decision and the principles involved.

NOTE.—For a full history and discussion of the Act of Congress above referred to, see "Two Republics," pp. 801–826.

CHAPTER VII.

THE PEOPLE'S RIGHT OF APPEAL.

IN their opposition to the establishment of "Christianity, general Christianity," in Virginia, and to the making of that a "Christian State," James Madison and the good people of Virginia declared that "one of the noblest characteristics of the [then] late Revolution" was in the fact that "the freemen of America did not wait till usurped power had strengthened itself by exercise, and entangled itself in precedents. They saw all the consequences in the principle, and they avoided the consequences by denying the principle." They also said that they themselves "revered this lesson too much soon to forget it." The American people ought yet to revere this lesson too much *ever* to forget it.

In the matter of a national religion, a religious despotism, by means of this "Christian nation" decision, it is too late to avoid the consequences by denying the principle; because the principle is already established. The people were given no opportunity to deny the principle. It was sprung upon them without their knowledge, and in spite of the constitutional barriers which they had set up in, as they supposed, eternal denial of the principle. For this reason it is too late to escape the consequences by denying the principle; but *it is not too late to escape the consequences by reversing the decision.*

It is not too late for this if only the people will think enough upon the question to see that all the consequences are in the principle; and that these consequences will certainly follow if the principle is left undisputed, if the decision is left standing as the meaning of the Constitution. It is not too late, if only the people will see this, and awake to the reality of the issue, and reverse the decision; and with one voice repudiate it, even in the words in which United States Senator William Pitt Fessenden denounced the famous Dred Scott decision, as "utterly at variance with all truth, utterly destitute of all legal logic, founded on error, and unsupported by anything resembling argument."[1]

For "the people of these United States are the rightful masters of both congresses and courts, not to overthrow the Constitution, but to overthrow the men who pervert the Constitution."—*Abraham Lincoln.*[2]

The right OF THE PEOPLE of the United States TO APPEAL from any decision of the Supreme Court of the United States, upon any constitutional question, upon any question involving the meaning or the interpretation of the Constitution, IS AN INALIENABLE RIGHT.

This proposition will probably be disputed by many judges, by many lawyers, and certainly by almost all the archbishops, bishops, preachers, and priests throughout the land; while the great majority of the people will doubtless be surprised at it, and wonder whether it is true. Yet it is not only the veritable truth, but it is the very life principle of a free government— which is only saying that it is the life principle of the government of the United States as a free government.

The inalienable right of the people to appeal from, to sit in judgment upon, and to correct, any action of the President or the Congress of the United States, is recognized and acted

---

[1] Blaine's "Twenty Years of Congress," Vol. I, p. 133.

[2] Speech "To the Kentuckians," Cincinnati, Ohio, September, 1869. "Political Speeches and Debates," p. 507. I give these double references so that anyone who has *any* copy of Lincoln's speeches may readily find the passage. The copy that I use is the one advertised at the end of this book.

upon by the people. But the right of the people to do likewise respecting the decisions of the Supreme Court touching constitutional questions, has been largely forgotten. And there is a vast combination in the United States scheming against the liberties of the people, whose members sincerely desire that this right shall be forgotten by the people in its exercise and in its existence. For this reason, if for no other, the knowledge of this right of the people needs to be revived as fully as possible.

The government of the United States, and, therefore, the Supreme Court as a coördinate branch of the government, is not self-existent; it was created. It did not spontaneously spring into existence of itself full formed; in all its parts it *was made*, as certainly as any other piece of machinery was ever made. It was created *by the people* of the United States; and, like any other creature, it is the subject not the master of its creator. "We, the people of the United States," made the government of the United States, and *in that* made the Supreme Court of the United States as a coördinate branch thereof; and "we, the people of the United States," therefore by this very fact are "the rightful masters," and not the servants of this thing which they have made; and as such the people have the inalienable right to sit in final judgment upon any act of the government of the United States.

"We, the people of the United States, *in order to form* a more perfect union," in order to form that which is the government of the United States, ordained and established "this Constitution." This Constitution is the charter of the nation's existence. This Constitution is the sole depository of all the authority of the government of the United States in all three of the coördinate branches thereof. This Constitution, therefore, is the sole depository of all the authority of the Supreme Court, and of all the authority that that court can ever rightly exercise. To this Constitution that court owes its existence, and all the accompaniments of that existence. And as "we, the people," established and ordained this Constitution which gives to the court its very existence and all the authority that it ever can rightly have, it follows that "we, the people," have ever the inalienable right of final judgment and correction of any and every decision of that court touching any question as to the meaning of the Constitution which "we, the people," have ordained and established.

The authority of the Supreme Court is delegated and not absolute. Decisions of the Supreme Court, therefore, are not final in all things, because the people have not delegated *all their rights*. In the Constitution the people have declared and established that—

"The enumeration in the Constitution of certain rights shall not be construed to *deny* or *disparage* others *retained by the people*."[3]

Again: The Supreme Court, being but a creature of the Constitution, must be subject to the Constitution. Having been created by the people, through the Constitution, it is bound by the limitations prescribed by the people in the Constitution. In the Constitution the people have declared that—

"The powers not delegated to the United States by the Constitution, nor prohibited by it to the States, *are reserved* to the States respectively, or *to the people*."[4]

As *the people* made the Constitution with the delegation *only of certain* rights to be exercised by the government, it follows conclusively that *the people* are the supreme authority in the United States, and the source of final appeal in all questions of their reserved rights. And "prudent jealousy" in the guardianship of these rights against encroachment on the part of the government or any of the branches thereof is the first duty of the people of the United States; and religious right is the chief of all these reserved rights no less than the

---

[3] Ninth amendment.   [4] Tenth amendment.

chief of all natural rights. "I insist that if there is anything which it is the duty of the whole people to never intrust to any hands but their own, that thing is the preservation and perpetuity of their own liberties and institutions."—*Abraham Lincoln.*[5]

This is sufficient as to the principle in the abstract, as the principle inheres in the very nature of a limited constitution. Yet, as with many persons the statement of a principle, however clear, is insufficient without proof from authorities, we shall now cite the very best authorities as to the correctness of the principle.

First, we have the authority of one of the makers of the Constitution:—

"It must be granted that a bad administration may take place. What is then to be done?—The answer is instantly found: Let the Fasces be lowered before—*the supreme sovereignty of the people.* It is their duty to watch, and their right to take care, that the Constitution be preserved, or, in the Roman phrase on perilous occasions— to provide that the republic receive no damage."

"When one part [of the government], without being sufficiently checked by the rest, abuses its power to the manifest danger of public happiness; or when the several parts abuse their respective powers so as to involve the commonwealth in the like peril; *the people* must restore things to that order from which their functionaries have departed. If *the people* suffer this living principle of watchfulness and control to be extinguished among them, they will assuredly, not long afterwards, experience that of *their* 'temple' 'there shall not be left one stone upon another, that shall not be thrown down.' "—*John Dickinson, pamphlet on The Federal Constitution, 1788.*[6]

Secondly, we have the authority of Thomas Jefferson. In 1820 a gentleman by the name of Jarvis sent to Jefferson a book that he had written, entitled "The Republican." In his acknowledgment of the present, Jefferson called the author's

---

[5] Speech on The Missouri Compromise, Peoria, Ill., October 16, 1854. "Political Speeches and Debates," p. 24.

[6] "Federalist and Other Constitutional Papers," p. 796.

attention to "a very dangerous doctrine" that seemed to be inculcated in the book. His words upon the point, and it is the very point which is here under consideration, are as follows:—

"You seem, in pages 84 and 148, to consider the judges as the ultimate arbiters of all constitutional questions,—a very dangerous doctrine indeed, and one which would place us under the despotism of an oligarchy. Our judges are as honest as other men, and not more so. They have, with others, the same passions for party, for power, and the privilege of their corps. Their maxim is, '*Boni judicis est ampliare jurisdictionem;*' and their power is the more dangerous as they are in office for life, and are not responsible, as the other functionaries are, to the elective control. The Constitution has erected no such single tribunal, knowing that, to whatever hands confided, with the corruptions of time and party, its members would become despots." [1]

Thirdly, we have the authority of Abraham Lincoln. With direct reference to this point he paraphrased the above statement from Jefferson as follows:—

"Jefferson said that 'judges are as honest as other men, and not more so.' And he said, substantially, that 'whenever a free people should give up in absolute submission to any department of government, retaining for themselves no appeal from it, their liberties were gone.'" [8]

Again: In his first inaugural address, March 4, 1861, Lincoln stated the case as follows:—

"I do not forget the position assumed by some, that constitutional questions are to be decided by the Supreme Court; nor do I deny that such decisions must be binding in any case upon the parties to a suit, *as to the object of that suit*, while they are also entitled to a very high respect and consideration in all parallel cases by all other departments of the government; and while it is obviously possible that such deci-

[1] "Jefferson's Correspondence," Vol. VII, p. 177. Quoted also by Abraham Lincoln in his speech at Springfield, Ill., July 17, 1858, "Political Speeches and Debates," p. 43.

[8] Debate with Douglas, Galesburg, Ill., October 7, 1858, "Political Speeches and Debates," p. 362.

sion may be erroneous in any given case, still the evil effect following it, *being limited to that particular case*, with the chance that it
may be overruled and never become a precedent for other cases, can
better be borne than could the evils of a different practice.

"At the same time the candid citizen must confess that, if the policy of the government upon vital questions affecting the whole
people is to be irrevocably fixed by the decisions of the Supreme
Court the instant they are made, as in ordinary litigation between
parties in personal action, *the people will have ceased to be their own
rulers*—having to that extent practically resigned their government
into the hands of that eminent tribunal. Nor is this view any assault
upon the court or the judges."—*Id., pp. 535, 536.*

Fourthly, we have the authority of George Bancroft, the
historian of the Constitution. Mr. Bancroft wrote the standard
and authoritative history of the United States up to the time of
the making of the Constitution, and then wrote the "History
of the Formation of the Constitution" itself. And in this latter history, in discussing "The Federal Judiciary," he makes
the following statement concerning the Supreme Court, which
is also only an extension of the principles laid down by Alexander Hamilton in his discussion of the Judiciary in the *Federalist, No. LXXVIII.*

"The Supreme Court was to be the 'bulwark of a limited constitution against legislative encroachments.' ["Federalist," LXXVIII.]
A bench of a few, selected with care by the President and Senate of
the nation, seemed a safer tribunal than a multitudinous assembly
elected for a short period under the sway of passing currents of
thought, or the intrepid fixedness of an uncompromising party.
There always remains danger of erroneous judgments, arising from
mistakes, imperfect investigation, the bias of previous connections,
the seductions of ambition, or the instigations of surrounding opinions, and *a court from which there is no appeal* is apt to forget circumspection in its sense of security.

"The passage of a judge from the bar to the bench does not necessarily divest him of prejudices, nor chill his relations to the particular political party to which he may owe his advancement, nor blot out
of his memory the great interests which he may have professionally
piloted through doubtful straits, nor quiet the ambition which he is

not required to renounce, even though his appointment is for life, nor cure predilections which sometimes have their seat in his inmost nature.

"But the Constitution retains the means of protecting itself against the errors of partial or interested judgments. In the first place, the force of a judicial opinion of the Supreme Court, in so far as it is irreversible, *reaches only the particular case in dispute;* and to this society submits, in order to escape from anarchy in the daily routine of business.

"To the decision on an underlying question of constitutional law *no such finality attaches.* To endure, it must be right. If it is right, it will approve itself to the universal sense of the impartial. A judge who can justly lay claim to integrity will never lay claim to infallibility, but with indefatigable research will add, retract, and correct, whenever more mature consideration shows the need of it. The court is itself inferior and subordinate to the Constitution; it has only a delegated authority, and every opinion contrary to the tenor of its commission *is void*, except as settling the case on trial.

"The prior act of a superior must be preferred to the subsequent act of an inferior; otherwise it might transform the limited into an unlimited constitution. When laws clash, the latest law is rightly held to express the corrected will of the Legislature; but *the Constitution is the fundamental code*, the law of laws; and where there is a conflict between the Constitution and a decision of the court, the original permanent act of the superior outweighs the later act of the inferior, and retains its own supreme energy unaltered and unalterable except in the manner prescribed by the Constitution itself.

"To say that a court, having once discovered an error, should yet cling to it because it has once been delivered as its opinion, is to invest caprice with inviolability and make a wrong judgment of a servant outweigh the Constitution to which he has sworn obedience. An act of the Legislature at variance with the Constitution is pronounced void; *an opinion of the Supreme Court at variance with the Constitution is equally so.*"[9]

This passage is worthy of more extended notice.

(a) "The Supreme Court was to be the bulwark against legislative encroachments" upon the rights of the people. This was the purpose of the founders of that tribunal. But

---

[9] Bryce, Vol. II, pp. 201–203.

did the people erect no bulwark against judicial encroach-ments? Or did they suppose that supreme judges were so decidedly infallible that there was no possibility of their en-croaching even unconsciously? Did they think it impossible for that Court to make a mistake?—Nothing of the kind. They knew that even supreme judges, being only men, are just like other men, having the same weaknesses and the same liability to mistakes as other men, and therefore being as lia-ble as legislators to mistake the meaning of the Constitution and to encroach upon the rights of the people. And knowing that "a court *from which there is no appeal* is apt to forget circumspection in its sense of security," and is thereby only the more apt to make mistakes and encroachments—knowing this, the people, while setting the Supreme Court as the bul-wark against legislative encroachments, retained to themselves the right of final appeal, judgment, and decision upon the deci-sions of the court touching all questions of the Constitution.

(*b*) "Where there is *a conflict* between the Constitution and a decision of the court," etc. But if every decision of the Supreme Court is final in all respects; and if said decisions are to be accepted as final as to the meaning of the Constitution; then it would be impossible that there ever could be any such thing as a conflict between the Constitution and a decision of the court.

Yet, as it is expressly declared in the Constitution that the people have reserved certain rights and powers exclusively to themselves, and so have forbidden the Supreme Court any jurisdiction in these, it is clearly possible for a conflict to be made between the Constitution and a decision of the court. And where there is a conflict there must of necessity be some authority to decide. And as the people made both the Con-stitution and the court; and as the people stand outside of and above both the Constitution and the court; it is perfectly plain that in all cases of conflict between the Constitution and the

Supreme Court, the right of final judgment and decision lies with *the people* as *an inalienable right.*

(*c*) The court "has only a delegated authority, and every opinion contrary to the tenor of its commission is void." But if every decision of the court is to be accepted as final in all respects, how would it be possible for any opinion ever to be void? And even though it were possible, how could the fact of its being void ever be discovered? It is true that the court has only a delegated authority, and that every opinion contrary to the tenor of its commission, that is, every opinion contrary to the tenor of the Constitution, *is void.* And it is equally true that it lies with the people, who delegated this authority, to discover and to disregard and set aside *as void* every such opinion. And this prerogative lies with the people as their inalienable right.

(*d*) "An act of the Legislature at variance with the Constitution is pronounced void. An opinion of the Supreme Court at variance with the Constitution is equally so." An act of the Legislature at variance with the Constitution is pronounced void *by the Supreme Court.* But when an opinion of the Supreme Court is at variance with the Constitution, whose prerogative is it to pronounce this void and to treat it so?—Clearly this is the prerogative and right of the people.

It is here said, and repeated, that every such opinion of the court "*is void.*" This is true; and if such decisions were completely ignored by everybody, and so left meaningless and void as they are, they could never do any harm. But it is hardly possible that there could ever be a decision in which nobody would have sufficient personal interest to seek to make it of force as far as possible; and every decision, void or otherwise, always stands as a matter of record to be taken up by interested parties and used as a precedent upon which to carry any principle involved, to its fullest extent in real factitive law. For this reason it is incumbent upon the people to see that every such decision is so positively pronounced void, and regarded so by themselves—the supreme and ultimate authority —that it shall not be cited even as a precedent.

For that such is the authority and the inalienable right of the people is certainly made clear both by the principle and by the authorities cited in this chapter.

There is another excellent statement of this principle, which, though not bearing exactly the force of national authority, is well worthy to be set down here. It is in every respect true, and shows how this subject presents itself to a disinterested mind. Here it is:—

"How and by whom, in case of dispute, is the validity or invalidity of a statute to be determined?—Such determination is to be effected by setting the statute side by side with the Constitution, and considering whether there is a discrepancy between them. Is the purpose of the statute one of the purposes mentioned or implied in the Constitution? Does it in pursuing that purpose contain anything which violates any clause of the Constitution? Sometimes this is a simple question which an intelligent layman may answer; more frequently it is a difficult one, which needs not only the subtlety of a trained lawyer, but a knowledge of former cases which have thrown light on the same or a similar point. In any event it is an important question, whose solution ought to proceed from a weighty authority. It is a question of interpretation, that is, of determining the true meaning both of the superior law [the Constitution] and of the inferior law [the statute], so as to discover whether they are inconsistent. Now the interpretation of laws belongs to courts of justice."

"How is the interpreting authority restrained? If the American Constitution is capable of being so developed by this expansive interpretation, what security do its written terms offer to the people and to the States? . . . There stands above and behind the Legislature, the executive, *and the judiciary*, ANOTHER POWER, that of public opinion. The President, Congress, and the courts are all, the two former directly, the latter practically, *amenable to the people*. . . . If the people approve the way in which these authorities are interpreting and using the Constitution, they go on; if the people disapprove, they pause, or at least slacken their pace. . . . The people have, of course, much less exact notions of the Constitution than the legal profession or the courts. But . . . they are sufficiently attached to its general doctrines, they sufficiently prize the protection it affords them against their own impulses, to censure any interpretation which palpably departs from the old lines."—*Bryce, American Commonwealth, chapter 23, par. 13, 14; chapter 33, par. 20, 22.*

Certainly the Supreme Court, in the "Christian nation" decision, has palpably enough departed from the old lines for its interpretation to deserve this censure of the people. The question now is, Are the people indeed sufficiently attached to this great leading doctrine of the Constitution to censure this interpretation that subverts that doctrine? This decision on that point is void. Will the people declare and treat it so?

CHAPTER VIII.

NATIONAL PRECEDENT ON RIGHT OF APPEAL.

As before remarked, there are some who, in addition to the principle, desire authority. The authority has been given. Yet there are still others who, in addition to both the principle and the authority, desire *precedent* before they can be fully satisfied of the correctness of a position, and particularly such a position as is held in this discussion. And, fortunately for all, this position is supported by every kind of evidence that any person may desire. It is supported by the firm evidence of the national *principle*, by the satisfactory evidence of national *authority*, and by the final evidence of national *precedent*.

The question still under discussion is *the right of the people* to appeal from and to reverse any decision of the Supreme Court of the United States touching any matter as to the meaning or interpretation of the Constitution.

There are two notable examples of national precedent on this subject,—one in the action of each of the two great political parties of the nation's history, the Democratic and the Republican parties.

First, during President Jackson's administration the Supreme Court decided that Congress could charter a National Bank, and that such bank was constitutional. President Jackson "asserted that he, as president, would not be bound to hold a National Bank to be constitutional, even though the Court had decided it to be so," and, accordingly, vetoed the Act of Congress for a recharter. "The whole Democratic party revolted against that decision" of the Court, and "reduced the decision to an absolute nullity."[1]

Secondly, the Supreme Court of the United States once rendered a decision on the slavery question in which a specific interpretation of the Constitution was made in favor of slavery as a national institution, and such interpretation declared to be the meaning and intent of the Constitution. The decision was endorsed by a large number of people, and it was ably defended in open and public discussion for several years by one of the leading men of the nation, a United States senator at the time—Stephen A. Douglas. Yet against all this, that decision was openly attacked, first in comparative obscurity and under great reproach, then in a larger field, and finally before the whole nation, by Abraham Lincoln; *and the decision was reversed by the people of the United States.*

That decision was, and ever since has been known as,

THE DRED SCOTT DECISION.

As this precedent is so marked, so apt, so undeniable, so universally known, and withal so perfect a parallel with the "Christian nation" decision, it will be discussed here as fully as the question demands.

In noticing the "Christian nation" decision in previous chapters reference has been made more than once to the close parallel between it and the Dred Scott decision. For this reason the Dred Scott decision is of double value in this discussion, (*a*) in that it is such an undeniable national precedent as to the right of the people to appeal from a Supreme Court decision; and (*b*) in that the exact parallel between it and the "Christian nation" decision serves to set in the strongest possible light the perfect absurdity of the "Christian nation" decision throughout.

[1] See speeches of Abraham Lincoln at Springfield, Ill., June 26, 1857, and July 17, 1858, "Political Speeches and Debates," pp. 43, 156.

We shall therefore first set down the parallel between these two decisions in such a way that no one can fail to see it.   Next we shall cite the arguments made in defense of the Dred Scott decision and those made against it, pointing out the application of both to the "Christian nation" decision, though indeed the application is so plain as scarcely to be mistakable.

The main point of the Dred Scott decision was the recognition of slavery as a national institution within the meaning and intent of the Constitution.   And from the notice already given to the Christian nation decision it is perfectly clear that *its* main point is the recognition of the "Christian religion" as a national institution within the meaning and intent of the Constitution.   The logic of the one made this a slave nation, as the logic of the other makes this a "Christian nation."

No one denied that, under the Constitution, slavery was a *State* institution and a State question in such States as had it or chose to have it; the question involved in the Dred Scott decision was whether it was a *national* institution.   Likewise no one can deny that, under the Constitution as it was originally made, religion was a State institution and a State question in such States as had it or chose to have it; the question involved in the Christian nation decision is whether it is a *national* institution.

The task therefore before the Dred Scott court was to show that slavery was, and was intended to be, included in the Constitution of the United States as a national affair; just as the task before the Christian nation court was to show that "Christianity, general Christianity," is, and was intended to be, included in the Constitution of the United States as a national affair.

The Dred Scott court sought to acccomplish its task, *not* by the examination of the Constitution itself, nor by an examination of the proceedings of the conventions wherein it was made or the words and works of the men who made it—all this was left out; but by citing the history of European nations, the legislation of the Colonies, the Declaration of Independence (!), and the legislation of the States, precisely as the "Christian nation" court sought to accomplish its task. From this evidence the Dred Scott court drew the conclusion that "the right of property in a slave is distinctly and expressly affirmed in the Constitution; precisely as the Christian nation court, from parallel evidence, and by parallel method, has drawn the conclusion that the "meaning" of the language of the Constitution is that "this is a Christian nation." Neither Madison, Jefferson, nor yet Washington is as much as named in the Dred Scott decision, any more than in the Christian nation decision.

The Dred Scott court made as its leading statement the proposition that at the time of the adoption of the Constitution—

"They [the negro race] had for more than a century been regarded as beings of an inferior order, and altogether unfit to associate with the white race, either in social or political relations, and so far inferior that they had no rights which the white man was bound to respect; and the negro might justly be reduced to slavery for his [the white man's] benefit."

The Christian nation court made as its leading statement the proposition that—

"This is a religious people. This is historically true. From the discovery of this continent to the present hour there is a single voice making this affirmation."

To prove its proposition that such is the meaning and intent of the Constitution—

The Dred Scott court said:—	The Christian nation court said:—
[1]	[1]
"The public history of every European nation displays it in a	"The commission to Christopher Columbus prior to his sail

manner too plain to be mistaken.
. . . And in no nation was
this opinion more firmly fixed or
more uniformly acted upon than
by the English government and
English people. . . .

The opinion thus entertained
and acted upon in England was
naturally impressed upon the Colonies they founded on this side
of the Atlantic."

westward, is from Ferdinand and
Isabella, etc. . . . The first
colonial grant, that made to Sir
Walter Raleigh, in 1584, was
from 'Elizabeth, by the Grace of
God, of England, Fraunce, and
Ireland, queene, defender of the
faith,' etc. . . . The first
charter of Virginia, granted by
King James I. . . . Lan-
guage of similar import may be
found in the subsequent charters
of that Colony from the same king.
. . . In language more or less
emphatic is the establishment of
the Christian religion declared to
be one of the purposes of the
grant."

[2]

"Accordingly, a negro of the
African race was regarded by
them [the Colonies] as an article
of property, and held and bought
and sold as such in every one of
the thirteen Colonies which
united in the Declaration of Independence, and afterwards
formed the Constitution of the
United States. . . . The legislation of the different Colonies
furnishes positive and indisputable proof of this fact. It would
be tedious . . . to enumerate
the various laws passed upon
this subject. . . . As a sample of the legislation . . .
the province of Maryland, in
1717, passed a law, etc.
. "The other colonial law to
which we refer was passed by
Massachussetts in 1705," etc.[2]

[2]

"The celebrated compact
made by the pilgrims in the *Mayflower*, 1620, recites, etc.

"The fundamental orders of
Connecticut, under which a provisional government was instituted in 1638, 1639, commence
with this declaration, etc.

"In the charter of privileges
granted by William Penn to the
province of Pennsylvania, in 1701,
it is recited," etc.

---

[2] The Christian nation court could have obtained from this same law of Massachusetts additional valuable (?) evidence in favor of its theory; for twice in this act the
definite phrase "Christian nation" is used. See decision, Appendix D.

[3]

"The language of the Declaration of Independence is equally conclusive."

[4]

"When we look to the condition of this race in *the several States* at the time. . . . And we may here again refer . . . to the plain and unequivocal language of the laws of the several States. . . . Their statute books are full of provisions relating to this class," etc.

"Thus Massachusetts, in 1786," etc.

"So, too, in Connecticut, 1774, 1784, 1833."

"By the laws of New Hampshire, collected and finally passed in 1815, . . . a subsequent collection made in 1855."

"In 1822 Rhode Island, in its revised code, . . . reënacted in its revised code of 1844."

[5]

"It would be impossible to enumerate . . . the various laws marking the condition of this race. . . . In addition to those already referred to, it is sufficient to say that *Chancellor Kent, whose accuracy and research* no one will question, states," etc.

[3]

"Coming nearer to the present time, the Declaration of Independence recognizes, etc."

[4]

"If we examine the constitutions of *the various States* we find in them a constant recognition of religious obligations. Every constitution of every one of the forty-four States contains language which either directly or by clear implication recognizes," etc.

"The Constitution of Illinois, 1870," etc.

"The Constitution of Indiana, 1816," etc.

"The Declaration of Rights of the Constitution of Maryland, 1867," etc.

"Or like . . . the Constitution of Massachusetts, 1780," etc.

"Or . . . the Constitution of Mississippi, 1832," etc.

"Or . . . the Constitution of Delaware, 1776."

[5]

"While, because of a general recognition of this truth, the question has seldom been presented to the courts, yet we find that in Updegraph *vs.* the Commonwealth, it was decided that 'Christianity, general Christianity, is, and always has been, a part of the Common Law of Pennsylvania. . . . And in the People *vs.* Ruggles, *Chancellor Kent, the great commentator* on American law, . . . said," etc.

[6]

"They [these laws] . . . are a faithful index to the state of feeling towards the class of persons of whom they speak. . . . They show that a perpetual and impassable barrier was intended to be erected between the white race and the one which they had reduced to slavery, and governed as subjects with absolute and despotic power. . . .

"*We refer to these historical facts* for the purpose of showing the fixed opinions concerning that race, upon which the statesmen of that day spoke and acted. It is necessary to do this, *in order to determine* whether the general terms used in the Constitution of the United States as to the rights of man and the rights of the people was intended to include them, or to give to them or their posterity the benefit of any of its provisions."

"Now, as we have already said in an earlier part of this opinion, *the right of property in a slave is distinctly and expressly affirmed in the Constitution.*"

[6]

"Even the Constitution of the United States . . . contains in the first amendment a declaration common to the constitutions of all the States. . . . There is no dissonance in these declarations. There is a universal language pervading them all, having one meaning; they affirm and reaffirm that this is a religious nation. These are not individual sayings, declarations of private persons; they are organic utterances; they speak the voice of the entire people."

"*These*, and many other matters which might be noticed, *add a volume* of unofficial declarations to the mass *of organic utterances* that THIS IS A CHRISTIAN NATION."

In view of these quotations, no man can deny that the Dred Scott decision and the Christian nation decision are in principle and in method exactly parallel. And as certainly as the Dred Scott decision established slavery as a national institution, so certainly the Christian nation decision establishes "the Christian religion" as a national institution. According to the plain words of the Dred Scott decision, slavery is absolutism and despotism. This is the truth; and it is no less the truth that any governmental establishment of "the Christian religion" is also sheer absolutism and despotism. Slavery is civil despotism; established religion is religious despotism. Of the former Abraham Lincoln said: "When the white man governs himself, that is self-government; but when he governs himself and also another man, that is more than self-government—that is despotism."[3] And of the latter say we: When any man chooses to be religious for himself, that is religious freedom; but when any man proposes to be religious for himself and also for another man, that is less than religious freedom—that is religious despotism. As certainly therefore as the Dred Scott decision, in nationalizing slavery, established a national *civil* despotism, if that decision had not been reversed, so certainly the Christian nation decision, in nationalizing "the Christian religion," establishes a national *religious* despotism, if this decision shall not be reversed.

Undoubtedly the real bearing of the Dred Scott decision in all its parts was more clearly seen by Abraham Lincoln than by any other man in the United States. The leadership of the opposition to the decision therefore naturally fell to him, while, from whatever cause, the defense of the decision devolved upon United States Senator Stephen A. Douglas. And not only does the parallel hold good as between these two decisions in themselves, but it continues throughout the discussion of the two decisions—the main arguments made in defense of the Dred Scott decision, or in apology for it, are precisely the ones that are now made in support of the Christian nation decision,

---

[3] Missouri Compromise Speech, before referred to.

or in apology for it, while every argument made against the Dred Scott decision is equally valid and lies with full force against the Christian nation decision. Indeed, in many instances the mere insertion of the words "Christian nation" instead of the words "Dred Scott," and the words "religion" or "religious despotism" in place of the word "slavery," will make whole pages of Lincoln's speeches as applicable and as powerful against the Christian nation decision and its bearing as they were against the Dred Scott decision and its bearing.

Of course these arguments pro and con. cannot be given or even indicated here in detail. The main ones, however, even at some length, may properly be here set down, because it is in forgetting this history that this vital principle of the nation is forgotten. And let it not be forgotten that in reproducing this matter here, the sole object is to demonstrate the utter weakness of the "Christian nation" decision and of the arguments in its favor, and, on the other hand, to demonstrate the perfect propriety, and, indeed, the necessity of uncompromising opposition to that decision, upon national principle, upon national authority, and upon national precedent.

The arguments reproduced here as once made in behalf of the Dred Scott decision, are in very substance, and largely in very words, the arguments, and the only ones, that are now made or that can be made in behalf of the Christian nation decision. And the answer to these arguments in the former case are exactly our answers now in this latter case. The decisions and the arguments in favor of it were invalid in the former case, and so they are in the latter case, while the opposition and the arguments thereof, being proper, sound, and constitutional against the former decision, so they are also against the latter decision.

FOR AND AGAINST THE DECISIONS.

The former decision was finally delivered about the beginning of the year 1857. It made a great commotion, and the opposition was instant and open and emphatic. Against this opposition the affirmative—Senator Douglas—in behalf of the decision declared:—

"The courts are the tribunals prescribed by the Constitution and created by the authority of the people to determine, expound, and enforce the law. Hence, whoever resists the final decision of the highest judicial tribunal, aims a deadly blow at our whole republican system of government—a blow which, if successful, would place all our rights and liberties at the mercy of passion, anarchy, and violence. I repeat, therefore, that if resistance to the decision of the Supreme Court of the United States in a matter like the points decided in the Dred Scott case, clearly within their jurisdiction as defined by the Constitution, shall be forced upon the country as a political issue, it will become a distinct and naked issue between the friends and enemies of the Constitution—the friends and the enemies of the supremacy of the laws."[4]—*Political Speeches and Debates, p. 43.*

To this the opposition—Abraham Lincoln, Springfield, Ill., June 26, 1857—replied:—

"And now as to the Dred Scott decision. That decision declares two propositions—first, that a negro cannot sue in the United States courts; and, secondly, that Congress cannot prohibit slavery in the Territories. . . . Judge Douglas . . . denounces all who question the correctness of that decision, as offering violent resistance to it. But who resists it? Who has, in spite of the decision, declared Dred Scott free, and resisted the authority of his master over him?

"Judicial decisions have two uses—first, to absolutely determine the case decided; and, secondly, to indicate to the public how other similar cases will be decided when they arise. For the latter use they are called 'precedents' and 'authorities.'

"We believe as much as Judge Douglas (perhaps more) in obedience to, and respect for, the judicial department of the government. . . . But we think the Dred Scott decision is erroneous. We know the court that made it, has often overruled its own decisions, and we shall do what we can to have it overrule this. We offer no resistance

---

[4] I have been unable to find the complete speech in which this was said. It is therefore taken from Lincoln's speech at Springfield, Ill., June 26, 1857, just as there it stands. Douglas's speech was made "two weeks" before this.

to it. . . . It is not resistance, it is not factious, it is not even disrespectful, to treat it as not having yet quite established a settled doctrine for the country.   But Judge Douglas considers this view awful."
—*Political Speeches and Debates, pp. 42, 43.*

In 1858 Lincoln and Douglas were rival candidates for the United States senatorship; and the Dred Scott decision was the leading issue.   Friday evening, July 9, Senator Douglas made a speech in Chicago, in which, noticing Lincoln's speech upon his nomination for senator, he said:—

"The other proposition discussed by Mr. Lincoln in his speech, consists in a crusade against the Supreme Court of the United States on account of the Dred Scott decision.   On this question also I desire to say to you unequivocally, that I take direct and distinct issue with him.   I have no warfare to make on the Supreme Court of the United States, either on account of that or any other decision which they have pronounced from that bench.   The Constitution of the United States has provided that the powers of government (and the constitution of each State has the same provision) shall be divided into three departments—Executive, Legislative, and Judicial.   The right and the province of expounding the Constitution and construing the law are vested in the judiciary established by the Constitution.   As a lawyer, I feel at liberty to appear before the court and controvert any principle of law while the question is pending before the tribunal; but when the decision is made, my private opinion, your opinion, all other opinions, must yield to the majesty of that authoritative adjudication.

"I wish you to bear in mind that this involves a great principle, upon which our rights, our liberty, and our property all depend.   What security have you for your property, for your reputation, and for your personal rights, if the courts are not upheld, and their decisions respected when once fairly rendered by the highest tribunal known to the Constitution?

"I do not choose, therefore, to go into any argument with Mr. Lincoln in reviewing the various decisions which the Supreme Court has made, either upon the Dred Scott case or any other.   I have no idea of appealing from the decision of the Supreme Court upon a constitutional question to the decisions of a tumultuous town meeting.   I am aware that once an eminent lawyer of this city, now no more, said that

11

the State of Illinois had the most perfect judicial system in the world, subject to but one exception, which could be cured by a slight amendment, and that amendment was to so change the law as to allow an appeal from the decisions of the Supreme Court of Illinois, on all constitutional questions, to justices of the peace.

"My friend, Mr. Lincoln, who sits behind me, reminds me that that proposition was made when I was judge of the Supreme Court. Be that as it may, I do not think that fact adds any greater weight or authority to the suggestion. It matters not with me who was on the bench, whether Mr. Lincoln or myself, whether a Lockwood or a Smith, a Taney or a Marshall; the decision of the highest tribunal known to the Constitution of the country must be final till it is reversed by an equally high authority. Hence, I am opposed to this doctrine of Mr. Lincoln by which he proposes to take an appeal from the decision of the Supreme Court of the United States, upon this high constitutional question, to a Republican caucus sitting in the country. Yes, or any other caucus or town meeting, whether it be Republican, American, or Democratic. I respect the decisions of that august tribunal. I shall always bow in deference to them. I am a law-abiding man. I will sustain the Constitution of the country as our fathers have made it. I will yield obedience to the laws whether I like them or not, as I find them on the statute book. I will sustain the judicial tribunals and constituted authorities in all matters within the pale of their jurisdiction as defined by the Constitution."—*Id., pp. 69, 70.*

The next night, July 10, 1858, Lincoln spoke in reply to Douglas, and upon this point said:—

"Another of the issues he says that is to be made with me is upon his devotion to the Dred Scott decision, and my opposition to it.

"I have expressed heretofore, and I now repeat my opposition to the Dred Scott decision; but I should be allowed to state the nature of that opposition, and I ask your indulgence while I do so. What is fairly implied by the term Judge Douglas has used, 'resistance to the decision'? I do not resist it. If I wanted to take Dred Scott from his master, I would be interfering with property, and that terrible difficulty that Judge Douglas speaks of, of interfering with property, would arise.   But I am doing no such thing as that; but all that I am doing is refusing to obey it as a political rule.   If I were in Congress, and a vote should come up on a question whether slavery should be prohibited in a new territory, in spite of the Dred Scott decision I would vote that it should.

"That is what I should do.   Judge Douglas said last night that before the decision he might advance his opinion, and it might be contrary to the decision when it was made, but after it was made, he would abide by it until it was reversed.   Just so!   We let this property abide by the decision, but we will try to reverse that decision.   We will try to put it where Judge Douglas would not object, for he says he will obey it until it is reversed.   Somebody has to reverse that decision, since it was made, and we mean to reverse it, and we mean to do it peaceably.

"What are the uses of decisions of courts?—They have two uses.   As rules of property they have two uses.   First, they decide upon the question before the court.   They decide in this case that Dred Scott is a slave; nobody resists that.   Not only that, but they say to everybody else that persons standing just as Dred Scott stands, are as he is.   That is, they say that when a question comes up upon another person, it will be so decided again, unless the court decides in another way, unless the court overrules its decision.   Well, we mean to do what we can to have the court decide the other way.   That is one thing we mean to try to do.

"The sacredness that Judge Douglas throws around this decision is a degree of sacredness that has never been before thrown around any other decision.   I have never heard of such a thing.   Why, decisions apparently contrary to that decision, or that good lawyers thought were contrary to that decision, have been made by that very court before.   It is the first of its kind; it is an astonisher in legal history; it is a new wonder of the world.   It is based upon falsehood in the main as to facts; allegations of facts upon which it stands are not facts at all in many instances, and no decision made on any question—the first instance of a decision made under so many unfavorable circumstances—thus placed, has ever been held by the profession as law, and it has always needed confirmation before the lawyers regarded it as settled law.   But Judge Douglas will have it that all hands must take this extraordinary decision, made under these extraordinary circumstances, and give their vote in Congress in accordance with it, yield to it, and obey it in every possible sense."—*Id.*, *84, 85.*

Again: In a speech at Bloomington, Illinois, July 16, 1858, Senator Douglas said:—

"I therefore take issue with Mr. Lincoln directly in regard to this warfare upon the Supreme Court of the United States. I accept the decision of that court as it was pronounced. Whatever my individual opinions may be, I, as a good citizen, am bound by the laws of the land as the Legislature makes them, as the court expounds them, and as the executive officer administers them. I am bound by our Constitution as our fathers made it, and as it is our duty to support it. I am bound as a good citizen to sustain the constituted authorities, and to resist, discourage, and beat down, by all lawful and peaceful means, all attempts at exciting mobs, or violence, or any other revolutionary proceedings, against the Constitution and the constituted authorities of the country."—*Id.*, *pp. 108, 109.*

The next night, July 17, at Springfield, Illinois, Lincoln replied and said:—

"Now as to the Dred Scott decision, for upon that he makes his last point at me. He boldly takes ground in favor of that decision.

"This is one-half the onslaught, and one-third of the plan, of the entire campaign. I am opposed to that decision in a certain sense, but not in the sense which he puts on it. I say that in so far as it decided in favor of Dred Scott's master, and against Dred Scott and his family, I do not propose to disturb or resist the decision.

"I never have proposed to do any such thing. I think that in respect for judicial authority my humble history would not suffer in comparison with that of Judge Douglas. He would have the citizen conform his vote to that decision; the member of Congress, his; the President, his use of the veto power. He would make it a rule of political action for the people and all the departments of the government. I would not. By resisting it as a political rule, I disturb no right of property, create no disorder, excite no mobs."—*Id., p. 155.*

Once more: In the debate at Galesburg, Illinois, October 7, 1858, between them, Douglas said:—

"Why this attempt then to bring the Supreme Court into disrepute among the people? It looks as if there was an effort being made to destroy public confidence in the highest judicial tribunal on earth. Suppose he succeeds in destroying public confidence in the court, so that the people will not respect its decisions, but will feel at liberty to disregard them and resist the laws of the land, what will he have gained? He will have changed the government from one of laws into that of a mob, in which the strong arm of violence will be substituted for the decisions of the courts of justice. He complains because I do not go into an argument reviewing Chief Justice Taney's opinion, and the other opinions of the different judges, to determine whether their reasoning is right or wrong on the questions of law. What use would that be? He wants to take an appeal from the Supreme Court to this meeting, to determine whether the questions of law were decided properly. He is going to appeal from the Supreme Court of the United States to every town meeting, in the hope that he can excite a prejudice against that court, and on the wave of that prejudice ride into the Senate of the United States when he could not get there on his own principles or his own merits." —*Id., pp. 372, 373.*

And in the debate at Quincy he said:—

"He [Lincoln] tells you that he does not like the Dred Scott decision. Suppose he does not; how is he going to help himself? He says he will reverse it. How will he reverse it? I know of but one mode of reversing judicial decisions, and that is by appealing from the inferior to the superior court. But I have never yet learned how or where an appeal could be taken from the Supreme Court of the United States! The Dred Scott decision was pronounced by the highest tribunal on earth. From that decision *there is no appeal this side of heaven.*"—*Id., pp. 396, 397.*

In the Quincy, Illinois, debate, October 13, 1858, upon this Lincoln said:—

"We oppose the Dred Scott decision in a certain way, upon which I ought perhaps to address you a few words. We do not propose that when Dred Scott has been decided to be a slave by the court, we, as a mob, will decide him to be free. We do not propose that when any other one, or one thousand, shall be decided by that court to be slaves, we will in any violent way disturb the rights of property thus settled; but we nevertheless do oppose that decision as a political rule which shall be binding on the voter to vote for nobody who thinks it wrong, which shall be binding on the members of Congress, or the President, to favor no measure which does not actually concur with the principles of that decision. We do not propose to be bound by it as a political rule in that way, because we think it lays the foundation not merely of enlarging and spreading out what we consider an evil, but it lays the foundation for spreading that evil into the States themselves. We propose so resisting it as to have it reversed if we can, and a new judicial rule established upon this subject."—*Id., p. 384.*

THE MEANING OF THE DECLARATION.

Another leading point in defense of the decision, was the necessity of maintaining the correctness of the use that the court had made of the Declaration of Independence. The court had argued as follows:—

"The language of the Declaration of Independence is equally conclusive. It begins by declaring. . . . It then proceeds to say: 'We hold these truths to be self-evident: that all men are created equal; that they are endowed by their Creator with certain unalienable rights; that among them are life, liberty, and the pursuit of happiness; that to secure these rights, governments are instituted deriving their just powers from the consent of the governed.'

"The general words above used would seem to embrace the whole human family, and if they were used in a similar instrument at this day, would be so understood. But it is too clear for dispute that the enslaved African race were not intended to be included, and formed no part of the people who framed and adopted this Declaration, for if the language as understood in that day would embrace them, then the conduct of the distinguished men who framed the Declaration of Independence would have been utterly and flagrantly inconsistent with the principles they asserted; and instead of the sympathy of mankind, to which they confidently appealed, they would have deserved and received universal rebuke and reprobation.

"Yet the men who framed this Declaration were great men—high in literary acquirements—high in their sense of honor, and incapable of asserting principles inconsistent with those on which they were acting.   They perfectly understood the meaning of the language they used, and how it would be understood by others; and they knew that it would not in any part of the civilized world be supposed to embrace the negro race, which by common consent had been excluded from civilized governments and the family of nations, and doomed to slavery."

In support of this view of the Supreme Court that "all men" did not include the negro, Senator Douglas argued thus:—

"No man can vindicate the character, motives, and conduct of the signers of the Declaration of Independence except upon the hypothesis that they referred to the white race alone, and not to the African, when they declared all men to have been created equal."—*Quoted by Lincoln, Springfield, Ill., speech, June 26, 1857; Id , p. 48.*

"I believe the Declaration of Independence, in the words 'all men are created equal,' was intended to allude only to the people of the United States, to men of European birth or descent, being white men; that they were created equal, and hence that Great Britain had no right to deprive them of their political and religious privileges; but the signers of that paper did not intend to include the Indian or the negro in the Declaration, for if they had, would they not have been bound to abolish slavery in every State and Colony from that day?"—*Springfield, Ill., speech, July 17, 1858; Id., p. 139.*

The answer to this division will be clearer, and its pertinency to the Christian nation decision more readily discerned, by separating it according to the two points made.   For both these points—the perversion of the plain words of the Declaration, and the drawing of those who made it, into this perversion—are equally the mode of the Christian nation decision and its defenders.

First, to the idea that the men of the Revolution actually meant the words "all men" to exclude the negro, or else laid themselves open to "universal rebuke and reprobation," Lincoln replied:—

"Chief Justice Taney, in his opinion in the Dred Scott case, admits that the language of the Declaration is broad enough to include the whole human family; but he and Judge Douglas argue that the authors of that instrument did not intend to include negroes, by the fact that they did not at once actually place them on an equality with the whites. Now this grave argument comes to just nothing at all by the other fact that they did not at once, or ever afterward, actually place all white people on an equality with one another. And this is the staple argument of both the chief justice and the senator for doing this obvious violence to the plain, unmistakable language of the Declaration.

"I think the authors of that notable instrument intended to include all men, but they did not intend to declare all men equal in all respects. They did not mean to say all were equal in color, size, intellect, moral development, or social capacity. They defined with tolerable distinctness in what respects they did consider all men created equal—equal 'with certain inalienable rights, among which are life, liberty, and the pursuit of happiness.' This they said, and this they meant. They did not mean to assert the obvious untruth that all were actually enjoying that equality, nor yet that they were about to confer it immediately upon them. In fact, they had no power to confer such a boon. They meant simply to declare the right, so that the enforcement of it might follow as fast as circumstances should permit."—*Springfield, Ill., Speech, June 26, 1857; Id., pp. 47, 48.*

"I do not propose, in regard to this argument drawn from the history of former times, to enter into a detailed examination of the historical statements he has made. I have the impression that they are inaccurate in a great many instances—sometimes in positive statement—but very much more inaccurate by the suppression of statements that really belong to the history. But I do not propose to affirm that this is so to any very great extent, or to enter into any very minute examination of his historical statements. I avoid doing so upon this principle—that if it were important for me to pass out of this lot in the least period of time possible, and I came to that fence, and saw by a calculation of my known strength and agility that I could clear it at a bound, it would be folly for me to stop and consider whether I could or not crawl through a crack. So I say of the whole history contained in his essay,[5] where he endeavored to link the men of the Revolution to popular sovereignty. It only requires an effort to leap out of it, a single bound to be entirely successful. If you read it over you will find that he quotes here and there from documents of the revolutionary times, tending to show that the people of the Colonies were desirous of regulating their own concerns in their own way. . . .

"Now, however this history may apply, and whatever of his argument there may be that is sound and accurate or unsound and inaccurate, if we can find out what these men did themselves do upon this very question of slavery in the Territories, does it not end the whole thing? If, after all this labor and effort to show that the men of the Revolution were in favor of his popular sovereignty, and his mode of dealing with slavery in the Territories, we can show that these very men took hold of that subject, and dealt with it, we can see for ourselves how they dealt with it. *It is not a matter of argument or inference, but we know what they thought about it.*

"It is precisely upon that part of the history of the country that one important omission is made by Judge Douglas. He selects parts of the history of the United States upon the subject of slavery, and treats it as the whole. . . . There was another part of our political history, made by the very men who were the actors in the Revolution, which has taken the name of the 'Ordinance of '87.' Let me bring that history to your attention. In 1784, I believe, this same Mr. Jefferson drew up an ordinance for the government of the country upon which we now stand, or, rather, a frame or draft of an ordinance for the government of this country, here in Ohio, our neighbors in Indiana, us who live in Illinois, our neighbors in Wisconsin and Michigan. In that ordinance, drawn up not only for the government of that Territory, but for the Territories south of the Ohio River, Mr. Jefferson *expressly provided for the prohibition of slavery.*

"Judge Douglas says, and perhaps is right, that that pro-

---

[5] Senator Douglas had published an essay in *Harper's Magazine*, which is immediately referred to here.

vision was lost from that ordinance. I believe that is true.
When the vote was taken upon it, a majority of all present in
the Congress of the confederation voted for it; but there were
so many absentees that those voting for it did not make the
clear majority necessary, and it was lost. But three years after
that the Congress of the confederation were together again,
and they adopted a new ordinance for the government of this
Northwest Territory, not contemplating territory south of the
river, for the States owning that territory had hitherto refrained
from giving it to the general government; hence they made
the ordinance to apply only to what the government owned.
In that, the provision excluding slavery *was inserted and passed
unanimously*, or, at any rate, it passed and became a part of
the law of the land. Under that ordinance we live. . . .

"Not only did that ordinance prevail, but it was constantly
looked to whenever a step was taken by a new Territory to
become a State.   Congress always turned their attention to it,
and in all their movements upon this subject, they traced their
course by that Ordinance of '87. When they admitted new
States they advised them of this ordinance as a part of the
legislation of the country. They did so because they had
traced the Ordinance of '87 throughout the history of the
country. Begin with the men of the Revolution, and go down
for sixty entire years, and until the last scrap of that Territory
comes into the Union in the form of the State of Wisconsin,
everything was made to conform with the Ordinance of '87,
excluding slavery from that vast extent of country.

"I omitted to mention in the right place that the Constitution of the United States was in process of being framed when
that ordinance was made by the Congress of the Confederation; and one of the first acts of Congress itself, *under the new
Constitution itself*,[6] was to give force to that ordinance by putting power to carry it out in the hands of the new officers
under the Constitution, in place of the old ones, who had been
legislated out of existence by the change in the government
from the confederation to the Constitution. Not only so, but
I believe Indiana once or twice, if not Ohio, petitioned the
general government for the privilege of suspending that provision and allowing them to have slaves. A report made by
Mr. Randolph, of Virginia, himself a slaveholder, was directly

---

[6]See pages 104, 124 this book.

against it, and the action was to refuse them the privilege of violating the Ordinance of '87.

"This period of history, which I have run over briefly, is, I presume, as familiar to most of this assembly as any other part of the history of our country. I suppose that few of my hearers are not as familiar with that part of history as I am, and I only mention it to recall your attention to it at this time. And hence I ask how extraordinary a thing it is that a man who has occupied a position on the floor of the Senate of the United States, who is now in his third term, and who looks to see the government of this whole country fall into his own hands, pretending to give a truthful and accurate history of the slavery question in this country, should so entirely ignore the whole of that portion of our history, the most important of all. Is it not a most extraordinary spectacle that a man should stand up and ask for any confidence in his statements who sets out as he does with portions of history, calling upon the people to believe that it is a true and fair representation when the leading part and controlling feature of the whole history is carefully suppressed?"[7]

"But the mere leaving out is not the most remarkable feature of this most remarkable essay. His proposition is to establish that the leading men of the Revolution were for his great principle of nonintervention by the government in the question of slavery in the Territories, while history shows that they decided, in the cases actually brought before them, in exactly the contrary way, and he knows it.[8] Not only did they so decide at that time, but they stuck to it during sixty years, through thick and thin, *as long as there was one of the revolutionary heroes upon the stage of political action. Through their whole course, from first to last, they clung to freedom.*

"And now he asks the community to believe that the men of the Revolution were in favor of his great principle, when we have the naked history that they themselves dealt with this very subject matter of his principle, and utterly repudiated his principle, acting upon a precisely contrary ground. It is as impudent and absurd as if a prosecuting attorney should stand up before a jury and ask them to convict A as the murderer of B, while B was walking alive before them."—*Speech, Columbus, Ohio, September, 1859; Id., pp. 469-473.*

[7] See pages 130-132 this book.
[8] See pages 88-108 this book.

In another speech touching the history here referred to, he closed his reference with these words:—

"Thus, with the author of the Declaration of Independence, the policy of prohibiting slavery in the new territory originated. Thus, away back of the Constitution, in the pure, fresh, free breath of the Revolution, the State of Virginia and the National Congress put that policy in practice."—*Peoria, Ill., October 16, 1854; Id., p. 3.*

Secondly, to the idea that the Declaration could be used by such interpretation in the interests of despotism, Lincoln replied:—

"Now, I ask you in all soberness if all these things, if indulged in, if ratified, if confirmed and endorsed, if taught to our children, and repeated to them, do not tend to rub out the sentiment of liberty in the country, and to transform this government into a government of some other form?[9]

"Those arguments that are made, that the inferior race are to be treated with as much allowance as they are capable of enjoying; that as much is to be done for them as their condition will allow—what are these arguments? They are the arguments that kings have made for enslaving the people in all ages of the world. You will find that all the arguments in favor of kingcraft were of this class; they also bestrode the necks of the people, not that they wanted to do it, but because the people were better off for being ridden. That is their argument, and this argument of the Judge is the same old serpent that says, You work, and I eat; you toil, and I will enjoy the fruits of it.

"Turn it whatever way you will, whether it come from the mouth of a king, as an excuse for enslaving the people of his

---

[9] Another thing that makes this discussion on the Declaration pertinent to the Christian nation decision and to our times, is the fact that the partisans of that decision have attacked that other material principle of the Declaration—governments derive their just powers from the consent of the governed. On this, at Chautauqua Assembly, 1889, the president of the American Sabbath Union said:—

"Governments do *not* derive their just powers from the consent of the governed."

And in the same year, in a religio-political convention in Sedalia, Missouri, another of the leaders of that company said:—

" I do not belive that governments derive their just powers from the consent of the governed; and so the object of this movement is to change that feature of our fundamental law."—*See Two Republics, pp. 727, 728, edition of 1895.*

country, or from the mouth of men of one race as a reason for enslaving the men of another race, it is all the same old serpent; and I hold, if that course of argumentation that is made for the purpose of convincing the public mind that we should not care about this, should be granted, it does not stop with the negro. I should like to know if, taking this old Declaration of Independence, which declares that all men are equal upon principle, and making exceptions to it, where will it stop? If one man says it does not mean a negro, why not another say it does not mean some other man? If that Declaration is not the truth, let us get the statute book in which we find it and tear it out. Who is so bold as to do it? If it is not true let us tear it out. [Cries of No! no!] Let us stick to it, then let us stand firmly by it, then."—*Chicago Speech, July 10, 1858; Id., p. 90.*

"They meant to set up a standard maxim for free society, which should be familiar to all, and referred to by all, constantly looked to, constantly labored for, and, even though never perfectly attained, constantly approximated, and thereby constantly spreading and deepening its influence and augmenting the happiness and value of life of all people of all color everywhere. The assertion that 'all men are created equal' was of no practical use in affecting our separation from England; and it was placed in the Declaration, not for that but for future use. Its authors meant it to be, as, thank God, it is now proving itself, a stumbling block to all those who, in after time, might seek to turn a free people back into the hateful paths of despotism. They knew the proneness of prosperity to breed tyrants, and they meant when such should reappear in this fair land and commence their vocation, they should find left for them at least one hard nut to crack."—*Springfield, Ill., Speech, June 26, 1857; Id , p. 48.*

"In those days our Declaration of Independence was held sacred by all, and thought to include all; but now, to aid in making the bondage of the negro [and now the consciences of all, A. T. J.] universal and eternal, it is assailed and sneered at, and construed, and hawked at, and torn, till, if its framers could rise from their graves, they could not at all recognize it."—*Id., p. 46.*

"DICTA" AND "DECISION."

Another plea, which, however, was rather in the shape of an apology for the Dred Scott decision, was that all that part against which the great objection was made was mere "*obiter dicta*," [10] that is, things said only by the way, or in passing; that it was "extra-judicial," and therefore of no real force in law, and so there was no need of paying any particular attention to it nor of raising any opposition against it. This plea Lincoln defined as "a little quibble among lawyers between the words 'dicta' and 'decision,'" [11] and replied to it as follows:—

"I know the legal arguments that can be made,—that after a court has decided that it cannot take jurisdiction in a case, it then has decided all that is before it, and that is the end of it. A plausible argument can be made in favor of that proposition; but I know that Judge Douglas has said in one of his speeches that the court went forward, *like honest men as they were*, and decided all the points in the case. If any points are really extra-judicially decided because not necessarily before them, then this one as to the power of the Territorial Legislature to exclude slavery is one of them, as also the one that the Missouri Compromise was null and void. They are both extra-judicial, or neither is, according as the court held that they had no jurisdiction in the case between the parties, because of want of capacity of one party to maintain a suit in that court.

"I want, if I have sufficient time, to show that the court did *pass its opinion;* but that is the only thing actually done in the case. If they did not decide, they showed what they were

---

[10] Even Bryce, at this late day, sanctions this view ("Am. Com.," chapter 24, par. 5 and note; and chapter 53, par. 15, note.). But however that may be as to the Dred Scott decision, there is no kind of ground for any such view fairly to be taken as to the "Christian nation" decision.

[11] His exact words are: "I undertake to give the opinion, at least, that if the Territories attempt by any direct legislation to drive the man with his slave out of the Territory, or to decide that his slave is free because of his being taken in there, or to tax him to such an extent that he cannot keep him there, the Supreme Court will unhesitatingly decide all such legislation unconstitutional as long as that Supreme Court is constructed as the Dred Scott Supreme Court is.' The first two things they have already decided, except that there is a little quibble among lawyers between the words 'dicta' and 'decision.' They have already decided that the negro cannot be made free by territorial legislation."— *Columbus, O., Speech, 1859; Id., pp. 475, 476.*

ready to decide whenever the matter was brought before them. What is that opinion? After having argued that Congress had no power to pass a law excluding slavery from a United States Territory, they then used language to this effect, That inasmuch as Congress itself could not exercise such a power, it followed as a matter of course that it could not authorize a territorial government to exercise it; for the territorial Legislature could do no more than Congress could do. Thus it expressed its opinion emphatically against the power of a territorial Legislature to exclude slavery, leaving us in just as little doubt upon that point as upon any other point they really decided."—*Jonesboro, Ill., Debate, September 15, 1858; Id., pp. 271, 272.*

And again:—

"There is no sort of question that the Supreme Court has decided that it is the right of the slaveholder to take his slave and hold him in the Territory; and saying this, Judge Douglas himself admits the conclusion. He says, 'If this is so, this consequence will follow;' and because this consequence would follow, his argument is, 'The decision cannot, therefore, be that way—that would spoil my popular sovereignty, and it cannot be possible that this great principle has been squelched out in that extraordinary way. It might be, if it were not for the extraordinary consequences of spoiling my humbug.' "— *Columbus, O., Speech, 1859, Id., p. 477.*

IS IT ONLY THEORY?

Another plea, akin to this "little quibble," was that, even admitting the points against which the opposition was contending, to be really a part of the decision itself, after all it was merely an abstract question of no moment whatever in any practical way. This view was stated by Senator Douglas thus:—

"Mr. Lincoln says that this Dred Scott decision destroys the doctrine of popular sovereignty, for the reason that the court has decided that Congress has no power to prohibit slavery in the Territories, and hence he infers that it would decide that the territorial Legislatures could not prohibit slavery there. I will not stop to inquire whether the court will carry the decision that far or not.   It would be interesting *as a matter of theory*, but of *no importance in practice.*"—*Springfield, Ill., Speech, July 17, 1858; Id., pp. 134, 135.*

"It matters not what way the Supreme Court may hereafter decide as to *the abstract question* whether slavery may, or may not, go into a territory under the Constitution. . . . Hence, no matter what the decision of the Supreme Court may be on *that abstract question,* etc."—*Freeport, Ill., Debate, August 27, 1858; Id., pp. 213, 214.*

To this, Lincoln replied thus:—

"He says this Dred Scott case is a very small matter at most—that it has no practical effect; that at best, or, rather, I suppose, at worst, it is but an abstraction.   I submit that the proposition that the thing which determines whether a man is free or a slave is rather *concrete* than *abstract.*   I think you would conclude that it was if your liberty depended upon it, and so would Judge Douglas if his liberty depended upon it." —*Springfield, Ill., Speech, July 17, 1858; Id., p. 157.*

"A decision of the Supreme Court is made, by which it is declared that Congress, if it desires to prohibit the spread of slavery into the Territories, has no constitutional power to do so.   Not only so, but that decision lays down principles which, if pushed to their logical conclusion,—I say pushed to their logical conclusion, would decide that the constitutions of free States, forbidding slavery, are themselves unconstitutional. Mark me, I do not say the judges said this, and let no man say I affirm the judges used these words; but I only say it is my opinion that what they did say, if pressed to its logical conclusion, will inevitably result thus. . . .

"Take it just as it stands, and apply it as a principle; extend and apply that principle elsewhere; and consider where it will lead you.   . . .   I say, if this principle is established, . . . when this is done, where this doctrine prevails, the miners and sappers will have formed public opinion for the slave trade. They will be ready for Jeff. Davis and Stephens and other leaders of that company to sound the bugle for the revival of the slave trade *for the second Dred Scott decision,* for the flood of slavery to be poured over the free States, while we shall be here tied down and helpless and run over like sheep."— *Columbus, O., Speech, 1859; Id., pp. 460, 478, 480.*

Such were the main pleas and the answers thereto, upon the merits of the Dred Scott decision. And we say again that every one of these pleas, in very substance, and almost in the very words, is now held and urged in behalf of the Christian nation decision. And the answers of Abraham Lincoln to those pleas in support of that decision in that day, are precisely our answers to these same pleas in support of this decision in this our day. No less than he in that case, do we oppose this decision now and appeal from it. No more than he in that case, do we in this case propose to disturb any right of property, create any disorder, or excite any mobs. No less than he in that case, are we in this case "working on the plan of the founders of the government," and "fighting it upon these original principles—fighting it in the Jeffersonian, Washingtonian, and Madisonian fashion." No more now than then ought the people to allow themselves to be made helpless and tied down and run over like sheep.

The people in that day arose in their right and reversed that decision, and thus added the force of national precedent to that of national principle and national authority, upon the right of the people to appeal from any Supreme Court decision touching any constitutional question. Will *the people* in this our day realize the danger of the religious despotism which lurks in this decision as did they in that day the danger of the civil despotism that lay in that decision, and again arise in their right—their right by fundamental principle, by national authority, and by national precedent—and reverse this decision?

12

CHAPTER IX.

THE BUGLERS, THE MINERS AND SAPPERS.

IT is certain that there was a powerful party interested in the maintenance of the Dred Scott decision in its principle of the nationalization of slavery, and who were ready to push that principle to the utmost extent of the logic of it.

It is certain that there is now in the United States *two* powerful combinations intensely interested in the maintenance of the principle of the Christian nation decision nationalizing "the establishment of the Christian religion," and determined to push the force of that decision to the fullest extent of all the logic that its principle can be made to bear. After the rendering of the decision of the Supreme Court that "this is a Christian nation" within the meaning of the Constitution, it were impossible that there should not be *at least* two bodies anxious to put themselves upon the nation as the Christianity most becoming to the Christian nation. Let governmental recognition of religion be once established, and there will always be organizations of religion to take advantage of it and turn the power and influence of it to their own aggrandizement. And the more sects there are in the country, and the more worldly these are, the more of such aspirants there will certainly be, each one being in a certain sense obliged to secure possession of the governmental recognition and power, so as to be safe from the oppression of such of the others as might obtain it; so as to be exempt, without persecution, from doing homage to such other one.

The first of these combinations, and the one of most importance practically, is THE PAPACY.

I.

WHAT THE PAPACY IS DOING.

In a previous chapter there has been pointed out how completely the principle of this decision is the papal principle only. The Papacy herself sees this, and is making great use of it. It would be surprising if she did not.

In the discussions which led up to the making of the national Constitution with the specific exclusion of religion from the notice of the national government, it was not without reason that our fathers pointedly inquired, "Who does not see that the same authority which can establish Christianity, in exclusion of all other religions, may establish with the same ease any particular sect of Christians in exclusion of all other sects?"—*P. 98.*

They knew full well that, as certainly as "Christianity" were established as the governmental religion, so certainly some particular sect of "Christians" would worm, or crowd, itself into the place of recognition and authority *as the "Christianity"* recognized and established, and this to the exclusion of all other sects, because it would be in some way decided by "authority" that that particular phase of "Christianity" was more in harmony with the intent of the law than any other.

Thus they saw that any recognition of "Christianity" would inevitably bring forth a decision of some kind as to "what is Christianity," and what form of the profession is most entitled to the name and the favor of the government, as contemplated in the act of establishment or the form of recognition. And knowing this, they further and truly said that "it is impossible for the magistrate to adjudge the right of preference among the various sects that profess the Christian faith, without erecting a claim to infallibility, which would lead us back to the Church of Rome."—*Pp. 86, 87.*

They saw that the domination of Rome must be the sure result of any governmental recognition of religion. It was clearly the intent of the makers of the national government to save this country from the domination of Rome. It was, therefore, to accomplish this, as well as from love of the right of the people, that in their establishment of the national Constitution they did it with the positive prohibition of any recognition of religion, and particularly "the Christian religion."

The Papacy still lives. She still lives, and is as thoroughly ambitious of governmental power as she ever was, and even more so, if such a thing were possible. And as the government of the United States has done the very thing which the makers of the government said that it were impossible to do without leading back to the Church of Rome, it is proper to look about us and see if there are now any signs of this result from this action on the part of the government.

As the Papacy still lives, as it is true that the Papacy "learns much and forgets nothing," and as it is her boast that she never changes, it will be instructive to glance at what she did once in such a case.

WHAT THE CATHOLIC CHURCH ONCE DID.

In the beginning of the fourth century, in the Roman Empire, the Catholic Church was a powerful ecclesiastical organization, the leaders and managers of which were "only anxious to assert the government as a kind of sovereignty for themselves."[1] Constantine and Licinius, as joint emperors, issued the Edict of Milan, reversing the persecuting edicts of Diocletian, and granting "liberty and full freedom to the Christians to observe their own mode of worship," granting, "likewise, to the Christians and to all, the free choice to follow

---

[1] Eusebius, "Ecclesiastical History," Book VIII, chapter 1.

that mode of worship which they may wish;" "that each may have the privilege to select and to worship whatsoever divinity he pleases;" and commanding that the churches and church property which had been confiscated by Diocletian should be restored to "the whole body of Christians," "and to each conventicle respectively." [2]

This was all just and proper enough, and innocent enough, in itself and on its face, *if that had been all there was to it;* but behind it there lay this ecclesiastical organization, ambitious to assert the government as a kind of sovereignty for itself. This ecclesiastical organization, the Catholic Church, claimed at that time, as ever since, to be the legitimate and only true representative and depositary of Christianity in the world. And no sooner had the Edict of Milan ordered the restoration of property *to the Christians* than it was seized upon by the church leaders and made an issue by which to secure the imperial recognition and the legal establishment of *the Catholic Church.*

The rule had long before been established that all who did not agree with the bishops of the Catholic Church were necessarily heretics, and not Christians at all. It was now claimed by the Catholic Church that, therefore, none such were entitled to any benefit from the edict restoring property *to the Christians.*

In other words, the Catholic Church disputed the right of any others than Catholics to receive property or money under the Edict of Milan, by disputing their right to the title of Christians. And by this issue the Catholic Church forced an imperial decision as to *who were Christians.* And, under the circumstances, by the power and influence which she held and by what she had already done with these in behalf of Constantine, it was a foregone conclusion, if not the concerted plan, that this decision would be in favor of the Catholic Church.

---

[2] *Id.*, Book X, chapter 5.

Consequently, Constantine's edict to the proconsul, directing the restoration of the property, contained these words:—

"It is our will that when thou shalt receive this epistle, if any of those things belonging to *the Catholic Church* of the Christians in the several cities or other places, are now possessed either by the decurions, or any others, these thou shalt cause immediately to be restored to their churches. Since we have previously determined that whatsoever *these same churches* before possessed should be restored to them."

Nor was it enough that the emperor should decide that all these favors were for " the Catholic Church of the Christians;" he was obliged next to decide *which was the Catholic Church.* This question was immediately raised and disputed, and in consequence an edict was drawn from Constantine, addressed to the same proconsul (of the province of Africa), in which were these words:—

"It is my will that these men, within the province intrusted to thee in the Catholic Church, *over which Cæcilianus presides*, who give their services to *this* holy religion, and whom they commonly call clergy, shall be held totally free and exempt from all public offices," etc.

The party over which Cecilianus presided in Africa was the party which was in communion with the bishop of Rome. As these only were favored, the other party drew up a long series of charges against Cecilianus, and sent them to the emperor, with a petition that he would have the case examined by the bishops of Gaul. Constantine was in Gaul at the time, but instead of having the bishops of Gaul examine into the case alone, he commissioned three of them to go to Rome and sit with the bishop of Rome in council to decide the case. Constantine sent a letter, with copies of all the charges and complaints which had been lodged with him, and in this letter to *the bishop of Rome*, with other things he said this:—

"Since it neither escapes your diligence that I show such regard for the holy Catholic Church that *I wish you*, upon the whole, *to leave no room* for *schism or division*."

This council of course confirmed the emperor's word that the Catholic Church in Africa was indeed the one over which Cecilianus presided. The other party appealed from this decision and petitioned that another and larger council be called to examine the question. Another council was called, composed of almost all the bishops of Constantine's dominions. This council likewise confirmed the emperor's word and the decision of the former council. Then the opposing party appealed from the decision of the council to the emperor himself. After hearing their appeal, he sustained the action of the councils and reaffirmed his original decision. Then the opposing party rejected not only the decisions of the councils but the decision of the emperor himself.

Then Constantine addressed a letter to Cecilianus, bestowing more favor upon what he now called "*the legitimate* and *most holy* Catholic religion," and empowering him to use the civil power to compel the opposing party—the Donatists—to submit. This portion of his letter is in the following words:—

"*Constantine Augustus to Cæcilianus, bishop of Carthage:*

"As we have determined that in all the provinces of Africa, Numidia and Mauritania, something should be granted to certain ministers of *the legitimate and most holy* Catholic religion to defray their expenses, I have given letters to Ursus, the most illustrious lieutenant governor of Africa, and have communicated to him that he shall provide to pay to your authority three thousand folles [about one hundred thousand dollars].[3] . . .

"And as I have ascertained that some men, who are of no settled mind, wished to divert the people from the most holy Catholic Church, by a certain pernicious adulteration, I wish thee to understand that I have given, both to the proconsul Anulinus and to Patricius, vicar-general of the prefects, when present, the following injunctions: That, among all the rest, *they should particularly pay the necessary attention to this,* nor should by any means tolerate that this should be over-

---

[3] The Catholic Church gets nearly *four* hundred thousand dollars *annually*, from the national treasury of the United States to-day.

looked. Wherefore, *if thou seest any of these men* persevering in this madness, *thou shalt*, without any hesitancy, *proceed to the aforesaid judges, and report it to them, that they may animadvert upon them, as I commanded them, when present.*"

Thus, no sooner was it decided what was "*the legitimate* and most holy Catholic Church," than the civil power was definitely placed at the disposal of that church, with positive instructions to use that power in compelling conformity to the new imperial religion.   Persecution was begun at once.   The Donatist bishops were driven out, and Constantine commanded that their churches should be delivered to the Catholic party. Nor was this done at all peacefully.   "Each party recriminated on the other; but neither denies the barbarous scenes of massacre and license which devastated the African cities.   The Donatists boasted of their martyrs; and the cruelties of the Catholic party rest on their own admission; they deny not, they proudly vindicate, their barbarities; 'Is the vengeance of God to be defrauded of its victims?' they cried."—*Milman, History of Christianity, Book III, chapter 1, paragraph 5 from the end.*

And the government by becoming a partisan had lost the power to keep the peace.   The *civil power*, by becoming a party to *religious controversy*, had lost the power to prevent *civil violence* between *religious factions*.

Nor was this thing long in coming.   It all occurred within *less than four years.*   The Edict of Milan was issued in the month of March, A. D. 313.   Before that month expired the decision was rendered that the imperial favors were for the Catholic Church only.   In the autumn of the same year—313 —the first council sat to decide which was the Catholic Church. In the summer of 314 sat the second council on the same question.   And in 316 the decree was sent to Cecilianus empowering him to distribute that money to the ministers of "the legitimate and most holy Catholic religion," and to use the civil power to force the Donatists to submit to the decision of the councils and the emperor.

The Edict of Milan, March, 313, named "the whole body of Christians" as the beneficiaries, without any qualification or any sectarian designation.   Before the expiration of that month, the provisions of the edict were confined to "the *Catholic Church* of the Christians" alone.   In the autumn of the same year, when the emperor wrote to the bishop of Rome, appointing the first council, he defined the established church as "the *holy* Catholic Church."   The following summer, 314, when he called the second council, he referred to the doctrine of the Catholic Church as embodying the "*most* holy religion." And when it had been decided which party represented this "most holy religion," then in 316 his letter and commission to Cecilianus defined it as "the *legitimate and* most holy Catholic religion."

Nor was this all.   While this was going on, also about the year 314, the first edict in favor of Sunday was issued, though it was blended with "Friday."   It ordered that on Friday and on Sunday "no judicial or other business should be transacted, but that God should be served with prayers and supplications, and in 321 Friday observance was dropped and Sunday alone was exalted by the famous Sunday-rest law of Constantine; all in furtherance of the ambition of the ecclesiastics to assert the government as a kind of sovereignty for themselves.   In 323, by the direct and officious aid of the Catholic Church, Constantine succeeded in defeating Licinius and making himself sole emperor.   No sooner was this accomplished than the *religious liberty* assured to "the Christians" by the Edict of Milan, like the provisions of the same edict restoring confiscated property to the Christians, *was* by a public and express edict *limited to Catholics alone.*   This portion of that decree runs as follows:—

"*Victor Constantinus Maximus Augustus, to the heretics:—*

"Understand now, by this present statute, ye Novatians, Valentinians, Marcionites, Paulians, ye who are called Cataphrygians, and all ye who devise and support heresies by means of your private assemblies, with what a tissue of falsehood and vanity, with what destructive and venomous errors, your doctrines are inseparably interwoven; so that through you the healthy soul is stricken with disease, and the living becomes the prey of everlasting death. . . .

"Forasmuch, then, as it is no longer possible to bear with your pernicious errors, we give warning by this present statute that none of you henceforth presume to assemble yourselves together. We have directed, accordingly, that you should be deprived of all the houses in which you are accustomed to hold your assemblies; and our care in this respect extends so far as to forbid the holding of your superstitious and senseless meetings, not in public merely, but in any private house or place whatsoever. Let those of you, therefore, who are desirous of embracing the true and pure religion, take the far better course of entering the Catholic Church, and uniting with it in holy fellowship, whereby you will be enabled to arrive at the knowledge of the truth. . . .

"It is an object worthy of that prosperity which we enjoy through the favor of God, to endeavor to bring back those who in time past were living in the hope of future blessing, from all irregularity and error, to the right path, from darkness to light, from vanity to truth, from death to salvation. And in order that this remedy may be applied with effectual power, we have commanded (as before said), that you be positively deprived of every gathering point for your superstitious meetings; I mean all the houses of prayer (if such be worthy of the name) which belong to heretics, and that these be made over without delay to the Catholic Church; that any other places be confiscated to the public service, and no facility whatever be left for any future gathering; in order that from this day forward none of your unlawful assemblies may presume to appear in any public or private place. Let this edict be made public."

Thus *in less than eleven years* from the issuing of the Edict of Milan, the Catholic Church stood in full and exclusive possession of the authority of the empire both in the rights of property and the right to worship under the profession of Christianity, and with a specific and direct commission to use that power and authority to compel the submission of "heretics." Thus was *made* the Papacy—the beast of Revelation 13: 1–10—and all that ever came in its career from that day to this has been but the natural and inevitable growth of the power and the prerogatives which were then possessed and claimed by the Catholic Church.

And it all came from the Edict of Milan bestowing governmental favors upon "the Christians." No man can fairly deny that in the Edict of Milan and the religio-political intrigue that lay behind it, there was contained the whole Papacy. No man can successfully deny that the Edict of Milan, though appearing innocent enough upon its face, contained the whole Papacy, or that the things that followed in the ten years up to 323, which we have sketched, were anything else than the logical and inevitable development of the evil that lay wrapped up in that.

So much for the experience of the Papacy. And in view of this experience we may here ask a question that is worthy of the most serious consideration by the American people. If a thing appearing so just and innocent as does the Edict of Milan could so easily be made by the Catholic Church of that day to produce such a world of mischief in so short a time, and be a curse to the world forever after; then, under the hand of the Papacy as at this day, what must be the result of this decision of the Supreme Court of the United States which has not, in any sense, any appearance of justice or innocence?

THE CATHOLIC CHURCH TO-DAY.

It is proper now to inquire whether there are any evidences of a purpose to act now in this case as she did in the former. And in response to this inquiry it must be said that there exists a series of facts of which the very least that can be said is that it is dangerously suggestive. These facts shall be set down here, without any note or comment, in the order of their occurrence from the date of the Supreme Court "Christian nation" decision, up to the latest dates before this book goes to press.   Here they are:—

1. February 29, 1892, the Supreme Court of the United States declared it to be the "meaning" of the Constitution of the United States that it is "the voice of the entire" people of this nation, speaking in "organic utterances," that "this is a religious nation," and that "this is a Christian nation."

2. July 11, 1892, there was published in this country, in the New York *Sun*, a letter from the Vatican announcing the plans of Leo XIII. respecting the United States, and through this the world.   In this letter it said:—

"What the church has done in the past for others, she will now do for the United States. . . . Like all intuitive souls, he hails in the United American States, and in their young and flourishing church, the source of new life for Europeans.   He wants America to be powerful, in order that Europe may regain strength from borrowing a rejuvenated type. . . . If the United States succeed in solving the many problems that puzzle us, *Europe will follow her example*, and this outpouring of light will mark a date in the history not only of the United States, but of ALL HUMANITY."

3. In October, 1892, Francis Satolli, Archbishop of Leponto, was sent to this country as the personal representative of the pope, ostensibly to represent the pope's interest in the Columbian Exposition, but in reality to be permanent apostolic delegate at the capital of the nation, with assurance under the seal of "the fisherman's ring" that whatever he does shall be confirmed by the pope.

4. September 5, 1893, at the World's Catholic Congress, Chicago, this same Satolli delivered to "the Catholics of America" the following message from Leo XIII.:—

"In the name of Leo XIII. I salute the great American republic; and I call upon the Catholics of America to go forward, in one hand bearing the book of Christian truth, and in the other the Constitution of the United States. . . . Bring your fellow-countrymen, *bring your country*, into immediate contact with that great secret of blessed-ness—Christ and his church. . . . Here you have a country which will repay all effort not merely tenfold, but aye! a hundred-fold. And this no one understands better than the immortal Leo. *And he charges me*, his delegate, to speak out to America words of hope and blessing, words of joy. Go forward! in one hand bearing the book of Christian truth—the Bible—and in the other the Consti-tution of the United States."

5. A few days later, September 24, 1893, Prof. Thos. O'Gorman, of the Catholic University, Washington, D. C., having been announced in the published program to read a paper at the World's Parliament of Religions on "The Rela-tion of the Catholic Church to America," changed the title to "The Relation of *Christianity* to America," and declared that "by right of discovery and possession, dating back almost nine hundred years, America is Christian;" cited evidences in proof of "an acquaintance between America and the church in times when the only Christianity in existence was Catholic;" and declared that this is "a nation that shall find its perfection in *Catholic* Christianity."

6. October 18, 19, 1893, the jubilee of Cardinal Gibbons' was celebrated at Baltimore. The night of the 18th Arch-bishop Ireland delivered a panegyric in which he exclaimed:—

"I preach the new, the most glorious crusade. Church and age! *Unite them* in mind and heart, in the name of humanity, in the name of God. Church and age! . . . Monsignor Satolli, the church, and the age. *Rome is the church; America is the age.*"

And at the banquet the night of the 19th, the archbishop again spoke to the following purpose:—

"I do not know whether or not you appreciate the full value of *the union* you see typified here to-night,—the union of the Catholic Church and America; the fraternity between the church and the non-Catholics of the nation. The Vice President of the United States comes here and takes his seat alongside the cardinal. The spirit of fraternity *between church and state* thus typified, is the result of the work of our American Cardinal."

7. September 21, 1894, a dispatch announcing the return of Bishop Keane from Rome gave the following words of an interview with him:—

"The policy of the pope, in view of the late overtures in Italy, is *the union of the church with* the great democratic powers of the future —that is, *America* and France. This is his hope, and toward it all his remarkable energies are bent."

Three days later, September 24, the newspaper dispatches stated that Bishop Keane was "the bearer of a rescript from Pope Leo XIII.," of which the import was the following:—

"The papal rescript elevates the United States to *the first rank* as *a Catholic nation.* Heretofore this country has stood before the church as a missionary country. It had no more recognition officially at Rome than had China. . . . By the new rescript the country is freed from the propaganda and is *declared to be a Catholic country.* . . . The importance, not only to Catholics, but to all citizens of the United States, of this radical change in the relations to Rome of the church in America, can scarcely be overestimated."

8. A letter from the Vatican, dated October 14, 1894, to the New York *Sun,* republished in the *Catholic Standard* (Philadelphia) of November 3, says:—

"The United States of America, it can be said without exaggeration, are the chief thought of Leo XIII. in the government of the Roman and universal Catholic Church; for he is one of the choice intellects of the Old World who are watching the starry flag of Washington rise to the zenith of the heavens. A few days ago, on receiving an eminent American, Leo XIII. said to him, 'But the United States are the future; we think of them incessantly.' . . . This ever-ready sympathy has its base in the fundamental interests of the holy see, in a peculiar conception of the part to be played and the position to be held by the church and the Papacy in the times to come. . . . That is why Leo XIII. turns all his soul, full of ideality, to what is improperly called his American policy. It should be rightly called his Catholic universal policy."

9. In his encyclical of January 6, 1895, to the hierarchy in America, Leo XIII. himself speaks, and says:—

"We highly esteem and love exceedingly the young and vigorous American nation, in which we plainly discern latent forces for the advancement alike of civilization and of Christianity." "The fact that Catholicity with you is in good condition, nay, is even enjoying a prosperous growth, is by all means to be attributed to the fecundity with which God has endowed his church; . . . but she would bring forth more abundant fruits, if, in addition to liberty, she enjoyed *the favor of the laws and the patronage of the public authority.*"

10. The *Catholic Mirror* (Baltimore) of March 2, 1895, reported a sermon by "Father" Lyons, of that city, delivered Sunday evening, February 24, 1895, in which he said:—

"It is strange that a rule which requires a Supreme Court to give final decisions on disputed points in our Constitution, should be abused and slandered when employed by the Catholic Church. Citizens and others may read the Constitution, but they are not allowed to interpret it for themselves, but must submit to the interpretation given by the Superior [Supreme(?)] Court. The Bible is the constitution of the Catholic Church, and while all are exhorted to read this divine Constitution, the interpretation of its true meaning must be left to the Superior Court of the church founded by Christ. The decision of our federal Supreme Court is final; the decision of the superior court of the church is final also, and, in virtue of the divine prerogative of inerrancy granted the church, infallible. The church has not, does not, and cannot, permit the violation of God's commandments in any case whatsoever."

11. March 11, 1895, the New York *Advertiser* printed a dispatch of March 10, from San Francisco, as follows:—

"SAN FRANCISCO, March 10.

"Private advices received here give an interesting and important communication from Mgr. Satolli to officials in Guatemala, concerning that country's following the course of Nicaragua in sending to Rome an envoy extraordinary and minister plenipotentiary.

"In the course of the document reference is made as to the propriety under the United States Constitution of official relations between Washington and Rome, and an interpretation given of that feature of the Constitution relative to the separation of Church and State. Mgr. Satolli's letter was written while negotiations were pending about four months ago. It refers at length to difficulties in church administra tion in Guatemala, and suggests that certain changes desired by the government should be accompanied by an equivalent of serious advantage to render less burdensome the condition of the church in Guatemala. The document then adds:—

" 'The condition of the Catholic Church in the United States, in whose Constitution was inserted the article of separation of the State from any religious sect, cannot escape our consideration. I might almost say it causes no surprise. If up to date no official relations exist between the government and the holy see, it is because the great majority of the population is anti-Catholic. In the meantime the church here is attaining possibly greater development and liberty than in other States.'

"It is stated that this is the first time, so far as is known, that Mgr. Satolli's mission has been extended outside of spiritual questions and has dealt with governmental subjects."

Now can any man read over this string of facts and deny that there is being carried on by the Papacy in the United States a fixed purpose to crowd herself into place in this nation as *the* " Christianity " of " this Christian nation " ? Can anyone fail to see that from the Supreme Court's interpretation of the Constitution to mean that " this is a Christian nation," she has caught the cue, and not only holds to that as true, but has begun to take upon herself the interpretation of the Constitution as it relates to " Christianity, general Christianity " ?

There is another fact to be set down here which will make this point yet more distinct. It is this: In the *Catholic World* for the month of September, 1871, there was printed a leading article, in which the Constitution of the United States was referred to in the following words:—

"As it is interpreted by the liberal and sectarian journals that are doing their best to revolutionize it, and is beginning to be interpreted by no small portion of the American people, or is *interpreted by the Protestant principle*, so widely diffused among us, . . . *we do not accept it*, or hold it to be *any government at all*, or as capable of performing any of the proper functions of government; and if it continues to be interpreted by the revolutionary principles of Protestantism, it is sure to fail. . . . Hence it is, we so often say that if the American republic is to be sustained and preserved at all, it must be by the rejection of the principle of the Reformation, and the acceptance of the Catholic principle by the American people."—*P. 736.*

Contrast that now with Leo's command by Satolli "to the Catholics of America" to "go forward" on their "hundred-fold" rewarded mission, "bearing in one hand the book of Christian truth—the Bible—and in the other *the Constitution of the United States;*" and inquire, What has caused this change of the attitude of Rome toward the Constitution?

The principle upon which the Constitution was founded in its total separation of religion from the notice of the national government, was definitely and intentionally the Protestant principle. In the discussions which led up to the making of the Constitution as it reads in this respect, and in the discussions upon the Constitution in the conventions which made it, we have seen that this point was especially dealt with and the Protestant principle was the one chosen and made the principle of the Constitution. In the documents of that time, and which are an essential part of the history of the Constitution, this, we have also seen, was the crucial point considered, and the Protestant principle was made the principle of the Constitution. In fact, it was plainly said not only that "it is impossible for the magistrate to adjudge the right of preference among the various sects which profess the Christian faith, without erecting a claim to *infallibility* which would *lead us back to the Church of Rome,*" but it was also said that "to judge for ourselves, and to engage in the exercise of religion agreeably to the dictates of our own consciences, is an unalienable right which, upon *the principles on which the gospel was first propagated* and THE REFORMATION FROM POPERY CARRIED ON, can never be transferred to another."

Therefore it is the undeniable truth of the only history on the question, that the Constitution of the United States was founded upon the Protestant principle. And while it was held

13

so, *no Catholic was ever commanded* by any pope to take that Constitution in one hand and the Bible in the other for any purpose under the sun.   On the contrary, they openly declared that so long as the Constitution was held to that principle Catholics did "not accept it," nor hold this government "to be any government at all."

But as soon as the Supreme Court of the United States had interpreted the Constitution by *the papal principle*—the principle of "the establishment of the Christian religion"— as soon as the Supreme Court thus rejected "the principle of the Reformation," and accepted "the Catholic principle"—

1. *Then it was*, and not till then, that there was published to the United States the purpose of Leo XIII., that what the church has done for other nations she will now do for the United States.

2. *Then it was*, and not till then, that Leo XIII., pope, sent his permanent apostolic delegate here in his name, to "call upon the Catholics of America to go forward, in one hand bearing the book of Christian truth and in the other the Constitution of the United States," upon their hundred-fold rewarded mission to bring this "country into immediate contact with the Church" of Rome.

3. Then it was that, in the World's Parliament of Religions, Professor O'Gorman, for the Catholic Church, claimed this country as Catholic, and which "must find its perfection in Catholic Christianity."

4. Then it was that Archbishop Ireland could proudly point out *the union* of the Catholic Church and the United States typified in the Vice President sitting at the right hand of the cardinal.

5. Then it was that it could be announced as "the policy of the pope," "toward which all his remarkable energies are bent," to unite "the church and America."

6. Then it was that Leo XIII. could officially declare the

United States to be "a Catholic country," and elevate it "to the first rank as a Catholic nation."

7. Since that it is that the United States has become "the chief thought" in "the government of the Roman and universal Catholic Church," in the carrying out of "his Catholic universal policy."

8. Then it was that Leo himself could openly call for "the favor of the laws and the patronage of the public authority" to the Catholic Church.

9. Then it was, and merely the consequence, too, that the Papacy could set forth the doctrine that in interpreting the Constitution "the decision of the Supreme Court is final," and that *the people* "may read the Constitution, but they are not allowed to interpret it, but must submit to the interpretation given by the Supreme Court."

10. And thus it is that Satolli can now take it upon himself to interpret the Constitution in its new relationship to religion, and set forth that the Constitution in its separation of government and religion meant *only* the "separation of the State from any *religious* SECT"—the very doctrine of the Christian nation court and its decision.

As it is certainly nothing else than the *Catholic* Bible, which Leo through Satolli has commanded the Catholics of America to "take in one hand," so certainly also is it nothing else than the *Catholic* Constitution of the United States that he has commanded them to take in the other hand. As "so long as that Constitution was interpreted by the Protestant principle the Catholics did not accept it," and now they are all commanded to accept it and use it, equally with the Catholic Bible, in their mission to bring this country into immediate contact with the Papacy, it follows inevitably that to the satisfaction of the Papacy that Constitution has been interpreted according to the papal principle. And as they themselves say and that its interpretation is final, this proves conclusively that the decision of the Supreme Court of the United States interpreting the Constitution to mean that this is a Christian nation, is the cause of this change in the attitude of the Papacy toward the Constitution, and is the foundation of this series of facts in the course of the Papacy in crowding itself upon the country as the "Christianity" of this "Christian nation."

Thus does it stand as clear as though it were in letters of fire that in its decision that "this is a Christian nation," the Supreme Court of the United States accomplished, to the satisfaction of the Papacy, precisely the thing that the Papacy had long demanded, viz., "the rejection of the principle of the Reformation, and the acceptance of the Catholic principle," in the interpretation of the national Constitution.

Thus, *in principle*, the work of our governmental fathers has been undone. The barrier which they set up against the nation's being led back to the Church of Rome has been broken down, and that church has already entered upon the consequential task of leading the nation back to that iniquitous goal.

The all-important question now is, Will the American people receive, or support, or submit to, this "rejection of the principle of the Reformation and the acceptance of the Catholic principle" as the principle of the interpretation of the Constitution of the United States?

II.

WHAT PROTESTANTISM IS DOING.

The other combination which is determined to push the "Christian nation" decision to the fullest extent of the logic of it, is THE COMBINED PROTESTANTISM of the country.

Probably the reader has already asked himself, What is Protestantism doing all this time? Well, Protestantism, *to be true to its name* and vital principles, *ought* with one voice to be protesting against this Christian nation decision in every conceivable shape.   For the celebrated Protest which gave to the Reformation the title of *Protestantism* is decidedly against it:—

"The principles contained in the celebrated Protest of the 19th of April, 1529, constitute *the very essence of Protestantism.* Now this Protest opposes two abuses of man in matters of faith; the *first* is the intrusion of the civil magistrate; and the *second,* the arbitrary authority of the church.   Instead of these abuses Protestantism sets the power of conscience above the magistrate, and the authority of the word of God above the visible church.   In the first place, it rejects the civil power in divine things, and says with the apostles and prophets, 'We must obey God rather than man.'   In the presence of Charles the Fifth it uplifts the crown of Jesus Christ."—*D'Aubigne History of the Reformation, Book XIII, chapter 6, par. 18.*

This is what Protestantism *ought* to be doing now in this case, but the fact is that, instead of this, that which stands for Protestantism in this country is the most persistent caller for the intrusion of the civil magistrate in matters of faith; and is no less strenuous in its assertion of the arbitrary authority of the church, than the Papacy itself.   And in all this that which stands for Protestantism in this country is the greatest aid that the Papacy has in her mischievous purposes upon the country.   From the day that the decision of the Supreme Court was made public and obtainable, the leaders of " Protestantism " in the country have been using it for all that it could be made to be worth, to crowd upon the government the recognition and maintenance of " the Christian religion."

For twenty-nine years there had been an organized effort by professed Protestants to have the Christian religion established as the national religion by *a constitutional amendment.* Beginning in 1863 this organization had gathered to itself in close alliance the Woman's Christian Temperance Union (1886), the Prohibition party (1887), the American Sabbath Union (1888), and the Young People's Society of Christian

Endeavor; so that when (in 1892) the decision was published that "this is a Christian nation," and that this is the meaning of the Constitution as it is, without any amendment, there was this whole combination ready to accept it and glad to use it to further their purposes.[4]

Undoubtedly the very first use that was ever made of the decision, outside of the case at bar, was when, in the month of April, 1892, the president of the American Sabbath Union took it in his hand and went before committees of the United States Senate and House of Representatives, recited its "argument," and demanded the closing of the World's Fair on Sunday by Congress, "because this is a Christian nation."

The *Pearl of Days*, the official organ of the American Sabbath Union, May 7, 1892, declared that this decision—

'Establishes clearly the fact that our government is Christian. *This decision is vital to the Sunday question in all its aspects*, and places that question among the most important issues now before the American people. . . . And this important decision rests upon the fundamental principle that religion is imbedded in the organic structure of the American government—a religion that recognizes, *and is bound to maintain, Sunday* as a day for rest and worship."

The *Christian Statesman*, always the official organ of the National Reform Association, and then the mouthpiece of the whole combination, in the issue of May 21, 1892, said:—

"'Christianity is the law of the land. 'This is a Christian nation.' —*U. S. Supreme Court, February 29, 1892.* The Christian church,

---

[4] In this the many sects of popular Protestantism are acting strictly together. For there is sufficient antagonism between Protestantism and Catholicism to give to all the divisions of Protestantism a form of unity, in opposition to the designs of the Papacy upon the country. It is true that the Protestant combination were willing to join hands, and did so, with the Catholics, to secure their aid in getting the government committed to religion. But this was done with the idea that the governmental power should be controlled by the Protestants when it should be obtained. Now, however, that the thing has been done, and the "Protestants" see Rome pushing herself to the front everywhere and taking control of all, they are crying loudly against "the encroachments of Rome." This, though, is nothing else than the same old cry of "Stop, thief," for, as will be seen, they are doing their utmost to carry off all the spoil for themselves. For a full history of this combination see "Two Republics," pp. 699-732.

therefore, has rights in this country.   Among these is the right to one day in seven protected from the assaults of greed, the god of this world, that it may be devoted to worship of the God of heaven and earth."

And in preparation for Thanksgiving day the same year, the *Christian Statesman* of November 19, 1892, came out with the following, which tells all of that part of the story that needs to be told.   We print it just as it there appeared, titles and all:—

CHRISTIAN POLITICS.

THE SUPREME COURT DECISION.

THE GREATEST OCCASION FOR THANKSGIVING.

[Department edited by Wm. Wier, Washington, Pa., District Secretary of the National Reform Association.]

" 'This is a Christian nation.'   That means Christian government, Christian laws, Christian institutions, Christian practices, Christian citizenship.   And this is not an outburst of popular passion or prejudice.   Christ did not lay his guiding hand there, but upon the calm, dispassionate supreme judicial tribunal of our government.   It is the weightiest, the noblest, the most tremendously far-reaching in its consequences of all the utterances of that sovereign tribunal.   And that utterance is for Christianity, for Christ.   ' A Christian nation!'   Then this nation is Christ's nation, for nothing can be Christian that does not belong to him.   Then his word is its sovereign law.   Then the nation is Christ's servant.   Then it ought to, and must, confess, love, and obey Christ.   All that the National Reform Association seeks, all that this department of Christian politics works for, is to be found in the development of that royal truth, ' This is a Christian nation.'   It is the hand of the second of our three great departments of national government throwing open a door of our national house, one that leads straight to the throne of Christ.

" Was there ever a Thanksgiving day before that called us to bless our God for such marvelous advances of our government and citizenship toward Christ?

" 'O sing unto the Lord a new song, for he hath done marvelous things; his right hand and his holy arm hath gotten him the victory. Sing unto the Lord with the harp and the voice of a psalm.'

                                                  "WILLIAM WEIR."

With these views of the decision, they made a determined onslaught upon Congress to secure definite national legislation in behalf of religion, using the Sunday closing of the World's Fair as the means by which to obtain the recognition of the Christian religion on the part of Congress. Finding other methods inadequate to accomplish their purpose soon enough to please them, they resorted to open threats of political perdition to all in Congress who should refuse to do their will. These threats were so offensive that both Senator Sherman and Senator Vest on the floor of the Senate rebuked them as an abuse of the right of petition. A sample of these threatening petitions, which were sent up to Congress from the churches all over the country, is the following, sent up by certain Presbyterian Churches in New York. It reads thus:—

"*Resolved*, That we do hereby pledge ourselves and each other, that we will from this time henceforth refuse to vote for or support for any office or position of trust, any member of Congress, either senator or representative, who shall vote for any further aid of any kind to the World's Fair except on conditions named in these resolutions." [5]

This effort was successful. Congress yielded to the demand, and enacted the required legislation, and this, too, *distinctly as religious* legislation, setting up Sunday by national law as "the *Christian* sabbath."

The record of that transaction is as follows. In the *Congressional Record* of July 10, 1892, page 6614, is this report:—

"MR. QUAY.—On page 122, line 13, after the word 'act' I move to insert:—

"'And that provision has been made by the proper authority for the closing of the Exposition on the sabbath day.'

"The reasons for the amendment I will send to the desk to be read. The secretary will have the kindness to read from the book of law I send to the desk, the part inclosed in brackets.

"THE VICE PRESIDENT.—The part indicated will be read.

"The secretary read as follows:—

---

[5] *Congressional Record*, May 25, 1892, p. 5144.

" ' Remember the Sabbath day to keep it holy. Six days shalt thou labor and do all thy work; but the seventh day is the Sabbath of the Lord thy God; in it thou shalt not do any work, thou, nor thy son, nor thy daughter, thy manservant, nor thy maidservant, nor thy cattle, nor thy stranger that is within thy gates; for in six days the Lord made heaven and earth, the sea, and all that in them is, and rested the seventh day; wherefore the Lord blessed the Sabbath day, and hallowed it.' "

The foregoing is all that was said or done in relation to the question that day. The next legislative day, however, the question was taken up and discussed. The debate was opened by Senator Manderson, of Nebraska. And in the *Record* of July 12, pages 6694, 6695, 6701, we read as follows:—

"The language of this amendment is that the Exposition shall be closed on the 'sabbath day.' I submit that if the senator from Pennsylvania desires that the Exposition shall be closed upon Sunday, this language will not necessarily meet that idea. . . .

"The word 'sabbath day' simply means that it is a rest day, and it may be Saturday or Sunday, and it would be subject to the discretion of those who will manage this Exposition whether they should close the Exposition on the last day of the week, in conformity with that observance which is made by the Israelites and the Seventh-day Baptists, or should close it on the first day of the week, generally known as the Christian sabbath. It certainly seems to me that this amendment should be adopted by the senator from Pennsylvania, and, if he proposes to close this Exposition, that it should be closed on the first day of the week, commonly called Sunday. . . .

"Therefore I offer an amendment to the amendment, which I hope may be accepted by the senator from Pennsylvania, to strike out the words 'Exposition on the sabbath day,' and insert 'mechanical portion of the Exposition on the first day of the week, commonly called Sunday.' . . .

" MR. QUAY.—I will accept the modification so far as it changes the phraseology of the amendment proposed by me in regard to designating the day of the week on which the Exposition shall be closed.

" THE VICE PRESIDENT.—The senator from Pennsylvania accepts the modification in part, but not in whole. . . .

" MR. HARRIS.—Let the amendment of the senator from Pennsylvania, as modified, be reported.

"THE VICE PRESIDENT.—It will be again reported.

"THE CHIEF CLERK.—On page 122, line 13, after the word 'act' it is proposed to amend the amendment of the committee by inserting:

"'And that provision has been made by the proper authority for the closing of the Exposition on the first day of the week, commonly called Sunday.'"

This amendment was afterward further amended by the insertion of the proviso that the managers of the Exposition should sign an agreement to close the Fair on Sunday before they could receive any of the appropriation; but this which we have given is the material point.

All of this the House confirmed in its vote accepting the Senate amendments. Besides this, the House had already, on its own part, by a vote of 131 to 36, adopted Sunday as the "Christian sabbath," and by a vote of 149 to 11 explicitly rejected the Sabbath itself. Indeed, the way the matter came up, the House by this vote practically decided that the seventh day is not the Sabbath. See *Congressional Record*, proceedings of May 25, 26, 1892.

Such is the official record; now let us study the principle. The makers of the Constitution said that " it is impossible for the magistrate to adjudge the right of preference among the various sects professing the Christian faith without erecting a claim to infallibility which would lead us back to the Church of Rome."

The first thing to be noticed in this record is that Congress did precisely this thing—it did adjudge the right of preference among sects that profess the Christian faith. The Seventh-day Baptists and their observance of the seventh day as the Sabbath of the commandment quoted were definitely named *in contrast* with those who observe " the first day of the week, generally known as the Christian Sabbath," with reference to the commandment quoted. And the preference was adjudged in favor of the latter.

Now the Seventh-day Baptists are a sect professing the

Christian faith. The original Sabbath commandment was quoted word for word from the Scriptures. The words of that commandment, as they stand in the proceedings of Congress, say "the seventh day is the Sabbath." The Seventh-day Baptists, a sect professing the Christian faith, observe the very day—the seventh day—named in the scripture quoted in the *Record*. There are other sects professing the Christian faith who profess to observe the Sabbath of this same commandment by keeping "the first day of the week, commonly called Sunday," and hence it is that that day is "generally known as the Christian sabbath." These facts were known to Congress, and were made a part of the record. Then upon this statement of facts as to the difference among sects professing the Christian faith, touching the very religious observance taken up by Congress, the Congress did deliberately and in set terms *adjudge the right of preference* between these sects professing the Christian faith. Congress did adjudge the right of preference in favor of those sects which observe "the first day of the week, generally known as the Christian sabbath," as against the plainly named sect which observes the day named in the commandment which Congress quoted from the Bible. Thus the Congress of the United States did the very thing which the fathers of the nation declared it "impossible" to do "without erecting a claim to infallibility, which would lead us back to the Church of Rome."

Let us follow this proceeding a step or two further, and see how certainly it does lead to Rome. From the official record it is as plain as anything can be that the Congress of the United States, in its official capacity, did take it upon itself to interpret the Scripture. It did in legislative action put an interpretation upon the commandment of God. Congress quoted the commandment bodily, which from God commands the observance of the Sabbath day, and which definitely names the day—the seventh day—to be observed. Congress then declared that the word "sabbath day" "means" so and so, and that it ."may be" one day or another, "Saturday or Sunday," and upon this, did decide which day it should be, namely, "the first day of the week, commonly called Sunday." This is as clearly an interpretation of the Bible as was ever made on earth.

How, then, does this interpretation stand as respects the testimony of the Bible itself? Let the word witness: "When the Sabbath *was past*, Mary Magdalene, and Mary the mother of James, and Salome, had bought sweet spices, that they might come and anoint him. And *very early* in the morning, *the first day of the week*, they came unto the sepulcher at the rising of the sun." Mark 16: 1, 2. Thus the plain word of God says that "the Sabbath *was past*" before the first day of the week came at all—yes, before even the "very early" part of it came. But, lo! the Congress of the United States officially decides that the Sabbath *is* the first day of the week. Now, when the word of God plainly says that the Sabbath *is past* before the first day of the week comes, and yet Congress says that the first day of the week *is* the Sabbath, which is right?

Nor is the word of God indefinite as to what this distinction refers. Here is the word as to that: "That day [the day of the crucifixion] was the preparation, and *the Sabbath* drew on. And the women also, which came with Him from Galilee, followed after, and beheld the sepulcher, and how His body was laid. And they returned, and prepared spices and ointments; and rested the Sabbath day *according to the commandment*. Now upon the *first day of the week*, very early in the morning, they came unto the sepulcher, bringing the spices which they had prepared, and certain others with them." Luke 23: 54–56; 24: 1. Here it is plainly shown that the Sabbath day according to the commandment and the first day of the week are two separate and distinct days entirely. And yet Congress gravely defines that "the Sabbath day" "may be one or the other"! The word of God plainly says that the Sabbath day *according to the commandment is past* before the first day of the week comes at all. And yet Congress declares that the first day of the week is itself the Sabbath! Which is right? Is the Lord able to say what he means? or is it essential that his commandments shall be put through a course of congressional procedure and interpretation in order that his meaning shall reach the people of the United States? And, further, are not the people of the United States capable of finding out for themselves what the meaning of the word of God is? or is it so that it is necessary that Congress should be put between God and the people, so as to insure to them the true and divine meaning of his word?

Whether these questions be answered one way or the other, it is certain that this is precisely the attitude which has been assumed by the Congress of the United States. Whatever men may believe, or whatever men may say, as to the right or the wrong of this question, there is no denying the fact that Congress has taken upon itself to interpret the Scripture for the people of the United States. This is a fact. It has been done. *Then where is the difference between this assumption and that of the other pope?* The Roman pope assumes the prerogative of interpreting the Scripture for the people of the whole world. Congress has assumed the prerogative of interpreting the Scripture for the people of the United States. Where is the difference in these claims—except, perhaps, in this, that whereas the claim of the Roman pope embraces the whole world, the claim of this congressional pope embraces only the United States. There is not a shadow of difference in principle.[6]

---

[6] And yet there is hardly room for even this distinction, because this interpretation by Congress was intended to include, and to be of force upon, all the nations that took part in the World's Fair, and these were expected to be all the nations of the world. So that, practically, the two claims are so nearly alike that it is only another illustration of the truth that there is no possibility of measuring degrees in the respective claims of rival popes. There are no degrees in infallibility anyhow. That the Fair was not closed on Sunday out of respect to this interpretation, does not alter the fact that Con-

Thus the very first step lands Congress and the country decidedly upon Roman ground; and the next step, which will certainly be taken sooner or later, will lead to the domination of the Church of Rome itself. For, note: This thing was crowded upon Congress by the church combination, professedly Protestant. It was *their* view, their interpretation, of the Scripture that was adopted by Congress, and put into the law. In other words, these professed Protestant churches had enough "influence" upon Congress to secure the decision of *this* question in their favor. And as soon as it was done, they gladly and loudly proclaimed that "this settles the sabbath question." Now, all questions between Catholics and these Protestants, even, are not entirely settled. One of these, for instance, is this very question of Sunday observance—not, indeed, *whether* it shall be observed, but *how* it shall be observed. Let this or any other question be disputed between them, and all the Catholic Church has now to do is to bring enough "influence" to bear upon Congress to get the question decided in *her* favor, and there you have it! The whole nation is then delivered bodily over into subjection to Rome.

And when it shall have been done, no Protestant who has, or has had, anything to do with this Sunday-law movement, can ever say a word. For if the action of Congress settles a religious question when it is decided in their favor, they can never deny that such action as certainly settles a religious question when it is decided in favor of the Catholic Church. If they accept, and require others to accept, such a decision of civil power when it suits *them*, they must likewise accept such a decision when it suits the Catholics. And this other thing will as certainly come as that this has already come. And thus the government and people of the United States will have been delivered into the hands of Rome by this blind procedure of apostate Protestantism. That which our fathers feared, and which they supposed they had forever prevented, will have come.

The decisive step toward this certain consummation has been taken by the combined " Protestantism " of the country in this successful demand upon the United States that Congress should interpret the Scripture, decide a religious dispute, and "settle" a religious question.   And this, too, was done by the use, and as the consequence, of the Supreme Court decision that " this is a Christian nation," which made the Constitution acceptable to the Papacy by " the rejection of the principle of the Reformation and the acceptance of the Catholic principle" as the "meaning" of the Constitution of the United States.

This, we repeat, the professed Protestantism of the country has done upon the basis, and in the use, of the " Christian nation" decision.   In their whole course in this matter, when any doubt or opposition was shown, they never failed to sound the merits of this Supreme Court decision—this was final and settled all questions.   The leading Methodist paper of the country, the New York *Christian Advocate*, in referring to the discussion of the question in Congress, said:—

"Every utterance upon this subject was in harmony with a late decision of the United States Supreme Court *whereby it is to be forever regarded as a settled principle* that this is a Christian nation."

And now the Papacy takes up the strain, and also declares that a decision of the Supreme Court interpreting the Constitution "is final."   And just as soon as the Catholics can so "influence" Congress as to comply with the pope's published wish that *that* church shall enjoy "the favor of the laws and the patronage of the public authority," *then*, with the doctrine already fastened upon the country by Protestants that this Supreme Court decision is final, the whole nation will find itself fastened under the domination of Rome, whose decisions by the same rule "are also final and infallible."   Thus, and certainly, is the nation being steadily drawn toward Rome by the violation of the fundamental principle which our fathers established—by the doing of that thing which they truthfully declared impossible to be done " without erecting a claim to infallibility, which would lead us back to the Church of Rome."

And *this* is what the "Protestantism" of the country is doing in this crisis—doing all it possibly can to aid and confirm the monstrous evil. This universal and insidious SUNDAY-LAW ISSUE *in the hands of professed Protestants*, is the " miner and sapper" in this siege of the national power by Rome. And so diligently have they plied themselves in this and other like things that we have not space to mention, that all is on the verge of being ready for Rome to sound the bugle, spring the mine, and, in the confusion, seize the very citadel of the national power, and revive the old-time religious despotism with all its horrors, while the people of the United States will find themselves here tied down, and helpless, and run over like sheep.

There is another line of evidence that develops yet more clearly the present crisis, and makes more emphatic the fact that this crisis is imminent. This is presented in the next chapter.

CHAPTER X.

THE SUNDAY-LAW MOVEMENT IN THE FOURTH CENTURY, AND ITS PARALLEL IN THE NINETEENTH.

A TITLE for this chapter equally good with the above would be, The Making of the Papacy and the Perfect Likeness to It; for the professed Christian church did once obtain control of the civil power, and by that power compelled all to do her bidding. This was the making and the working of the Papacy. It is well to see how that was done, and to know the means by which it was done. And if we shall see the same things being done over again, in our day and country, we shall know what it implies. In 2 Thess. 2 : 1–4, 7, Paul wrote:—

"Now we beseech you, brethren, by the coming of our Lord Jesus Christ, and by our gathering together unto him, that ye be not soon shaken in mind, or be troubled, neither by spirit, nor by word, nor by letter as from us, as that the day of Christ is at hand. Let no man deceive you by any means; for that day shall not come, except there come a falling away first, and that man of sin be revealed, the son of perdition; who opposeth and exalteth himself above all that is called God, or that is worshiped; so that he as God sitteth in the temple of God, showing himself that he is God." "For the mystery of iniquity doth already work."

Speaking to the elders of the church at Ephesus, Paul makes known what is the secret, we might say the *spring*, of the Papacy. Acts 20 : 28–30. "Of your own selves shall men arise, speaking perverse things, to draw away disciples after them." He was here speaking to the elders of the churches— the bishops. Whether he meant that there would be among

14

these Ephesian bishops, individuals who would do this, or that the bishopric would be perverted from its true office, and would exalt itself to the full development of the Papacy, it matters not; for the words themselves express the fact as it was enacted in the history that followed. The bishopric of Rome finally developed into the Papacy, which is the embodiment of the "mystery of iniquity." This work, as he says, began by the bishops' speaking perverse things, to draw away disciples after them.

It became quite general about twenty years after the death of John. Says Mosheim:—

"The bishops augmented the number of religious rites in the Christian worship, by way of accommodation to the infirmities and prejudices both of Jews and heathen, in order to facilitate their conversion to Christianity." "For this purpose, they gave the name of *mysteries* to the institutions of the gospel, and decorated particularly the holy sacrament with that solemn title. They used in that sacred institution, as also in that of baptism, several of the terms employed in the heathen mysteries, and proceeded so far at length as to adopt some of the ceremonies of which those renowned mysteries consisted. This imitation began in the Eastern provinces; but after the time of Hadrian [emperor A. D. 117-138], who first introduced the mysteries among the Latins, it was followed by the Christians who dwelt in the western part of the empire. A great part, therefore, of the service of the church in this century, had a certain air of the heathen mysteries, and resembled them considerably in many particulars."—*Church History, cent. 2, part 2, chapter 4, par. 2, 5.*

Another means by which these ambitious bishops secured disciples to themselves in great numbers from among the heathen, was the adoption of *the day of the sun* as a festival day.

"The oldest, the most widespread, and the most enduring of all the forms of idolatry known to man, [is] the worship of the sun."— *T. W. Chambers, in Old Testament Student, January, 1886.*

And says Mosheim:—

"Before the coming of Christ all the Eastern nations performed divine worship with their faces turned to that part of the heavens where the sun displays his rising beams. This custom was founded upon a general opinion that God, whose *essence* they looked upon to be *light*, and whom they considered as being circumscribed within certain limits, dwelt in that part of the firmament from which he sends forth the sun, the bright image of his benignity and glory. The Christian converts, indeed, rejected this gross error [of supposing that God dwelt in that part of the firmament]; but they retained the ancient and universal custom of worshiping toward the east, which sprang from it. Nor is this custom abolished even in our times, but still prevails in a great number of Christian churches."—*Church History, cent. 2, part 2, chapter 4, par. 7.*

See also Eze. 8 : 16.   This was first adopted in connection with the Sabbath of the Lord; but after a while the paganized form of godliness crowded out the Sabbath entirely, and those were cursed who would observe it. By the beginning of the fourth century this apostasy had gained a prominence by which it could make itself felt in the political workings of the Roman Empire.   The ambitious bishops of the apostasy had at this time invented a theory of government which they determined to have recognized, which should make the civil power subordinate to the ecclesiastical.   Says Neander:—

" There had in fact arisen in the church a false theocratical theory, originating not in the essence of the gospel, but in the confusion of the religious constitutions of the Old and New Testaments, which . . . brought along with it an unchristian opposition of the spiritual to the secular power, and which might easily result in the formation of a sacerdotal State, subordinating the secular to itself in a false and outward way."—*Torrey's Neander, Boston, 1852, p. 132.*

The government of Israel was a true theocracy.   That was really a government of God.   At the burning bush, God commissioned Moses to lead his people out of Egypt.   By signs and wonders and mighty miracles multiplied, God delivered Israel from Egypt, and led them through the wilderness, and finally into the promised land.   There he ruled them by judges "until Samuel the prophet," to whom, when he was a child, God spoke, and by whom he made known his will.

In the days of Samuel, the people asked that they might have a king. This was allowed, and God chose Saul, and Samuel anointed him king of Israel. Saul failed to do the will of God, and as he rejected the word of the Lord, the Lord rejected him from being king, and sent Samuel to anoint David king of Israel; and David's throne God established forevermore. When Solomon succeeded to the kingdom in the place of David his father, the record is, "Then Solomon sat on the throne of the Lord as king instead of David his father." 1 Chron. 29 : 23. David's throne was the throne of the Lord, and Solomon sat on the throne of the Lord as king over the earthly kingdom of God. The succession to the throne descended in David's line to Zedekiah, who was made subject to the king of Babylon, and who entered into a solemn covenant before God that he would loyally render allegiance to the king of Babylon. But Zedekiah broke his covenant; and then God said to him:—

"Thou, profane wicked prince of Israel, whose day is come, when iniquity shall have an end, thus saith the Lord God: Remove the diadem, and take off the crown; this shall not be the same; exalt him that is low, and abase him that is high. I will overturn, overturn, overturn it; and it shall be no more, until he come whose right it is; and I will give it him." Eze. 21 : 25-27. See also Eze. 17 : 1-21.

The kingdom was then subject to Babylon. When Babylon fell, and Medo-Persia succeeded, it was overturned the first time. When Medo-Persia fell, and was succeeded by Grecia, it was overturned the second time. When the Greek Empire gave way to Rome, it was overturned the third time. And then says the word, "It shall be no more, until he come whose right it is; and I will give it him." Who is he whose right it is?—"Thou . . . shalt call his name Jesus. He shall be great, and shall be called the Son of the Highest; and the Lord God shall give unto him the throne of his father David; and he shall reign over the house of Jacob forever; and of his kingdom there shall be no end." Luke 1: 31–33. And while he was here as "that prophet," "a man of sorrows, and acquainted with grief," the night in which he was betrayed he himself declared, "My kingdom is not of this world."

Thus the throne of the Lord has been removed from this world, and will "be no more, until he come whose right it is," and then it will be given him. And *that time* is the end of this world, and the beginning of "the world to come." Therefore, while this world stands, a true theocracy can never be in it again. Consequently, from the death of Christ till the end of this world, every theory of an earthly theocracy is a false theory; every pretension to it is a false pretension; and wherever any such theory is proposed or advocated, whether in Rome in the fourth century, or anywhere else in any other century, it bears in it all that the Papacy is or that it ever pretended to be, —it puts a man in the place of God.

These theocratical bishops in the fourth century made themselves and their power a necessity to Constantine, who, in order to make sure of their support, became a political convert to the form of Christianity, and made it the recognized religion of the empire. And says Neander further:—

"This theocratical theory was already the prevailing one in the time of Constantine; and . . . the bishops voluntarily made themselves dependent on him by their disputes, and by their determination to make use of the power of the State for the furtherance of their aims."—*Idem.*

In these quotations from Neander, the whole history of the Papacy is epitomized. All that the history of the Papacy is, is only the working out of this theory. For the first step in the logic of a man-made theocracy, is a pope; the second step is the infallibility of that pope; and the third step is the Inquisition, to make his infallibility effective, as we will prove:—

First, a true theocracy being a government immediately directed by God, a false theocracy is a government directed by a man in the place of God. But a man governing in the place of God is a pope. A man ruling the world in the place of God is all that the pope has ever claimed to be. In the Encyclical of Leo XIII., of June, 1894, relating to the "reunion of Christendom," addressed "To the Princes and Peoples of the Universe," this pope assures them that "we hold the regency of God on earth." [1]

Second, a false theocracy being a professed government of God, he who sits at the head of it, sits there as the representative of God. He represents the divine authority; and when he speaks or acts officially, his speech or act is that of God. But to make a man thus the representative of God, is only to clothe human passions with divine power and authority. And being human, he is bound always to act unlike God; and being clothed with irresponsible power, he will sometimes act like the devil. Consequently, in order to make all his actions consistent with his profession, he is compelled to cover them all with the divine attributes, and make everything that he does in his official capacity the act of God.

This is precisely the logic and the profession of papal infallibility. It is not claimed that all the pope speaks is infallible; it is only what he speaks officially—what he speaks "from the throne." Under this theory, he sits upon that throne as the head of the government of God in this world. He sits there as the representative—the "regent"—of God. And when he speaks officially, when he speaks from the throne, he speaks as the representative of God. Therefore, sitting in the place of God, ruling from that place as the official representative of God, that which he speaks from the throne is the word of God, and must be infallible.

This is the straight logic of the false theocratical theory.

[1] The *Monitor* (Catholic), of San Francisco, has denied that "To the Princes and Peoples of the *Universe*" is a correct translation of the title of this Encyclical. But this is the translation as it stands in the official copy sent out by Cardinal Gibbons, and as it is published in the *Northwestern Chronicle*, July 20, 1894.

And if it is denied that the theory is false, there is logically no escape from accepting the papal system. The claims of the Papacy are not in the least extravagant, if the theory be correct.

Third, God is the moral governor. His government is a moral one, whose code is the moral law. His government and his law have to do with the thoughts, the intents, and the secrets of men's hearts. This must be ever the government of God, and nothing short of it can be the government of God. The pope then being the head of what pretends to be a government of God, and ruling there in the place of God, his government must rule in the realm of morals, and must take cognizance of the counsels of the heart. But being a man, how could he discover what were the thoughts of men's hearts, whether they were good or evil, that he might pronounce judgment upon them?—By long and careful experiment, and by intense ingenuity, means were discovered by which the most secret thoughts of men's hearts might be wrung from them, and that was by the Inquisition.

But the Inquisition was only the direct logic of the theocratical theory upon which the Papacy was founded. The *history of the Papacy* is only the logic of the theocratical theory upon which the Papacy was founded: First, a pope; then the infallibility of that pope; then the Inquisition, to make his infallible authority effective. And that is the logic of any theocratical theory of earthly government since Jesus Christ died.

This being the theory of the bishops, and their determination being "to make use of the power of the State for the furtherance of their aims," the question arises, What means did they employ to secure control of this power? *Answer—The means of Sunday laws.* They secured from Constantine the following Sunday law:—

"THE EMPEROR CONSTANTINE TO HELPIDIUS.

" On the venerable day of the sun let the magistrates and people living in towns rest, and let all workshops be closed. Nevertheless, in the country, those engaged in the cultivation of land may freely and lawfully work, because it often happens that another day is not so well fitted for sowing grain and planting vines; lest by neglect of the best time the bounty provided by Heaven should be lost. Given the seventh day of March, Crispus and Constantine being consuls, both for the second time." [A. D. 321.]

This was not the very first Sunday law that they secured; the first one has not survived. But though it has not survived, the *reason* for it has. Sozomen says that it was "that the day might be devoted with less interruption to the purposes of devotion." And this statement of Sozomen's is indorsed by Neander ("Church History," Vol. II, p. 298). This reason given by Sozomen reveals the secret of the legislation; it shows that it was in behalf of the church, and to please the church.

By reading the above edict, it is seen that they started out quite moderately. They did not stop *all* work; only judges, townspeople, and mechanics were required to rest, while people in the country might freely and lawfully work. The emperor paraded his soldiers on Sunday, and required them to repeat in concert the following prayer:—

"Thee alone we acknowledge as the true God; thee we acknowledge as ruler; thee we invoke for help; from thee have we received the victory; through thee have we conquered our enemies; to thee are we indebted for our present blessings; from thee also we hope for future favors; to thee we will direct our prayer. We beseech thee, that thou wouldst preserve our Emperor Constantine and his pious sons in health and prosperity through the longest life."

This Sunday law of A. D. 321 continued until 386, when—

"Those older changes effected by the Emperor Constantine were more rigorously enforced, and, in general, civil transactions of every kind on Sunday were strictly forbidden. Whoever transgressed was to be considered, in fact, as guilty of sacrilege."—*Neander, Id., p. 300.*

Then as the people were not allowed to do any manner of work, they would play, and, as the natural consequence, the circuses and the theaters throughout the empire were crowded every Sunday. But the object of the law, from the first one that was issued, was that the day might be used for the purposes of devotion, and the people might go to church. Consequently, that this object might be met, there was another step to take, and it was taken. At a church convention held at Carthage in 401, the bishops passed a resolution to send up a petition to the emperor, praying—

"That the public shows might be transferred from the Christian Sunday, and from feast days, to some other days of the week."—*Id.*

And the reason given in support of the petition was,—

"The people congregate more to the circus than to the church." —*Id., note 5.*

In the circuses and the theaters large numbers of men were employed, among whom many were church members. But, rather than to give up their jobs, they would work on Sunday. The bishops complained that these were compelled to work; they pronounced it persecution, and asked for a law to protect those persons from such "persecution." The church had become filled with a mass of people, unconverted, who cared vastly more for worldly interests and pleasures than they did for religion. And as the government was now a government of God, it was considered proper that the civil power should be used to cause all to show respect for God, whether or not they had any respect for him.

But as long as the people could make something by working on Sunday, they would work rather than go to church. A law was secured forbidding all manner of Sunday work. Then they would crowd the circuses and the theaters, instead of going to church. But this was not what the bishops wanted; this was not that for which all work had been forbidden. All work was forbidden in order that the people might go to church; but instead of that, they crowded to the circus and the theater, and the audiences of the bishops were rather slim. This was not at all satisfying to their pride; therefore the next step, and a logical one, too, was, as the petition prayed, to have the exhibitions of the circuses and the theaters transferred to some other days of the week, so that the churches and the theaters should not be open at the same time. For if both were open, the Christians(?), as well as others, not being able to go to both places at once, would go to the circus or the theater instead of to the church. Neander says:—

"Owing to the prevailing passion at that time, especially in the large cities, to run after the various public shows, it so happened that when these spectacles fell on the same days which had been consecrated by the church to some religious festival, they proved a great hindrance to the devotion of Christians, though chiefly, it must be allowed, to those whose Christianity was the least an affair of the life and of the heart."—*Id.*

Assuredly! An open circus or theater will always prove a great hindrance to the devotion of those "Christians" whose Christianity is the least an affair of the life and of the heart. In other words, an open circus or theater will always be a great hindrance to the devotion of those who have not religion enough to keep them from going to it, but who only want to use the profession of religion to maintain their popularity and to promote their selfish interests. On the other hand, to the devotion of those whose Christianity is really an affair of the life and of the heart, an open circus or theater will never be a particle of hindrance, whether open at church time or all the time. But those people had not enough religion or love of right to do what they thought to be right; therefore they wanted the State to take away from them all opportunity to do wrong, so that they could all be Christians. Satan himself could be made that kind of Christian in that way; but he would be Satan still.

Says Neander again :—

"Church teachers . . . were in truth often forced to complain that in such competitions the theater was vastly more frequented than the church."—*Id.*

And the church could not then stand competition; she wanted a monopoly.   And she got it.

This etition of the Carthage convention could not be granted at once, but in 425 the desired law was secured; and to this also there was attached the reason that was given for the first Sunday law that ever was made, namely:—

"In order that the devotion of the faithful might be free from all disturbance."—*Id., p. 301.*

It must constantly be borne in mind, however, that the only way in which "the devotion of the faithful" was "disturbed" by these things was that, when the circus or the theater was open at the same time that the church was open, the "faithful" would go to the circus or the theater instead of to church, and, *therefore*, their "devotion" was "disturbed." And of course the only way in which the "devotion" of such "faithful" ones could be freed from all disturbance, was to close the circuses and the theaters at church time.

In the logic of this theocratical scheme, there was one more step to be taken.   It came about in this way: First, the church had all work on Sunday forbidden, in order that the people might attend to things divine.   But the people went to the circus and the theater instead of to church.   Then the church had laws enacted closing the circuses and the theaters, in order that the people might attend to things divine.   But even then the people would not be devoted, nor attend to things divine, for they had no real religion.   The next step to be taken, therefore, in the logic of the situation, was to compel them to be devoted—to compel them to attend to things divine.   This was the next step logically to be taken, and it was taken. The theocratical bishops were equal to the occasion. They were ready with a theory that exactly met the demands of the case, and the great Catholic Church father and Catholic saint, Augustine, was the father of this Catholic saintly theory. He wrote:—

"It is indeed better that men should be brought to serve God by instruction than by fear of punishment, or by pain. But because the former means are better, the latter must not, therefore, be neglected. Many must often be brought back to their Lord, like wicked servants, by the rod of temporal suffering, before they attain to the highest grade of religious development."—*Schaff's Church History, Vol. II, sec. 27.*

Of this theory Neander remarks:—

"It was by Augustine, then, that a theory was proposed and founded which . . . . contained the germ of that whole system of spiritual despotism, of intolerance and persecution, which ended in the tribunals of the Inquisition."—*Church History, p. 217.*

The history of the Inquisition is only the history of the carrying out of this infamous theory of Augustine's. But this theory is only the logical sequence of the theory upon which the whole series of Sunday laws was founded.

Then says Neander:—

"In this way the church received help from the State for the furtherance of her ends."

This statement is correct. Constantine did many things to favor the bishops. He gave them money and political preference. He made their decisions in disputed cases final, as the decision of Jesus Christ. But in nothing that he did for them did he give them *power over those who did not belong to the church*, to compel them to act as though they did, *except in that one thing of the Sunday law.* Their decisions, which he decreed to be final, were binding only on those who voluntarily chose that tribunal, and affected none others. Before this time if any who had repaired to the tribunal of the bishops were dissatisfied with the decision, they could appeal to the civil magistrate.   This edict cut off that source of appeal, yet affected none but those who voluntarily chose the arbitration of the bishops.   But in the Sunday law power was given to the church to compel those who did not belong to the church, and who were not subject to the jurisdiction of the church, to obey the commands of the church.   In the Sunday law there was given to the church control of the civil power, that by it she could compel those who did not belong to the church to act as if they did.   The history of Constantine's time may be searched through and through, and it will be found that in nothing did he give to the church any such power, except in this one thing—the Sunday law.   Neander's statement is literally correct, that it was "in this way the church received help from the State for the furtherance of her ends."

Here let us bring together more closely the direct bearing of these statements from Neander.   First, he says of the carrying into effect of the theocratical theory of those bishops, that they made themselves dependent upon Constantine by their disputes, and "by their determination to use the power of the State for the furtherance of their aims."   Then he mentions the first and second Sunday laws of Constantine; the Sunday law of 386; the Carthage convention, resolution, and petition of 401; and the law of 425 in response to this petition; and then, without a break, and with direct reference to these Sunday laws, he says, "*In this way* the church received help from the State for the furtherance of her ends."

She started out with the determination to do it.   She did it, and "*in this way*" she did it.   And when she had secured control of the power of the State, she used it for the furtherance of her own aims, and that in her own despotic way, as announced in the inquisitorial theory of Augustine.   The first step logically and inevitably led to the last, and the theocratical leaders in the movement had the cruel courage to follow the first step unto the last, as framed in the words of Augustine, and illustrated in the history of the Inquisition.

LOOK ON THAT PICTURE, THEN ON THIS.

In a preceding chapter we have given *verbatim* the congressional Sunday measure, and have discussed some of its features. As we have seen, it was forced upon Congress by the churches, even under threats. What, then, is the purpose of those who are working so strenuously to have Sunday fixed in the law, whether national law or State law?

At Elgin, Illinois, November 8, 1887, there was held a Sunday-law convention, which was but the first in a series of events that ended only with the congressional recognition and establishment of Sunday as the national "Christian sabbath." The doctrines and acts of this convention are, therefore, proper evidence in this inquiry.

This convention was "called by the members of the Elgin Association of Congregational Ministers and Churches, to consider the prevalent desecration of the sabbath, and its remedy." It was well attended by prominent ministers. In that convention the following resolutions were passed:—

"*Resolved*, That we recognize the Sabbath as an institution of God, revealed in nature and the Bible, and of perpetual obligation on all men; and also as a civil and American institution, bound up in vital and historical connection with the origin and foundation of our government, the growth of our polity, and necessary to be maintained in order for the preservation and integrity of our national system, and, therefore, as having a sacred claim on all patriotic American citizens."

"The seventh day is the Sabbath of *the Lord thy God*," is what the commandment says, and that is *whose* it is. The word "sabbath" means rest. But the rest belongs to the one who rested. Who rested?—God. From what?—From the work of creation. "Remember the Sabbath day, to keep it holy," says the commandment.   It is religious entirely.   There is nothing either American or civil about it.   It is the Lord's, and it is holy.   If it is not kept holy, it is not kept at all. And being the Sabbath of the Lord—the Lord's day—it is to be rendered to the Lord, and not to Cæsar.   With its observance or nonobservance civil government can never of right have anything to do.   The second resolution was this:—

"*Resolved*, That we look with shame and sorrow on the non-observance of the sabbath by many Christian people, in that the custom prevails with them of purchasing sabbath newspapers, engaging in, and patronizing sabbath business and travel, and in many instances giving themselves to pleasure and self-indulgence, setting aside by neglect and indifference the great duties and privileges which God's day brings them."

That is a fact.   They ought to be ashamed of it.   But what do they do to rectify the matter?   Do they resolve to preach the gospel better, to be more faithful themselves in bringing up the consciences of the people, by showing them their duty in regard to these things?—Oh, no.   They resolve to do this:—

"*Resolved*, That we give our votes and support to those candidates or political officers who will pledge themselves to vote for the enactment and enforcing of statutes in favor of the civil sabbath."

Yes, they are ashamed and sorry that Christians will not act like Christians, morally and religiously; therefore they will compel them to act both morally and religiously by enforcing upon them a *civil* sabbath!   But if men will not obey the commandment of God without being compelled to do it by the civil law, then when they obey the civil law, are they obeying God? —They are not.   Do not these people, then, in that, put the civil law in the place of the law of God, and the civil government in the place of God?—They assuredly do.   And that is always the effect of such attempts as this.   It makes utter confusion of all civil and religious relations, and only adds hypocrisy to guilt, and increases unto more ungodliness.

There is another important consideration just here. They never intended to secure nor to enforce a civil Sunday, but a religious one wholly; for in all the discussions of that whole convention there was not a word said about a *civil* sabbath, except in two of these resolutions. In the discussions of the resolutions themselves everything was upon a religious basis. *There is no such thing as a civil sabbath*, and no man can argue three minutes in favor of Sunday or any other day as a civil sabbath without making it only what it is, religious wholly.

In a Sunday-law mass meeting held in Hamilton Hall, Oakland, Cal., in January, 1887, "Rev." Dr. Briggs, of Napa, Cal., said to the State:—

"You relegate moral instruction to the church, and then let all go as they please on Sunday, so that we cannot get at them."

And so they want the State to *corral* all the people on Sunday, that the preachers may get at them. That is what they wanted in the fourth century. They got it at last. The Sunday railway train must also be stopped, and for the same reason. In the Elgin convention Dr. Everts said:—

"The Sunday train is another great evil. They cannot afford to run a train unless they get a great many passengers, and *so break up a great many congregations*. The Sunday railroad trains are hurrying their passengers fast on to perdition. What an outrage that the railroad, that great civilizer, should destroy the Christian sabbath!"

It is not necessary to add any more statements, though whole pages of them might be cited; they are all in the same line. They all plainly show that the secret and real object of the whole Sunday-law movement is to get people to go to church. The Sunday train must be stopped because church members ride on it, and don't go to church enough. The

Sunday paper must be abolished because the people read it instead of going to church, and because those who read it and go to church too are not so well prepared to receive the preaching.

It was precisely the same way in the fourth century concerning the Sunday circus and theater. The people, even the church members, would go to these instead of to church; and even if any went to both, it must be confessed that the Roman circus or theater was not a very excellent dish to set down before a man to prepare him for hearing the word of God. The Sunday circus and theater could not afford to keep open unless they could have a great many spectators and so break up a great many congregations. And as they hurried the spectators fast on to perdition, they had to be shut on Sunday, so as to keep "a great many congregations" out of perdition.

It is exceedingly difficult to see how a Sunday circus in the fourth century could hurry to perdition any one who did not attend it; or how a Sunday train in the nineteenth century can hurry to perdition any one who does not ride on it. And if any are hurried to perdition by this means, who is to blame: the Sunday train, or the ones who ride on it? Right here lies the secret of the whole evil now, as it did in the fourth century: they blame everybody and everything else, even to inanimate things, for the irreligion, the infidelity, and the sin that lie in their own hearts.

Nor are they going to be content with a little. "Rev." W. F. Crafts, speaking before the United States Senate Committee, in April, 1888, in favor of the national Sunday law, said:—

"The law allows the local postmaster, if he chooses (and some of them do choose), to open the mails at the very hour of church, and so make the post office the competitor of the churches."

This same trouble was experienced in the fourth century, also, between the circus or the theater and the church. The

15

church could not stand competition. She would be content with nothing less than a monopoly, and she got it, precisely as these church managers are trying to get it. More than this, they want now, as they did then, the government to secure them in the enjoyment of a perpetual monopoly. At another point in the same speech Mr. Crafts referred to the proposed law as one for "protecting the church services from post office competition." Having secured the help of the government in confirming their monopolizing ambition, what then ?—Nothing short of a complete and perpetual monopoly will satisfy them. This is proved by Dr. McAllister's words at Lakeside, Ohio, July, 1887, as follows:—

"Let a man be what he may,—Jew, seventh-day observer of some other denomination, or those who do not believe in the Christian sabbath,—let the law apply to everyone, that there shall be no public desecration of the first day of the week, the Christian sabbath, the day of rest for the nation. They may hold any other day of the week as sacred, and observe it; but that day which is the one day in seven for the nation at large, let that not be publicly desecrated by anyone, by officer in the government, or by private citizen high or low, rich or poor."

There is much being said of the grasping, grinding greed of monopolies of many kinds; but of all monopolies on earth, the most grinding, the most greedy, the most oppressive the most conscienceless, is a religious monopoly.

THE NEW FALSE THEOCRATICAL THEORY.

A theocratical theory of government was the basis of the religious legislation in the fourth century; it is the same now. The Woman's Christian Temperance Union was, and is, one of the most active and influential bodies in the Sunday-law movement. The great majority of the "petitions" to Congress, except that of their seven-million-two-hundred-thousand-times-multiplied cardinal, were secured by the W. C. T. U. Official documents of that organization declare that—

"A true theocracy is yet to come, and the enthronement of Christ in law and lawmakers; hence I pray devoutly as a Christian patriot, for the ballot in the hands of women, and rejoice that the National Woman's Christian Temperance Union has so long championed this cause."—*Monthly Reading for September, 1886.*

And that—

"The Woman's Christian Temperance Union, local, State, national, and world-wide, has one vital, organic thought, one all-absorbing purpose, one undying enthusiasm, and that is that Christ shall be *this world's king*—yea, verily, THIS WORLD'S KING in its realm of cause and effect,—king of its courts, its camps, its commerce,—king of its colleges and cloisters,—king of its customs and its constitutions. . . . The kingdom of Christ must enter the realm of law through the gateway of politics. . . . We pray heaven to give them [the old parties] no rest . . . until they shall . . . swear an oath of allegiance to Christ in politics, and march in one great army up to the polls to worship God."—*President's Annual Address in Convention, Nashville, 1887.*

Not only this, but the W. C. T. U. is allied with the National Reform Association, whose declared object has ever been to turn this republic into a "kingdom of God." In the Cincinnati National Reform Convention, 1872, Prof. J. R. W. Sloane, D.D., said:—

"Every government by equitable laws is a government of God. A republic thus governed is of him, through the people, and is as truly and really a theocracy as the commonwealth of Israel."

By the expression "government by equitable laws" Mr. Sloane and the National Reformers generally, mean such a government as the National Reformers seek to have established. According to their theory, our government as the fathers made it is not a government by equitable laws, but is entirely founded upon infidel and atheistic ideas. Consequently they wanted the Constitution religiously amended, and framed upon their ideas, so that it should be a government by equitable laws, and as truly and really a theocracy as was the commonwealth of Israel.

The Sunday-law Association also holds much the same theory.   In the Elgin Sunday-law convention, Dr. Mandeville, of Chicago, said:—

"The merchants of Tyre insisted upon selling goods near the temple on the Sabbath, and Nehemiah compelled the officers of the law to do their duty, and stop it.   So we can compel the officers of the law to do their duty."

Now Nehemiah was ruling there in a true theocracy, a government of God; the law of God was the law of the land, and God's will was made known by the written word and by the prophets.   Therefore if Dr. Mandeville's argument is of any force at all, it is so only upon the claim of the establishment of a theocracy.   With this idea the view of Mr. Crafts agrees precisely, and Mr. Crafts was general secretary for the National Sunday-law Union, in their national campaign for national recognition of the Sunday.   He claims, as expressed in his own words, that—

"The preachers are the successors of the prophets."—*Christian Statesman, July 5, 1888.*

Now put these things together.   The government of Israel was a theocracy; the will of God was made known to the ruler by prophets; the ruler compelled the officers of the law to prevent the ungodly from selling goods on the Sabbath.   This government is to be made a theocracy; the preachers are the successors of the prophets; and they are to compel the officers of the law to prevent all selling of goods and all manner of work on Sunday.   This shows conclusively that these preachers intend to take the supremacy into their hands, officially declare the will of God, and compel all men to conform to it. This is why they must needs attack the Declaration of Independence, and declare that "governments do not derive their just powers from the consent of the governed."   This deduction is made a certainty by the words of Professor Blanchard in the Elgin convention:—

"In this work we are undertaking for the Sabbath, we are the representatives of God."

And the chief of these representatives of God will be but a pope again; because when preachers control the civil power as the representatives of God, a pope is a certainty.

These quotations prove, to a demonstration, that the whole theory upon which this religio-political movement is based, is identical with that of the fourth century, which established the Papacy. They show also that the means employed—Sunday laws—by which to gain control of the civil power to make the wicked theory effective, are identical with the means which were employed in the fourth century for the same purpose.

The next question is, Will they carry the theory into effect as they did in the fourth century and onward?

When they shall have stopped all Sunday work, and all Sunday papers, and all Sunday trains, in order that the people may go to church and attend to things divine, suppose that then the people fail to go to church or attend to things divine, will the religio-political managers stop there? Having done all this that the people may be devoted, will they suffer their good intentions to be frustrated, or their good offices to be despised? Will not these now take the next logical step, the step that was taken in the fourth century, and *compel* men to attend to things divine? If not, why not? Having taken all the steps but this, will they not take this?—Of course they will. Human nature is the same now as it was in the fourth century. Politics is the same now as it was then. And as for religious bigotry, it knows no centuries; it knows no such thing as progress or enlightenment; it is ever the same. And in its control of civil power, the cruel results are also ever the same.

In other words, when they get the power to oppress, will they use the power? A sufficient answer to this would seem to be the simple inquiry, If they do not intend to use the power, then why are they making such strenuous efforts to get it? But we are not left merely to this inquiry, nor yet to the argument, for an answer to the question; we have their own words. At a National Reform W. C. T. U. convention held at Lakeside, Ohio, in 1887, the following question was asked:

"Will not the National Reform movement result in persecution against those who on some points believe differently from the majority, even as the recognition of the Christian religion by the Roman power resulted in grievous persecution against true Christians?"

Answer, by Dr. McAllister:—

"Now notice the fallacy here. The recognition of the Roman Catholic religion by the State, made that State a persecuting power. Why?—Because the Roman Catholic religion is a persecuting religion. If true Christianity is a persecuting religion, then the acknowledgment of our principles by the State will make the State a persecutor. But if the true Christian religion is a religion of liberty, a religion that regards the rights of all, then the acknowledgment of those principles by the State will make the State the guardian of all men, and the State will be no persecutor. True religion never persecutes."

There is indeed a fallacy here; but it is not in the question; it is in the answer. That which made the Roman State a persecuting power, says the doctor, was its recognition of the Catholic religion, "which is a persecuting religion." But the Roman Catholic religion is not the only persecuting religion that has been in the world. Presbyterianism persecuted while John Calvin ruled in Geneva; it persecuted while the Covenanters ruled in Scotland; it persecuted while it held the power in England. Congregationalism persecuted while it had the power in New England. Episcopalianism persecuted in England and in Virginia. Every religion that has been allied with the civil power, or that has controlled the civil power, has been a persecuting religion; and such will always be the case.

Mr. McAllister's implied statement is true, that "true Christianity never persecutes;" but it is true only because true Christianity never will allow itself to be allied in any way with the civil power, or to receive any support from it.   It is true because true Christianity will never allow itself the possession of any power by which anybody could be persecuted.   The National Reform Association does propose to "enforce upon all, the laws of Christian morality;" it proposes to have the government adopt the National Reform religion, and then "lay its hand upon any religion that does not conform to it;" and it asserts that the civil power has the right "to command the consciences of men."   Now any such thing carried into effect as is here plainly proposed by that association, can never be anything else than persecution.

But Mr. McAllister affirms that the National Reform movement, if successful, would not lead to persecution, "because true religion never persecutes."   The doctor's argument amounts only to this: The National Reform religion is the true religion.   True religion never persecutes.   Therefore, to compel men to conform to the true religion,—that is, the religion that controls the civil power,—is not persecution!

In A. D. 556 Pope Pelagius called upon Narses to compel certain parties to obey the pope's command.   Narses refused, on the ground that it would be persecution.   The pope answered Narses' objection with this argument:—

"Be not alarmed at the idle talk of some, crying out against persecution, and reproaching the church, as if she delighted in cruelty, when she punishes evil with wholesome severities, or procures the salvation of souls. *He alone persecutes who forces to evil.* But to restrain men from doing evil, or to punish those who have done it, is not persecution, or cruelty, but love of mankind."—*Bower's History of the Popes, Pelagius, A. D. 556.*

Compare this with Dr. McAllister's answer, and find any difference in principle between them who can.   There is no difference.   The arguments are identical.   It is the essential spirit of the Papacy which is displayed in both, and in that of Pope Pelagius no more than in that of Dr. McAllister.

Another question, or rather statement, was this:—

" There is a law in the State of Arkansas enforcing Sunday observance upon the people, and the result has been that many good persons have not only been imprisoned, but have lost their property, and even their lives." [2]

Answer, by Dr. McAllister:—

" It is better that a few should suffer than that the whole nation should lose its sabbath."

This argument is identical with that by which the Pharisees in Christ's day justified themselves in killing him. It was said:—

" It is expedient for us, that one man should die for the people, and that the whole nation perish not." John 11 : 50.

And then says the record:—

" Then from that day forth they took counsel together for to put him to death." Verse 53.

The argument used in support of the claim of *right to use* this power, is identical with that used by the Papacy in inaugurating her persecutions; the argument in justification of the *use* of the power is identical with that by which the murderers of Jesus Christ justified themselves in accomplishing that wicked deed; and if anybody thinks that these men in our day, proceeding upon the identical theory, in the identical way, and justifying their proceedings by arguments identical with those of the Papacy and the murderous Pharisees,—if anybody thinks that these men will stop short of persecution, he has vastly more confidence in apostate humanity than we have.

We need not multiply evidences further to show that this whole religio-political Sunday-law movement of our day is of

---

[2] This same thing has gone on ever since—in Arkansas, Tennessee, Georgia, Maryland, and Massachusetts—and still continues. In the year 1894 more days were spent in jail by Sabbath-keeping Christians than there were days in the year. And at the time of writing this note, in 1895, eight men are in jail, and over thirty more under indictment. And all for "sabbath breaking." Later: These eight men were all pardoned at once by Governor Turney. But the prosecutions are still going on.

the same piece with that in the fourth century. The theory is the same; the means and the arguments are the same in both; and two things that are so precisely alike in the making, will be exactly alike when they are made. That in the fourth century made the Papacy; and this in the nineteenth century makes a living likeness of the Papacy.

Sunday has no basis whatever as a civil institution; it never had any. And the only basis it has, or ever had, as a *religious* institution, is the authority of the Papacy. This is both the law and the literal truth in the case.

It was perfectly in order, therefore, for Cardinal Gibbons to indorse a movement to give to Sunday the legal sanction and support of the United States Government, and thus secure the governmental recognition of *the authority of the Papacy.* The cardinal's indorsement has been heralded by the Sunday-law workers throughout the length and breadth of the land, as a mighty accession to the Sunday-law movement. And, as a matter of fact, it is a mighty accession; but to what purpose? The following letter from the cardinal to Mr. E. E. Franke, of Jersey City, N. J., will show:—

"CARDINAL'S RESIDENCE,
408 North Charles St., Baltimore, Md.,
October 3, 1889.

"DEAR MR. FRANKE: At the request of his eminence, the cardinal, I write to assure you that you are correct in your assertion that Protestants in observing the Sunday are following, not the *Bible*, which they take as their only rule of action, but the *tradition* of the church. I defy them to point out to me the word 'Sunday' in the Bible; if it is not to be found there, and it cannot be, then it is not the Bible which they follow in this particular instance, but tradition, and in this they flatly contradict themselves.

"The Catholic Church changed the day of rest from the last to the first day of the week, because the most memorable of Christ's works was accomplished on Sunday. It is needless for me to enter into any elaborate proof of the matter. They cannot prove their point from Scripture; therefore, if sincere, they must acknowledge that they draw their observance of the Sunday from tradition, and are therefore weekly contradicting themselves.

"Yours very sincerely,   M. A. REARDON."

This shows that it is *as a Roman Catholic*, securing honor to an institution of the Papacy, and thus to the Papacy itself, that Cardinal Gibbons has indorsed the national Sunday-law movement. The cardinal understands what he is doing a great deal better than Mr. Crafts, Mrs. Bateham, *et al.*, understand what they were doing. And, further, the cardinal understands what THEY are doing a great deal better than they themselves do. This also shows that those who signed the petition for a Sunday law, as the cardinal did, were honoring the Papacy, as the cardinal was.

How appropriate, therefore, it is that Cardinal Gibbons should indorse the national Sunday bill! How natural, indeed, that he should gladly add his name to the number of petitioners in support of the movement to secure legislation in the interests of the church! He knows just how his brethren in the fourth century worked the thing. He knows what the outcome of the movement was then, and he knows full well what the outcome of this movement will be now. He knows that the theory underlying this movement is identical with the theory which was the basis of that. He knows the methods of working are the same now as they were then. He knows that the means employed now to secure control of the civil power are identical with the means employed then, and he knows that the result must be the same. He knows that when religion shall have been established as an essential element in legislation in this government, the experience of fifteen hundred eventful years, and "the ingenuity and patient care" of fifty generations of statesmen, will not be lost in the effort to make the papal power supreme over all here and now, as was done there and then.

And this thing—this Catholic Sunday, this "miner and sapper" of a religious despotism, this "coach" of the Inquisition —this thing it is that the Congress of the United States has taken up from the combined "Protestantism" of the United States and interpreted into the commandment of God and fixed in the legislation of the nation as "the Christian sabbath"! In view of all these things, why should not Rome triumph?

And now the Catholic Church itself is taking the lead in enforcing respect for the Sunday by law. The *Northwestern Chronicle*, Archbishop Ireland's organ, April 5, 1895, announced the organization of a "Sunday-law Observance League," and prints an address to the W. C. T. U. and all friends of the American Sabbath, concluding with the following appeal:—

"All W. C. T. U.'s and Y.'s, churches, pastors, young people's societies, temperance organizations, Law and Order Leagues, and individuals, are called upon to help maintain our sabbath as a day of the Lord for the people, without regard to race, sex, or condition, for a day of rest and worship. To this end let us make sabbath observance week in Minnesota marked by sermons, public meetings, Sunday school exercises, distribution of literature, and prayer for the better enforcement of law against all infringement of the right of sabbath observance, and particularly against that arch-enemy of God and man, the saloon."

From the origin and history of Sunday laws, this was, of course, to be expected sooner or later. And now that this, as well as all the rest of the machinery of a religious despotism, has been made ready to her hand, it is not surprising that she assumes the leadership and sounds the bugle for the general advance.

CHAPTER XI.

THE Catholic Church claims infallibility. This claim springs directly, and logically too, from her claim of the prerogative of interpreter of the Scriptures.

As we have seen, the Congress of the United States has also assumed and exercised this prerogative. With Congress, as certainly as with the Papacy, the assumption of this prerogative carries with it the assertion of infallibility. This action, of itself, therefore, placed Congress directly upon Roman ground.

This action of Congress, however, was merely the legislative formula giving authority to the interpretation already determined upon by combined "Protestantism." This, therefore, was nothing else than the recognition, and the setting up, by "Protestantism" in the United States, of a human tribunal charged with the interpretation of Scripture, with the authoritative enforcement of that interpretation by governmental power. This proceeding, therefore, placed the combined "Protestantism" of the country altogether and thoroughly upon papal ground.

If this thing had been done by the Papacy; if she had thus forced herself and her interpretation of Scripture upon Congress, and thus got her religious notions fixed in the law to be forced upon the people; there could be no surprise at it. In so doing the Papacy would have been only acting according to her own native character, and carrying out her avowed princi-

(238)

ples. But for professed Protestantism to do it, is in positive
contradiction of every principle that the term Protestantism
justly implies. Bryce's arraignment of Protestantism on this
point is well deserved, and is decidedly applicable here:—

"The principles which had led the Protestants to sever themselves
from the Roman Church should have taught them to bear with the
opinions of others, and warned them from the attempt to connect
agreement in doctrine or manner of worship with the necessary forms
of civil government. Still less ought they to have enforced that agreement by civil penalties, for faith, upon their own showing, had no
value save when it was freely given. A church which does not claim
to be infallible is bound to allow that some part of the truth may possibly be with its adversaries; a church which permits or encourages
human reason to apply itself to revelation, has no right first to argue
with people and then to punish them if they are not convinced.

" But whether it was that men only half saw what they had done;
or that, finding it hard enough to unrivet priestly fetters, they wel-
comed all the aid a temporal prince could give; the result was that
religion, or, rather, religious creeds, began to be involved with politics
more closely than had ever been the case before. Through the
greater part of Christendom wars of religion raged for a century or
more, and down to our own days feelings of theological antipathy
continue to affect the relations of the powers of Europe. In almost
every country the form of doctrine which triumphed associated itself
with the State, *and maintained the despotic system* of the Middle Ages,
while it forsook the grounds on which that system had been based.

" It was thus that there arose national churches, which were to be
to the several Protestant countries of Europe that which the Church
Catholic had been to the world at large; churches, that is to say, each
of which was to be coextensive with its respective State, was to enjoy
landed wealth and exclusive political privilege, and was to be armed
with coercive powers against recusants. It was not altogether easy
to find a set of theoretical principles on which such churches might be
made to rest; for they could not, like the old church, point to the
historical transmission of their doctrines; they could not claim to have
in any one man, or body of men, an infallible organ of divine truth;
they could not even fall back upon general councils, or the argument, whatever it may be worth, '*Securus indicat orbis terrarum.*'

" But in practice these difficulties were soon got over, for the dominant party in each State, if it was not infallible, was at any rate quite sure that it was right, and could attribute the resistance of other sects to nothing but moral obliquity. The will of the sovereign, as in England, *or the will of the majority*, as in Holland, Scandinavia, and Scotland, *imposed upon each country a peculiar form of worship*, and *kept up the practices* of medieval intolerance *without their justification*.

"Persecution, which might be at least excused in an infallible, Catholic, and apostolic church, was peculiarly odious when practiced by those who were not Catholic; who were no more apostolic than their neighbors; and who had just revolted from the most ancient and venerable authority, in the name of rights which they now denied to others. If union with the visible church by participation in a material sacrament be necessary to eternal life, persecution may be held a duty, a kindness to perishing souls. But if the kingdom of heaven be in every sense a kingdom of the spirit, if saving faith be possible out of one visible body and under a diversity of external forms, persecution becomes at once a crime and a folly.

"Therefore the intolerance of Protestants, if the forms it took were less cruel than those practiced by the Roman Catholics, was also far less defensible; for it had seldom anything better to allege on its behalf than motives of political expediency, or more often the mere headstrong passion of a ruler or a faction, to silence the expression of any opinions but their own. . . . And hence it is not too much to say that the ideas . . . regarding the duty of the magistrate to compel uniformity in doctrine and worship by the civil arm, may all be traced to the relation which that theory established between the Roman Church and the Roman Empire; to the conception, in fact, of an empire church itself."—*Holy Roman Empire, chapter 18, par. 8.*

This shows how certainly the professed Protestantism *and the Government* of the United States have put themselves upon papal ground.

THE PIVOT OF INFALLIBILITY.

Nor yet is this all. This prerogative of interpreting the Scripture was exercised by the professed Protestantism and the Congress of the United States, in the substitution of Sunday for the Sabbath of the Lord as it stands written in the commandment of God. And this is precisely the thing—the very point—upon which turns the argument for the validity of the claim of infallibility on the part of the Papacy.

The supreme point that marks the difference between Protestantism and the Papacy is, whether the Bible, and the Bible alone, or the Bible *and tradition*, is the true standard of faith and morals. "The Bible, and the Bible alone," is the claim of Protestantism. "The Bible *and tradition*" is the claim of Catholicism. And this term "tradition" in the Catholic system does not mean merely antiquity, "but *continuing inspiration.*" And this "continuing inspiration" is but another form of expression for "infallibility."

This question as to "the Bible and tradition" was not finally settled even for Catholicism until the Council of Trent. It was one of the leading questions of that council as between Protestantism and Catholicism; and it was in the settlement of the question as between these, that it was finally settled for the Catholic Church itself.

The very first question concerning the faith that was considered in the council was the one involved in this issue. There was a strong party, even of the Catholics, in the council, who were in favor of abandoning tradition and adopting *the Scripture only* as the standard of authority in faith and morals. This was so largely and so decidedly held in the council that the pope's legates wrote to him that there was "a strong tendency to set aside tradition altogether, and to make Scripture the sole standard of appeal."—*Encyclopedia Britannica, Trent, Council of*.

To do this, however, would certainly be to go a long way toward admitting the claims of the Protestants, and this would never do. This crisis, however, forced the ultra-Catholic portion of the council to find some way of convincing the others that "Scripture *and tradition*" was the only sure ground to stand upon. Although two decrees were passed April 8, 1546, favoring the view of "Scripture *and tradition*," yet this was not satisfactory. The question kept constantly recurring in the counsel; many of those who had sustained the decrees were very uneasy about it. Accordingly Dr. Holtzmann writes thus:—

" The council was unanimously of the opinion of Ambrosius Pelargus that at no price should any triumph be prepared for the Protestants to be able to say that the council had condemned the teachings of the old church. But this practice caused endless trouble, without ever giving good security. Indeed, it required for this crisis that ' almost divine sagacity' which the Spanish legate ceded to the synod on March 15, 1562. . . .

" Finally, at the opening of the last session, January 18, 1562, all scruples were cast aside; *the archbishop of Rheggio made a speech, in which he openly declared that tradition stood higher than the Bible.* For this reason alone the authority of the church could not be bound to the authority of the Scriptures, *because the former had changed the Sabbath into Sunday—not by the commandment of Christ, but solely by her own authority.* This destroyed the last illusion, and it was hereby declared *that tradition signified not so much antiquity, but rather continuing inspiration.*"—*Canon and Tradition, p. 263.*

This particular part of the archbishop's speech was as follows :—

"The condition of the heretics nowadays is such that they do not appeal to anything more than this [the Bible, and the Bible alone; the Scriptures, as in the written word, the sole standard in faith and morals], to overthrow the church under the pretext of following the word of God. Just as though the church—the body—were in conflict with the word of Christ; or as if the head could be against the body. Indeed, this very authority of the church is most of all glorified by the Holy Scriptures; for while on the one hand the church recommends the word of God, declaring it to be divine, and presenting it to us to read, explaining doubtful points and faithfully condemning all that runs counter thereto; on the other hand, *by the same authority, the church, the legal precepts of the Lord, contained in the Holy Scriptures, have ceased. The Sabbath,* the most glorious day in the law, *has been merged into the Lord's day.* . . . This day and similar institutions have not ceased in consequence of the preaching of Christ (for he says that he did not come to destroy the law, but to fulfill it); but yet they have been changed, and that *solely by the authority of the church*. Now, if this authority should be done away with (which would please the heretics very much), who would there be to testify for the truth and to confound the obstinacy of the heretics?"—*Id.*

There was no getting around this; for the Protestants' own confession of faith,—the Augsburg Confession, 1530,—had clearly admitted that "the observation of the Lord's day" had been appointed by "the church" only. As Dr. Holtzmann says, this argument "destroyed the last illusion," because as it was clear that in observing Sunday upon the appointment of the church, instead of the Sabbath which stood in the written commandment of the Lord himself, the Protestants themselves held *not* to "the Bible and the Bible alone," but to the Bible *and tradition*, with tradition above the Bible. By this fact and this argument, the uneasy minds in the council were set completely at rest, and the question as between "the Bible and the Bible alone," or "the Bible and tradition," was finally settled in the Catholic Church.

Therefore the papal position is constructed thus: (*a*) The Scripture *and tradition* is the faith of the Papacy; (*b*) tradition means "continuing inspiration;" (*c*) continuing inspiration means infallibility in matters of faith and morals; (*d*) and this is demonstrated in the fact of her having substituted Sunday for the Sabbath of the Lord in the written commandment. And thus it is that the substitution of Sunday for the Sabbath is the pivot upon which turns the validity of the argument as against Protestants, for the infallibility of the Papacy.

This shows how fully the Protestantism and the Congress of the United States put themselves upon papal ground, in their first essay in the exercise of the prerogative of authoritative interpreter of the Scripture. They did it precisely in the likeness of the Papacy by substituting Sunday for the Sabbath of the Lord as in the written commandment.

And this is why it is that the Papacy, in taking the advantage
16

which she has already taken, and in following it up to whatever extent that she may, is only acting straightforwardly upon her own native and abiding principles.   In this respect the Papacy is not in anywise to blame for what she has already done, nor for what she may do upon this basis in the times to come.   For assuredly if papal principles are to prevail, who is better qualified, who has a better *right*, to apply these principles than the Papacy herself?   Since the Government of the United States has been set bodily upon papal principles in the interpretation of the Constitution, in the authoritative interpretation of the Scriptures, and in the adoption of the very sign of papal infallibility itself, who, then, is so well qualified to guide the government and the nation in the new path, as is she who for nearly sixteen hundred years has steadily traveled that path?

THE ONE GREAT QUESTION NOW.

The conclusion of the whole matter, the sum of all that has been said, or that can be said, on the subject, is that the principles of the Government of the United States as regards religion and the State, are no longer American, but Roman; no longer Protestant, but papal; no longer Christian, but antichristian. And the question now to be decided by every man, woman, and child in the nation is whether they will be American, Protestant, and Christian, or whether they will be Roman, papal, and antichristian.   Every person is now absolutely shut up to the decision of this question.   The very course of events will force every soul to the decision of this question—each one for himself.   The people can no more escape this issue than they can get out of the world.

As the matter now stands, every person in the United States is shut up to just one of two things: Either to assent to governmental interpretations and interference in religious matters, or decidedly to protest against it; either to assent to that which has already been done, and to the like of which is to follow, to be plastered on, layer after layer, till the whole nation shall be groaning under the curse of a religious despotism equal to that of the Dark Ages, or else decidedly to protest against, and refuse any kind of assent to, that which has been done, which is being done, or any such that may follow in any shape whatever.

The historian of the Reformation has well remarked that "the establishment of a tribunal charged with the interpretation of the Bible, had terminated only in slavishly subjecting man to man in what should be most unfettered,—conscience and faith."—*D'Aubigne, Book XIII, chapter 6.* Revolt from this thing in the sixteenth century was the emancipation of mankind.

When the attempt was made, by means of a Supreme Court decision perverting the Constitution, to accomplish throughout the whole nation the enslavement of man to man in all his bodily interests—for even the slaveholder left free the conscience and faith of his slaves—uncompromising opposition to it was the emancipation of a whole race and the assured freedom of the nation.

And now, when by both these means—when by a Supreme Court decision perverting the Constitution, and the establishment of a tribunal charged with the interpretation of the Bible —this powerful attempt is made to bring about once more the enslavement of man to man in that which should be most unfettered, conscience and faith, nothing less than absolutely uncompromising opposition to this thing in every phase of it from beginning to end—can secure the liberty of the individual, of the nation, or of mankind.

And who can refuse uncompromisingly to oppose it? With the example of Christianity as it started in the world; of the Reformation as it arose in the sixteenth century; of the fathers who made this nation; of the opposition to, and not merely the reversal, but the annihilation of, the Dred Scott decision—with all this history and all these examples before us, which the conscience and better judgment of all men approve, how can any man hesitate to enlist all his energies of body, soul, and spirit, in uncompromising opposition to this monstrous evil so treacherously conceived and so powerfully maintained?

So much for the necessity of such opposition. But as this book is a study of the rights of the people, it will be proper here to set forth the rights by which the people, with courage, consistency, and righteousness, can inaugurate, and forever carry on, this uncompromising opposition.

DIVINE RIGHT.

It is the *divine right* of every man to believe or not believe, to be religious or not religious, as he shall choose for himself. God himself, in Jesus Christ, has said: " If any man hear my words, and believe not, I judge him not; for I came not to judge the world, but to save the world. He that rejecteth me, and receiveth not my words, hath one that judgeth him; the word that I have spoken, the same shall judge him in the last day." John 12 : 47, 48. Thus the God of heaven, the Author of Christianity, has left every soul free to believe or not believe, to receive or reject, his words, as the man may choose for himself. And when any man chooses not to believe, and chooses to reject his word, the Lord does not condemn him.

Whoever, therefore, would presume to exercise jurisdiction over the religious belief or observances of any man, or would compel any man to conform to the precepts of any religion, or to comply with the ceremonies of any religious body, or would condemn any man for not so complying, does in that thing put himself above Jesus Christ, and, indeed, above God, for he exercises a prerogative which God himself refuses to exercise.

The word of God is the word of life. To whomsoever that

word comes, whosoever heareth it, to him in that word there comes life from God—eternal life. Then he who rejects that word rejects life. He who rejects life does in that very thing choose death. And he who chooses death by the rejection of life does in that pass judgment of death upon himself. And so it stands written, "It was necessary that the word of God should first have been spoken to you; but seeing ye put it from you, and *judge yourselves* unworthy of everlasting life," etc. Acts 13:46. Thus it is that God judges no man for rejecting his word; and this is how it is that that word shall judge men in the last day. "In that day" that word of life will stand there as the witness to all that eternal life came to all, but was rejected, and nothing but death remains. And when the death is received, each one receives simply what he has chosen, and in that the God of love does not condemn, but is sorry instead.

Now to the Christian church is committed this word of life as she is sent into the world. She is to "preach the word." To her it is written, "Do all things without murmurings and disputings; that ye may be blameless and harmless, the sons of God, without rebuke, in the midst of a crooked and perverse nation, among whom ye shine as lights in the world; *holding forth the word of life.*" Phil. 2:14–16. Thus the true church is in the world "in Christ's stead" (2 Cor. 5:20), to hold forth, to bring to men, the word of life. In so doing she judges no one, she condemns no one, she sets at naught no one, for she "is subject unto Christ" in everything (Eph. 5:24), and he ever says, "If any man hear my words, and believe not, I judge [condemn] him not."

In this word Christ also establishes the divine right of every man, at his own free choice, to dissent from, and to disregard in every way, any doctrine, dogma, ordinance, rite, or institution of any church on earth. And no man can ever rightly be molested or disquieted in any way whatever in the free exercise of this divine right.

A SUBTLE SUBTERFUGE.

Professedly this right has always been recognized by both Catholicism and the different sects of Protestantism, but in nearly every instance the profession of recognition of the right has been only a pretense; for, while professing to recognize the right in one way, in another way, and by a sheer subterfuge, it has been denied and attempt made to sweep it entirely away. This subterfuge is for the church to get her dogmas or institutions recognized in the law, and then demand *obedience to the law*, throwing upon the dissenter the odium of "lawlessness and disrespect for the constituted authorities," while she poses as the champion of "law and order," the "conservator of the State, and the stay of society"!

Of all the hypocritical pretenses that were every employed, this is perhaps the subtlest, and is certainly the meanest. It flourished throughout the Middle Ages, when anything and everything that the church could invent was thus forced upon the people. Its slimy trail can be traced throughout the history of the "Protestant" sects, in thus forcing upon the people such peculiar institutions as were characteristic of the sect that could obtain control of the law. And now it is made to flourish again, by all the sects together, in thus forcing upon the people the one thing in which they are all agreed, and in which they have obtained control of the law,[1] the observance of Sunday, "the Christian sabbath," supported by such auxiliary organizations, such wheels within wheels, as the National Reform Association, the American Sabbath Union, the "Law and Order Leagues," the "Civic Federations," W. C. T. U., Y. M. C. A., Y. P. S. C. E., and so on through the rest of the alphabet.

[1] "By a sort of factitious advantage, the observers of Sunday have secured the aid of the civil law, and adhere to that advantage with great tenacity, in spite of the clamor for religious freedom and the progress that has been made in the absolute separation of Church and State. . . . And the efforts to extirpate the advantage above mentioned, by judicial decision in favor of a civil right to disregard the change, seem to me quite useless."—*U. S. Circuit Court.* See "Due Process of Law," pp. 31, 116.

Sunday, not only according to their own showing, but by every other fair showing that can be made, is a religious institution, a church institution, only. This they all know as well as they know anything. And yet every one of these organizations, principal or auxiliary, is working constantly to get this church institution fixed, and more firmly fixed, *in the law*, with penalties attached that are more worthy of barbarism than of civilization; and then, when anybody objects to it, they all cry out that "it is not a question of religion, it is simply a question of *law*. We are not asking any religious observance; all that we ask is *respect for law*"!!

The Christian, Protestant, and American answer to all this is that neither the Sunday institution nor any other religious or ecclesiastical institution, *has any right to a place in the law.* And even when it is put into the law, this does not take away the right of dissent. The divine right of dissent from religious or ecclesiastical institutions abides ever the same, whether the institution is out of the law or in the law. And when the institution is fixed in the law, the right of dissent then extends *to that law.* The *subterfuge* cannot destroy the *right.*

THE COURTS INDORSE THE SUBTERFUGE.

From the church organizations the courts have caught up this cry. And, though acknowledging that the Sunday institution is religious; that it is enacted and enforced at the will of the church; and that the logic of it is the union of Church and State; yet they insist that, as it is in the law, and the law is for the public good, no right of dissent can be recognized, but the dissenter "may be made to suffer for his defiance *by persecutions*, if you call them so, on the part of the great majority."[2]

This argument is as old as is the contest for the right of

---

[2] These are the very words of the United States Circuit Court for the western district of Tennessee, in August, 1891, and in behalf of Sunday, too. See "Due Process of Law," where the decision is printed in full.

the free exercise of religious belief. It was the very position occupied by Rome when the disciples of Christ were sent into the world to preach religious freedom to all mankind. Religious observances were enforced by the law. The Christians asserted and maintained the right to dissent from all such observances, and, in fact, from *every one* of the religious observances of Rome, and to believe religiously for themselves, though in so doing they totally disregarded the laws, which, on the part of the Roman State, were held to be beneficial to the population. Then, *as now*, it was held that, though religious belief was the foundation of the custom, yet this was no objection to it, because it had become a part of the legal system of the government, and was enforced by the State for its own good.[3] But Christianity *then* refused to recognize any validity in any such argument, and so it does now.

When Paganism was supplanted by the Papacy in the Roman Empire, the same argument was again brought forth to sustain the papal observances which were enforced by imperial law; and through the whole period of papal supremacy Christianity still refused to recognize any validity whatever in the argument.

Under the Calvinistic theocracy of Geneva the same argument was again used in behalf of religious oppression. In England the same argument was used against the Puritans and other dissenters in behalf of religious oppression there. In New England, under the Puritan theocracy, the same argument was used in behalf of religious oppression, and to justify the Congregationalists, who had control of legislation, in compelling the Baptists and the Quakers, under penalty of banish-

---

[3] "The pagan religion was, in truth, so closely interwoven with all the arrangements of civil and social life that it was not always easy to separate and distinguish the barely civil or social from the religious element. Many customs had really sprung from a religious source, whose connection, however, with religion had long been forgotten by the multitude, and, remembered only by a few learned antiquarians, lay too far back to be recalled in the popular consciousness."—*Neander, Church History, Vol. I, sec. 3, par. 17.*

ment and even of death, to conform to the religious observances of the Congregationalists.

" The rulers of Massachusetts put the Quakers to death and banished the Antinomians and·'Anabaptists,' *not* because of their religious tenets, but because of their *violations of the civil laws.* This is the justification which they pleaded, and it was the best they could make. Miserable excuse! But just so it is; wherever there is such a union of church and State, heresy and heretical practices are apt to become violations of the civil code, and are punished no longer *as errors in religion*, but infractions of the laws of the land. So the defenders of the Inquisition have always spoken and written in justification of that awful and most iniquitous tribunal."—*Baird's Religion in America, p. 94, note.*

In short, this argument—this " miserable excuse "—whether made by churches or by courts, is the same old serpent (Rev. 12: 9, 12, 14) that tortured the Christians to death under Pagan Rome; that burnt John Huss at Constance, and Michael Servetus at Geneva; that whipped and banished the Baptists, and banished and hanged the Quakers, in New England. Whether used by the Roman State and the Catholic Church, or by other States and other churches, in the early centuries or in these last years of the nineteenth century of the Christian era, that argument is ever the same old serpent, and Christianity has always refused to recognize any validity whatever in it, and it always will.

THE STATE A PARTISAN OF THE CHURCH.

We have proved by the express words of Christ the divine right of dissent in all religious things: that any man has the divine right to dissent from any and every religious doctrine or observance of any body on earth. So long as civil government keeps its place, and requires of men only those things which pertain to Cæsar,—things civil,—so long there will be neither dissent nor disagreement, but peace only, between the government and all Christian sects or subjects. But just as soon as civil government adopts any church institution and makes it a part of the law, it makes itself the partisan of a religious party, and sets itself up as the champion of religious observances. And just then this right of dissent in religious things is extended to the authority of the government, *in so far* as that authority is thus exercised. And so far there will be dissent on the part of every Christian in the government.

Let it be repeated: When the State undertakes to enforce the observance of any church ordinance or institution, and thus makes itself the champion and partisan of the church, then *the inalienable right* of men *to dissent from* CHURCH doctrines and to disregard church ordinances and institutions, *is extended to the "authority" of the* STATE in so far as it is thus exercised. The "authority" of the State in such case is just no authority at all; because no earthly government can ever by any pretext have any authority in matters of religion or religious observances.

Sunday observance is in itself religious, and religious only. The institution is wholly ecclesiastical. The creation of the institution was for religious purposes only. The first law of government enforcing its observance was enacted with religious intent; such has been the character of every Sunday law that ever was made, and such its character is now recognized to be by both churches and courts. It is therefore the divine right of every man utterly to ignore the institution, to disregard its observance, and to dissent from the authority which instituted or enjoins it. And when any State or civil government makes itself the partisan of the ecclesiastical body which instituted it, and the champion of the ecclesiastical authority which enjoins it, and enacts laws to compel men to respect it and observe it, that State does attempt to compel submission to church authority, and conformity to church discipline, and does thereby invade the inalienable right of dissent from church authority and church discipline. If the State can rightfully do this in one thing, it can do so in all; and therefore in doing this it does, in principle and in effect, destroy all freedom of religious thought and action. Men are thereby compelled either to submit to be robbed of their inalienable right of freedom of thought in religious things, or else to disregard the authority of the State. And no Christian, and no man of sound principle and honest conviction, will ever hesitate as to which of the two things he will do.

Thus it is clear that by *divine right* every man can, with courage, consistency, and righteousness, engage in uncompromising opposition to this movement to establish a national religious despotism.

THE NATURAL AND CONSTITUTIONAL RIGHT.

This is also *the natural right* of every man. On this read again paragraph 1 of the "Memorial and Remonstrance of the People of Virginia," page 95; the "Act Establishing Freedom of Religion in Virginia," page 90; and the points on pages 52–55.

This is also *the constitutional right* of every man in the United States. This has been demonstrated in chapter 5.

Here, however, is where the issue is joined. Here is where the crisis is reached. Because the Supreme Courts of all the States that have such laws have declared them to be constitutional;[4] a Circuit Court of the United States has declared that "persecution" in the States accordingly is "due process of law;" and the United States Supreme Court has declared that "the establishment of the Christian religion," is the meaning of the national Constitution, and that, accordingly, "this is a Christian nation." So far, therefore, as Supreme Courts are concerned—State and national—this constitutional right has been swept away.

---

[4] The Supreme Court of California first decided all such laws unconstitutional. Judge Stephen J. Field, now of the United States Supreme Court, was a member of the court and dissented. Afterward changes came in the court, Judge Field became chief justice, the question was brought up again, and such laws were declared to be constitutional. Then *the people* of California afterwards took up the question and annulled all such decisions by a majority of over 17,000.

As for the inferior courts in the States—the judges, justices, prosecuting attorneys, etc.—instead of reading the Constitution for themselves and supporting *it*, as they have taken a solemn oath to do, they take somebody else's reading of it and support somebody else's *interpretation of it*, while their own conscience, their own sober judgment, and the plain word of the Constitution, all tell them that such interpretation is clearly wrong.[5] They argue that as "the Supreme Court has decided that the law is constitutional, it is not for us to decide differently, whatever our own views of the case may be," etc.

General Jackson, when President of the United States, recognized no such doctrine. The Supreme Court declared to be

---

[5] There are noble exceptions to this course, though they are very, very few. One of these, such as every one ought to be, in a private letter dated December 22, 1891, writes as follows:—

"When I was—from 1878 to 1887—the Attorney General of —— I absolutely refused to make my office the medium through which to indict and punish men who toiled six days and then asserted their right to worship God under their own vine and fig tree, according to the dictates of conscience.

"The very moment the Legislatures of American States declare (and that declaration is carried into effect) that men shall (without reference to their creed) have one Sunday, and that the Sunday of modern Christianity, commonly known as the sabbath, shall be alike kept holy by every man under a penalty for its violation, you sound the death knell of American republicanism and open the way for a religious inquisition as infamous, devilish, and ungodly as was that of Italy. Our forefathers with prophetic vision saw the danger of commingling the affairs of Church and State, and, with a wisdom as consummate as it was politic, they laid the very foundation of this government upon the idea that religion should never have any part or identity with the civic machinery. . . .

"Ten or twelve years ago, when I was the owner and editor of the daily —— here (being Attorney General at the same time), the preachers howled from their pulpits on the duty of the Attorney General to rigidly enforce the Sunday law. I replied to their criticisms, and I think I got the best of the argument—at all events I did not yield my principles, and defied them to carry out the threat to impeach me. They did not do so; and from that day to this, the men of —— worship God in their own way, and each creed selects its own day. The churches are protected in their right to worship as they may deem proper; but the man who does not feel like going to church on Sunday, but prefers to do as seems best for himself, is allowed to go his way rejoicing, with none to make him afraid. All Sunday laws ought to be wiped from the statute books, and every man left free to pursue the line of worship dictated by his conscience.

"Oh, if it were possible to rebuild the public sentiment of this country, and model it after the plan of [Richard M.] Johnson, Jefferson, Washington, and the men of their day and generation!"

constitutional a law which, as such, fell to him for enforcement. Stern Old Hickory refused to enforce it. He argued, and rightly, that he had taken no oath to support Supreme Court decisions, or other people's interpretation of the Constitution, but *the Constitution itself*, and declared the American fundamental principle that—

"Each public officer who takes an oath to support the Constitution, swears that he will support it as he understands it, and not as it is understood by others."

The nation stood by General Jackson in this, and completely killed that decision, and the law which it pronounced constitutional. Again, the soundness of this principle, and the unsoundness of this position taken by the inferior courts, is seen from the following:—

"To whom does it belong to interpret the Constitution?—Any question arising in a legal proceeding as to the meaning and application of this fundamental law will evidently be settled by the courts of law. Every court is equally bound to pronounce, *and competent to pronounce*, on such questions, *a State court* no less than a Federal court; but as all the more important questions are carried by appeal to the Supreme Federal Court, it is practically that court whose opinion finally determines them."[6]

"The so-called 'power of annulling an unconstitutional statute' is a duty rather than a power, and a duty *incumbent on the humblest State court* when a case raising the point comes before it, no less than on the Supreme Federal Court at Washington. When, therefore, people talk, as they sometimes do, even in the United States, of the Supreme Court as 'the guardian of the Constitution,' they mean nothing more than that it is the final court of appeal, before which suits involving constitutional questions may be brought up by the parties for decision. In so far the phrase is legitimate. But the functions of the Supreme Court are the same in kind as those of all other courts, State as well as Federal. Its duty and theirs is simply to declare and apply the law; and when any court, *be it a State court of first instance*, or the Federal court of last instance, finds a law of lower authority [the Legislature] clashing with a law of higher authority [the Constitution],

[6] Final only as the particular case on trial, of course. See pp. 145, 146, 147.

Andrew Jackson

it must reject the former as being really no law, and enforce the latter.''
—*Bryce, American Commonwealth, Vol. I, pp. 374, 252.*

FAILURE OF THE SWORN AGENTS OF THE PEOPLE.

This is fundamental, American, constitutional ground. And it is not only a fearful thing, but a treacherous thing as well, for any officer, chosen by the people and therefore responsible to the people, to give his oath to the people to stand faithful to their instructions as given to him in the Constitution, and then ignore and abandon these instructions altogether, putting between himself and the people another set of the servants of the people— who, equally with himself, are responsible to the people— and adopt their interpretations instead of the plain words of the Constitution which he has given his oath to support. An illustration will be in place. The people of Tennessee in the Bill of Rights of their Constitution have said this:—

"SEC. 3. That all men have a natural and indefeasible right to worship Almighty God according to the dictates of their own conscience; that no man can, of right, be compelled to attend, erect, or support any place of worship, or to maintain any ministry against his consent; that *no human authority can, in any case whatever, control or interfere with the rights of conscience;* and that *no preference shall ever be given, by law, to any* religious establishment or *mode of worship.*"

Now to say that these instructions need to be *interpreted* is an insult to anybody who can read the English language. They need only to be accepted as they stand. Yet, in spite of these plain words, a Sunday law is on the statute books of that State, and the State Supreme Court has declared it to be constitutional, because "Christianity is part of the common law" of that State. Thus that Supreme Court by its *interpretation* has given *preference by* common *law* to the *Christian* mode of worship, in spite of the plain words that no such thing *shall ever* be done. The other courts and officers of the State who have sworn to support that *Constitution*, have, instead, adopted

and supported this *interpretation:* and for years Christian men
have been indicted by the dozen, and prosecuted, fined, and imprisoned solely for disregarding Sunday, which is a part of the
"Christianity" which by this interpretation is made part of the
common law of that State.

This is but a fair sample of the judicial situation in all the
States of the Union, with the exception of two or three at most.
And all on account of Supreme Court decisions strictly analogous to this, supported by officials who forget their oath to
support the Constitution, and, instead, blindly support decisions
which are absolutely subversive of the Constitution and of all
the rights of the people.

THE REMEDY.

When the servants of the people who have been selected
and sworn for the sole purpose of maintaining the constitutional provisions which the people have established for the
security of their rights, fail so completely to do what they have
been appointed to do, and really subvert the Constitution instead
of support it, then the right to do this themselves, in their own
proper persons, rests by a double tenure *with the people.*

First, it is always the right and just prerogative of the
people to set the actions of these servants alongside of the
Constitution and judge whether they have indeed supported it
or failed to support it. Remember the words of Dickinson,
quoted on page 144, that "the people must restore things to
that order from which their functionaries have departed;" and
of Wilson, on page 80, that "the supreme power resides in the
people, *and they never part with it;*" the words of Bryce,
quoted on pages 150, 151, that "the people censure any
interpretation which palpably departs from the old lines;"
and the words of Lincoln, quoted on page 141, that "the people of these United States are the rightful masters of both
Congresses and courts; not to overthrow the Constitution, but
to overthrow the men who pervert the Constitution."

This right rests always with the people, for them freely to exercise. But when the agents which they have appointed for the very purpose of detecting unconstitutional laws, and protecting the people from their injustice—when these agents themselves not only fail to do this, but actually aid in fastening unconstitutional statutes upon the people, then the right of the people to test the statutes by the Constitution, being "incapable of annihilation,"[7] returns to the people, and rests with them, by additional tenure, and it then *of right* devolves upon the people, themselves and for themselves, and each one for himself, to decide the case, declare such law unconstitutional and void, and treat it so in all their actions.

This is not to say, nor even to imply, that every man is at liberty to disregard, or disrespect, whatever action of the government he may not personally agree with. It *is* to say that it is absolutely incumbent on every citizen to be so well read in the Constitution and the Declaration that he shall know for himself the limitations upon the government, and act accordingly. Every citizen must hold *himself*, as well as *the government*, strictly to the Constitution. The Constitution is a limitation, not, indeed, upon the *power* of the people, except in the prescribed way, but upon the passions and caprices of the people. This is sound American principle. It is the fundamental principle of a government of the people. Let it not be forgotten that one of the chief fathers of this nation, Alexander Hamilton, in persuading the ratification of the Constitution, declared that—

"Justice is the end of government. It is the end of civil society. . . . In a society, under the forms of which the stronger faction can readily unite and oppress the weaker, anarchy may as truly be said to reign as in a state of nature, where the weaker individual is not secured against the violence of the stronger."—*Federalist LI.*

And another of these, James Madison, nobly said:—

---

[7] Declaration of Independence, par. 8.

17

"An *elective despotism* was not the government we fought for; but one which should not only be founded on free principles, but in which the powers of government should be so divided and balanced among several bodies of magistracy as that no one could transcend their legal limits."—*Federalist XLVIII.*

And when the agents of the people, appointed under the forms of constitutional government, take the very unconstitutional course that brings about just the anarchy and elective despotism here pointed out, then it is the right of the people, by this double tenure, to see to it that such unconstitutional laws and proceedings are disregarded, and the Constitution made to prevail. This is further sustained by authority. Let all read carefully the following passages, which are equally applicable to Legislatures and State constitutions as to Congress and the national Constitution:—

"The supreme law-making power is the people, that is, the qualified voters, acting in a prescribed way. The people have by their supreme law, the Constitution, given to Congress a delegated and limited power of legislation. Every statute passed under that power conformably to the Constitution, has all the authority of the Constitution behind it. Any statute passed which goes beyond that power is invalid and incapable of enforcement. It is in fact not a statute at all, because Congress in passing it was not really a law-making body, but a mere group of private persons.

"Says Chief Justice Marshall: ' The powers of the Legislature are defined and limited; and that those limits may not be mistaken or forgotten, the Constitution is written. To what purpose are powers limited, and to what purpose is that limitation committed to writing, if those limits may at any time be passed, by those intended to be restrained? The Constitution is either a superior, paramount law, unchangeable by ordinary means, or it is on a level with ordinary legislative acts, and, like any other acts, is alterable when the Legislature shall please to alter it. If the former part of the alternative be true, then a legislative act contrary to the Constitution *is not law*. If the latter part be true, then written constitutions are absurd attempts on the part of the people to limit a power in its own nature illimitable.' "

"A statute pasesd by Congress beyond the scope of its powers is of no more effect than a by-law made *ultra vires* by an English municipality."

"If the subordinate body attempts to transcend the power committed to it, and makes rules for other purposes or under other conditions than those specified by the superior authority, these rules are not law, but are null and void. Their validity depends on their being within the scope of the law-making power conferred by the superior authority, and as they have passed outside that scope they are invalid. . . . *They ought not to be obeyed or in any way regarded by the citizens*, because they are not law."

" Not merely Congress alone, but also Congress and the President conjoined [and the Supreme Court also—A. T. J.], are subject to the Constitution, and cannot move a step outside the circle which the Constitution has drawn around them. If they do, they transgress the law and exceed their powers. Such acts as they may do in excess of their powers are void, and may be, *indeed ought to be*, treated as void by the meanest citizen."—*Bryce, American Commonwealth, Vol. I, pp. 245, 246, 243, 36.*

It is impossible to demonstrate more clearly or to present more forcibly the truth that *the constitutional right* of the people is *absolute*, to disregard every Sunday law or other religious or ecclesiastical thing that is made a part of the common or any other law. And by this absolute constitutional right every person can, with courage, consistency, and righteousness, carry on uncompromising opposition to the religious despotism that is fastening itself upon the country.

STAND WITH ANYBODY THAT STANDS RIGHT.

There is another "argument" used by the movers for this religious despotism, to combat which requires no assurance of any particular right, but which does require more courage than a great many people are willing to show. That is the "argument" of sneers and jeers and denunciation—the ready application of the epithets "infidel," "atheist," "enemy of Christianity," "enemy of the government," "despiser of the flag," "traitor," "anarchist," and, above all, and to the mind

of those who use it worst of all, "*Seventh-day Adventist.*"[8]
Every person who would oppose the encroachments of this
religious despotism, on the only ground upon which it can be
successfully opposed, may expect to have these epithets hurled
at him and rained upon him.   True and righteous though
this opposition be by every possible count, yet this is what
those certainly meet from the church-combination, who do
make this opposition.   If anyone doubts this, only let him sincerely engage in it for a little while.

Yet all that is required to meet and defeat all this "argument" is only the courage of conviction, the courage of principle.   Jefferson, Madison, and those with them who in that
day engaged in this same cause, had to meet it.   When the
"Act Establishing Religious Freedom" was published in
Italian and French, and was distributed through Europe, as
related on page 104, Jefferson wrote home to Madison that it
had thus "been the best evidence of the falsehood of those
reports *which stated us to be in anarchy.*"— *Works, Vol. II,
pp. 55, 56.* ˙ And the stigma that is sought still to be put upon
Jefferson's memory as "an enemy of Christianity," is, more
than anything else, because of his opposition to that religious
despotism in that day.

Abraham Lincoln, in his opposition to a national despotism
sustained by a Supreme Court decision, was also, as we have
seen (p. 162), charged with being among "the enemies of the
Constitution," "the enemies of the supremacy of the laws,"
with aiming "a deadly blow at our whole republican form of

---

[8] An illustration, which is only a sample of this, appeared in the *Christian Statesman*, the organ of the "Protestant" combination in this work, of January 19, 1895.   In
the "Question Box" there appeared a question from some person in Minnesota, asking whether Protestant denominations, in their efforts to secure enforcement of
religious observances by law, were not making a "concession to the Papacy, an
acknowledgment of the principles of Romanism," and referring to Christ's words,
"My kingdom is not of this world," etc.   The first word in answer to this, by the
editor, is this: "We suspect that our correspondent is a Seventh-day Adventist.   At
all events, he is a sympathizer with the views of that body on civil government."

government," "which, if successful, would place all our rights and liberties at the mercy of passion, anarchy, and violence." Of him it was said, "There is no objection to him, except the monstrous revolutionary doctrines with which he is identified."[9] But, above all, he was charged with being an "Abolitionist." This word in that day, by those who so used it, was expressive of the lowest point in the scale which it was possible to reach. It was very difficult, indeed almost impossible, for such persons to obtain a hearing on any public platform. Senator Douglas once referred to them in a way that shows the popular estimate of them, by speaking of Lincoln's "following the example and lead of all the little Abolition orators who go around and lecture in the basements of schools and churches."—*First Speech in Ottawa Debate, Id., p. 173.*

And these ready charges, especially the reproach of "Abolitionist," did in many cases accomplish the purpose for which they were used in that day—they did smother the opposition of men who in their consciences knew that that despotism ought to be opposed, precisely as the like epithets—and especially that of "Seventh-day Adventist"—smother the opposition of many people who to-day in their consciences know that this despotism should be openly opposed. Abraham Lincoln's advice to all such persons in that day is equally applicable to-day and for all time. Here it is:—

"Some men, mostly Whigs, who condemn the repeal of the Missouri Compromise, nevertheless hesitate to go for its restoration lest they be thrown in company with the Abolitionist. Will they allow me, as an old Whig, to tell them, good-humoredly, that I think this is very silly? STAND WITH ANYBODY THAT STANDS RIGHT. Stand with him while he is right, and part with him when he goes wrong. . . . To desert such ground *because of any company* is to be less than a Whig, less than a man, less than an American."—*Peoria Speech, October 16, 1854, Id., pp. 28, 29.*

---

[9] Senator Douglas's speech at Springfield, Ill., July 17, 1858, "Political Speeches and Debates," p. 142.

So it may be fittingly said to-day, and on this mighty question.

There is no doubt that the Seventh-day Adventists do stand in uncompromising opposition to this approaching religious despotism, in every phase of it. They oppose it upon the principles set down in this book—upon the Jeffersonian, Madisonian, Washingtonian, and *Lincolnian* principles; upon genuine American, Protestant, and Christian principles. And in so doing they are absolutely in the right. And if it be true, as no doubt it is, that they have upon these principles made their opposition so effective as to deserve to be singled out by the miners and sappers and buglers of this religious despotism as the chiefest of all their opponents, then the more honor to them for it—they are absolutely in the right. And it is true here, too, that many men who condemn this encroachment of the religious power upon the civil, nevertheless hesitate openly to oppose it lest they be thrown in company with the Seventh-day Adventists. But let it be now also said to all: "*Stand with anybody that stands right*. Stand with him while he is right, and part with him when he goes wrong."

So to stand to-day upon this great issue is to defend the natural rights of mankind. It is to conserve the constitutional rights of the American people. It is to maintain pure Protestantism. It is to manifest true Christianity in the world. To desert such ground because of any company is to desert the company *and abandon the principles* of Lincoln, Washington, Madison, Jefferson, Martin Luther, and the Lord Jesus Christ. To desert such ground because of any company is to be less than a man, less than an American, less than a Protestant, less than a Christian.

CHAPTER XII.

RELIGIOUS RIGHT IN THE STATES.

It has been shown in chapter 5 how that, upon the victory of religious right in Virginia in 1787, and the nationalizing of those principles by the example and provisions of the national Constitution made in 1787-1789, "In every other American State oppressive statutes concerning religion fell into disuse." And that the statute of Virginia then established had since been incorporated—always in its principles and often in its very words—in every State constitution in the Union from that day to this.

This was not accomplished in a day, however, in the others of the original thirteen States. As also formerly stated, all the other States except Rhode Island had established religion in some form. This was so when the national Constitution was adopted. And being so, each State retaining control of its own peculiar institutions, the national Constitution was not made to prohibit State recognitions of religion, but only that "*Congress* shall make no law respecting an establishment of religion, or prohibiting the free exercise thereof." It was hoped indeed that the moral effect of the example of the national Constitution would lead to the extinction of the thing in all the States. But the difficulties attending the creation of a national power at all, were so great that it was essential to attend to this one paramount object, and not try to accomplish too much at once and directly, lest nothing at all be done. Abraham Lincoln's statement of the case as to slavery—the civil despotism—is so precisely the statement of the case as to established religion—religious despotism—that it could not be better defined; therefore we quote:—

"When our government was established we had the institution of slavery among us. We were in a certain sense compelled to tolerate its existence. It was a sort of necessity. We had gone through our struggle and secured our own independence. The framers of the Constitution found the institution of slavery amongst their other institutions at the time. They found that by an effort to eradicate it they might lose much of what they had already gained. They were obliged to bow to the necessity. . . . They did what they could, and yielded to necessity for the rest."—*Springfield, Ill., Speech, July 17 1858, Political Speeches and Debates, p. 160.*

Read "established religions" in place of "slavery" in this passage, and the case is perfectly stated as to that question also.

Thus the institution of slavery continued until, by a Supreme Court decision perverting the Constitution, an attempt was made to nationalize it, when it was abolished even in the States by the thirteenth amendment to the national Constitution, which runs thus:—

ARTICLE XIII.

"SECTION 1. Neither slavery nor involuntary servitude, except as a punishment for crime, whereof the party shall have been duly convicted, shall exist within the United States, or any place subject to their jurisdiction."

In order that this amendment might be effective in all its scope, it was essential that the basis of citizenship should be changed.

"If we were now to have a broader nationality as the result of our civil struggle, it was apparent to the mass of men, as well as to the publicist and statesman, that citizenship should be placed on unquestionable ground, on ground so plain that the humblest man who should inherit its protection would comprehend the extent and significance of his title."—*Blaine, Twenty Years of Congress, Vol. II, p. 311.*

Accordingly, the fourteenth amendment to the Constitution was adopted, the first section of which reads as follows:—

ARTICLE XIV.

"All persons born or naturalized in the United States, and subject to the jurisdiction thereof, are citizens of the United States, and of the State in which they reside. No State shall make or enforce any law which shall abridge the privileges or immunities of citizens of the United States; nor shall any State deprive any person of life, liberty, or property without due process of law, nor deny to any person within its jurisdiction the equal protection of the laws."

Before this amendment was adopted there was, *primarily*, no such thing as citizenship of the United States. Citizenship of the United States came, except to aliens, only as a *consequence* of citizenship of a State. The reason of this peculiar fact was that *the thirteen States* were all here as sovereign independencies *before* the United States Government was formed; and the people, being citizens of these States to begin with, when these very persons formed the national government they *became*, by that very process, citizens of the United States. And as there was no provision in the Constitution touching the subject with respect to any but aliens, the situation still remained the same—citizens of a State first, and, as a consequence of that, citizens of the United States. As stated by an authority in the time when the matter stood thus, it is as follows:—

"Citizenship, as we understand it, may be acquired in either of two ways,—by birth or by adoption, called, when applied to aliens, naturalization. After the Declaration of Independence, and before the adoption of the Constitution of the United States, the power of conferring citizenship by naturalization or otherwise, like all other sovereign powers, was in the several States. And as the power vested in Congress by that instrument applies to aliens only, and as all powers not delegated to Congress by the Constitution, nor prohibited to the States, are expressly reserved to the States respectively or to the people, the power of conferring citizenship on all persons not aliens, necessarily remains in the several States both as to persons born on their soil, and as to those born in other parts of the Union; and any person upon whom such rights are conferred becomes a citi-

zen of the State conferring them.   And every citizen of a State is,
ipso facto, a citizen of the United States."—*Law Reporter, June, 1857,
p. 14.*

As more fully stated by authority since it was changed, it is
as follows:—

" Before the adoption of this amendment, citizenship of the United
States was inferred from citizenship of some one of the States, for
there was nothing in the Constitution defining or even implying
national citizenship as distinct from its origination in, or derivation
from, a State.   It was declared in Article IV, section 2, of the Federal Constitution, that citizens of each State shall be entitled to all
the privileges and immunities of citizens of the several States; but
nothing was better known than that this provision was a dead letter
from its very origin.   A colored man who was a citizen of a northern
State was certain to be placed under the surveillance of the police if
he ventured south of the Potomac or the Ohio, destined probably to
be sold into slavery under State law, or permitted as a special favor
to return at once to his home.   A foreign-born citizen, with his certif-
icate of naturalization in his possession, had, prior to the war, no
guarantee or protection against any form of discrimination, or indignity, *or even persecution*, to which State law might subject him, as
has been painfully demonstrated at least twice in our history."

At that time any State could have as thorough-going an
establishment of religion as might be chosen, and persecute
without limit, and yet there was no refuge under the national
Constitution, because that document only said that "*Congress*
shall make no law respecting an establishment of religion or
prohibiting the free exercise thereof."   The Constitution did
not say that *no State* should do it; and as the powers not delegated to the United States, *nor prohibited by it to the States*,
are reserved to the States or to the people, it followed that
each State might do all this without restraint, at its own will.
The fourteenth amendment overturned this.   Further we
quote:—

" But this rank injustice and this hurtful inequality were removed
by the fourteenth amendment.   Its opening section settled all con-
flicts and contradictions on this question by a comprehensive decla-

ration which defined national citizenship, and gave to it *precedence of the citizenship of a State.* 'All persons born or naturalized in the United States and subject to the jurisdiction thereof are citizens of the United States, and of the States wherein they reside.' These pregnant words distinctly *reversed the origin and character of American citizenship.* Instead of a man being a citizen of the United States because he was a citizen of one of the States, he was now made a citizen of any State in which he might choose to reside because he was antecedently a citizen of the United States."—*Blaine, Twenty Years, Vol. II, pp. 312, 313.*

Every such person, then, being by the supreme law a citizen of the United States first of all, and this citizenship holding precedence of every other, it follows that all privileges, immunities, and rights secured to him by the national Constitution are likewise his first of all and take precedence of all others. This is as certainly true as it would be if there were no other citizenship known to the Constitution.

Now absolute freedom from any sort of an establishment of religion is an immunity, and exemption from every kind of law prohibiting the free exercise of religion is the privilege of every citizen of the United States; for it is written, "Congress shall make no law respecting an establishment of religion, or prohibiting the free exercise thereof." If there were no other citizenship known to the Constitution than citizenship of the United States, the only law-making power that could possibly affect the citizen would be Congress. The only government that could have anything to do with the citizen would be the United States Government, and Congress is forbidden to make any law respecting religion or that would interfere with the free exercise of religion. Therefore, absolute freedom from any such thing is a privilege and immunity of every citizen of the United States, by the Constitution.

And now the second sentence of section 1 of this fourteenth amendment declares that "*no State shall make or enforce any law* abridging the privileges or immunities of citizens of the United States." That is to say, that no State shall make any law, or enforce any law already made, which abridges, which restricts, which lessens, the privilege or immunity of any citizen of the United States to be absolutely free in things religious. It practically declares that "no State shall make any law respecting an establishment of religion, or prohibiting the free exercise thereof."

"Whatever one may claim as of right under the Constitution and laws of the United States by virtue of his citizenship, is a privilege of a citizen of the United States. Whatever the Constitution and laws of the United States entitle him to exemption from, he may claim an exemption in respect to. And such a right or privilege is abridged whenever the State law interferes with any legitimate operation of federal authority which concerns his interest, whether it be an authority actively exerted, or resting only in the express or implied command or assurance of the Federal Constitution or law."—*Cooley, Principles, p. 247; Quoted by Bryce, American Commonwealth, chapter 36, par. 22, note.*

Accordingly, this provision of the fourteenth amendment annihilates the force of every Sunday law, or other religious law, or law abridging the free exercise of religion, in every State in the Union. This is as plain a consequence as ever came or could come from any provision of law. It prohibits the persecution of any Seventh-day Adventist, Seventh-day Baptist, Jew, Protestant, Catholic, or anybody else, by any State law which interferes with the free exercise of his religion. This is the effect of the provision as it is in its plain reading. This is certain. And it is no less certain that the intent of those who made it was that this should be its effect. James G. Blaine was one of the leading spirits in the framing of this amendment, and, after remarking of the first provision of this section, that it "establishes American citizenship upon a permanent foundation, gives to the humblest man in the republic ample protection against any abridgment of his privileges and immunities by State law," and that "the first section of the constitutional amendment, which includes these invaluable provisions, *is in fact a new charter of liberty to the*

James G. Blaine

citizens of the United States," with the matter before quoted, he continues:—

"The consequences that flowed from this radical change in the basis of citizenship were numerous and weighty. Nor were these consequences left subject to construction or speculation. They were incorporated in the same section of the amendment. The abuses which were formerly heaped on the citizens of one State by the legislative and judicial authority of another State were rendered thenceforth impossible. The language of the fourteenth amendment is authoritative and mandatory: *'No State shall make or enforce any law abridging the privileges or immunities of citizens of the United States; nor shall any State deprive any person of life, liberty, or property without due process of law, nor deny to any person within its jurisdiction the equal protection of the laws.*

"Under the force of these weighty inhibitions, the citizen of foreign birth cannot be persecuted by discriminating statutes, nor can the citizen of dark complexion be deprived of a single privilege or immunity which belongs to the white man. *Nor can the Catholic, or the Protestant, or the Jew, be placed under ban or subjected to any deprivation of personal or religious right.*

"The provision is comprehensive and absolute, and sweeps away at once every form of oppression and every denial of justice. It abolishes *caste* and enlarges the scope of human freedom. It increases the power of the republic to do equal and exact justice to all its citizens, and curtails the power of the States to shelter the wrongdoer, or to authorize crime by a statute. To Congress is committed the authority to enforce every provision of the fourteenth amendment, and the humblest man who is denied the equal protection of the laws of the State can have his wrongs redressed before the supreme judiciary of the nation."—*Twenty Years of Congress, Vol. II, pp. 313, 314.*

Such is the statement, the pledge, and the security, of religious right in the States, according to the "weighty," "authoritative, and mandatory" provisions of the national Constitution.

It is true that each State constitution contains strong guaranties of the perfect freedom of religious right, yet the Legislatures have ignored them, and the State Supreme Courts have interpreted them away. It is true that the national

Constitution guarantees exemption from interference on the part of the government or any State, with the religious right of citizens of the United States; yet the supreme judiciary of the nation has interpreted into that Constitution "the establishment of the Christian religion" as the "meaning" thereof; Congress in its Sunday legislation has put in the national law the very religious idea that has been set up by the States; and the executive has approved it. Thus, so far, the national power, instead of maintaining the high dignity which the people had given it forever to protect the privileges and immunities of citizenship of the United States from invasion by the States, has abandoned its high station, and has gone down and actually joined the States in the invasion. Nevertheless,

THE RIGHT OF THE PEOPLE STILL ABIDES.

The Constitution as the people have made it, is still the voice and will of the people. It still guarantees privilege, immunity, and freedom, to citizens of the United States: only as the agencies appointed by the people to maintain these guaranties have failed to do it, the responsibility and the right now devolve upon the people themselves to see that it is done.

Slavery and established religions—twin despotisms—existed in the States at the time of the making of the nation. The makers of the nation, finding it impossible to do away with them without risking the loss of all, yielded to the necessity and left them standing as State institutions only. When by the Dred Scott decision and congressional legislation the attempt was made to nationalize one of these despotisms, the people arose in their majesty and reversed that decision and destroyed that despotism, and with it all other, even in the States. Now, however, the other despotism has reared its hateful head, and, by means of the "Christian nation" Supreme Court decision, and congressional legislation, *this* is sought to be nationalized. Will the people, yea, will not the people, rise once more in their majesty and reverse this decision and set the national power back again at the height and dignity where they placed it when they destroyed the other despotism?

This is the duty, this is the task, this is *the right* of the people of the United States. True, now as before, the wealth, the popularity, and the power of the country—the power of State and Church, and of Church and State united—are all against us. But God and the right are for us. And with the immortal Lincoln we must say:—

"*We* have to fight this battle upon principle, and upon principle alone. . . . So I hope those with whom I am surrounded have principle enough to nerve themselves for the task, and leave nothing undone that can be fairly done to bring about the right result."—*Springfield, Ill., July 17, 1858, Political Speeches and Debates, p. 145.*

Let us never rest until there is created such a public sentiment that every court will be ashamed to use the term "Christian nation." For "public sentiment is everything. With public sentiment, nothing can fail; without it, nothing can succeed. Consequently, he who moulds public sentiment, goes deeper than he who enacts statutes or pronounces decisions. He makes statutes and decisions possible or impossible to be executed."—*Id., p. 191.*

True, in the effort to create this public sentiment, we shall be unpopular; we shall be scoffed at; we shall be reviled; but in this we are right—absolutely and eternally right. Then let no one "be slandered from his duty by false accusations, nor frightened from it by menaces of dungeons. Let us have faith that right makes might; and in that faith let us to the end dare to do our duty as we understand it."—*Id., p. 527.*

Many times the people may refuse to listen, as at first, even in his own home town, they did to Abraham Lincoln against slavery. Once in 1855, in Springfield, Illinois, Lincoln was advertised to speak on the "Slavery Question." Mr. Herndon, his law partner, spread great posters through the town, employed a band to march the streets, and had the bells rung to have the people come. Not a soul came to hear—but

Herndon himself and the janitor of the building. Yet Lincoln made the following speech:—

"GENTLEMEN: This meeting is larger than I knew it would be, as I knew that Herndon and myself would come, but I did not know that anyone else would be here, and yet another has come—you, John Paine [the janitor].

"These are bad times, and seem out of joint. All seems dead, *dead*, DRAD; but the age is NOT yet dead. It liveth as sure as our Maker liveth. Under all this seeming want of life and motion, the world does move, nevertheless. Be hopeful. And now let us adjourn and appeal to the people."

So it is now said to every reader of this book: Let us appeal to the people. Yea, though they will not listen, still let us appeal to the people. It is the only right course. The people must do the work. Will the people awake, and arise, and assert, and maintain,

THE RIGHTS OF THE PEOPLE?

APPENDIX A.

THE DECLARATION OF INDEPENDENCE.

WHEN, in the course of human events, it becomes necessary for one people to dissolve the political bands which have connected them with another, and to assume, among the powers of the earth, the separate and equal station to which the laws of nature and of nature's God entitle them, a decent respect to the opinions of mankind requires that they should declare the causes which impel them to the separation.

We hold these truths to be self-evident, that all men are created equal; that they are endowed by their Creator with certain unalienable rights; that among these are life, liberty, and the pursuit of happiness. That to secure these rights, governments are instituted among men, deriving their just powers from the consent of the governed; that whenever any form of government becomes destructive of these ends, it is the right of the people to alter or to abolish it, and to institute a new government, laying its foundation on such principles, and organizing its powers in such form, as to them shall seem most likely to effect their safety and happiness. Prudence, indeed, will dictate that governments long established should not be changed for light and transient causes; and accordingly, all experience hath shown that mankind are more disposed to suffer, while evils are sufferable, than to right themselves by abolishing the forms to which they are accustomed. But when a long train of abuses and usurpations, pursuing invariably the same object, evinces a design to reduce them under absolute despotism, it is their right, it is their duty, to throw off such government, and to provide new guards for their future security. Such has been the patient sufferance of these Colonies, and such is now the necessity which constrains them to alter their former systems of government. The history of the present king of Great Britain is a history of repeated injuries and usurpations, all having, in direct object, the establishment of an absolute tyranny over these States. To prove this, let facts be submitted to a candid world:-

He has refused his assent to laws the most wholesome and necessary for the public good.

He has forbidden his governors to pass laws of immediate and pressing importance, unless suspended in their operation till his assent should be obtained; and, when so suspended, he has utterly neglected to attend to them.

He has refused to pass other laws for the accommodation of large districts of people, unless those people would relinquish the right of representation in the Legislature; a right inestimable to them, and formidable to tyrants only.

He has called together legislative bodies at places unusual, uncomfortable, and distant from the depository of their public records, for the sole purpose of fatiguing them into compliance with his measures.

He has dissolved representative houses repeatedly for opposing, with manly firmness, his invasions on the rights of the people.

He has refused, for a long time after such dissolutions, to cause others to be elected; whereby the legislative powers, incapable of annihilation, have returned to the people at large for their exercise, the State remaining, in the meantime, exposed to all the danger of invasion from without and convulsions within.

He has endeavored to prevent the population of these States, for that purpose obstructing the laws for the naturalization of foreigners, refusing to pass others to encourage their migration hither, and raising the conditions of new appropriations of lands.

He has obstructed the administration of justice, by refusing his assent to laws for establishing judiciary powers.

He has made judges dependent on his will alone for the tenure of their offices, and the amount and payment of their salaries.

He has erected a multitude of new offices, and sent hither swarms of officers to harass our people and eat out their substance

He has kept among us, in times of peace, standing armies, without the consent of our Legislature.

He has affected to render the military independent of, and superior to, the civil power.

He has combined, with others, to subject us to a jurisdiction foreign to our Constitution, and unacknowledged by our laws, giving his assent to their acts of pretended legislation:

For quartering large bodies of armed troops among us;

For protecting them, by a mock trial, from punishment for any murders which they should commit on the inhabitants of these States;

For cutting off our trade with all parts of the world;

For imposing taxes on us without our consent;

For depriving us, in many cases, of the benefits of trial by jury;

For transporting us beyond seas to be tried for pretended offenses;

For abolishing the free system of English laws in a neighboring province, establishing therein an arbitrary government, and enlarging its boundaries, so as to render it at once an example and fit instrument for introducing the same absolute rule into these Colonies;

For taking away our charters, abolishing our most valuable laws, and altering, fundamentally, the powers of our government;

For suspending our own Legislatures, and declaring themselves invested with power to legislate for us in all cases whatsoever.

He has abdicated government here, by declaring us out of his protection, and waging war against us.

He has plundered our seas, ravaged our coasts, burnt our towns, and destroyed the lives of our people.

He is, at this time, transporting large armies of foreign mercenaries to complete the works of death, desolation, and tyranny already begun, with circumstances of cruelty and perfidy scarcely paralleled in the most barbarous ages, and totally unworthy the head of a civilized nation.

He has constrained our fellow-citizens, taken captive on the high seas, to bear arms against their country, to become the executioners of their friends and brethren, or to fall themselves by their hands.

He has excited domestic insurrections among us, and has endeavored to bring on the inhabitants of our frontiers the merciless Indian savages, whose known rule of warfare is an undistinguished destruction of all ages, sexes, and conditions.

In every stage of these oppressions we have petitioned for redress in the most humble terms. Our repeated petitions have been answered only by repeated injury. A prince whose character is thus marked by every act which may define a tyrant is unfit to be the ruler of a free people.

Nor have we been wanting in attention to our British brethren. We have warned them, from time to time, of attempts made by their Legislature to extend an unwarrantable jurisdiction over us. We have reminded them of the circumstances of our emigration and settlement here. We have appealed to their native justice and magnanimity, and we have conjured them, by the ties of our common kindred, to disavow these usurpations, which would inevitably interrupt our connections and correspondence. They, too, have been deaf to the voice of justice and consanguinity. We must, therefore, acquiesce in the necessity which denounces our separation, and hold them, as we hold the rest of mankind, enemies in war, in peace friends.

We, therefore, the representatives of the United States of America, in General Congress assembled, appealing to the Supreme Judge of the world for the rectitude of our intentions, do, in the name and by the authority of the good people of these Colonies, solemnly publish and declare, That these United Colonies are, and, of right, ought to be, *free and independent States;* that they are absolved from all allegiance to the British crown, and that all political connection between them and the State of Great Britain is, and ought to be, totally dissolved; and that, as *free and independent States*, they have full power to levy war, conclude peace, contract alliances establish commerce, and to do all other acts and things which *independent States* may of right do. And, for the support of this Declaration, with a firm reliance on the protection of Divine Providence, we mutually pledge to each other our lives, our fortunes, and our sacred honor.

Massachusetts Bay.

JOHN HANCOCK,
SAMUEL ADAMS,
JOHN ADAMS,
ROBERT TREAT PAINE,
ELBRIDGE GERRY.

New Hampshire.

JOSIAH BARTLETT,
WILLIAM WHIPPLE,
MATTHEW THORNTON.

Rhode Island.

STEPHEN HOPKINS,
WILLIAM ELLERY.

New York.

WILLIAM FLOYD,
PHILIP LIVINGSTON,
FRANCIS LEWIS,
LEWIS MORRIS.

New Jersey.

RICHARD STOCKTON,
JOHN WITHERSPOON,
FRANCIS HOPKINSON,
JOHN HART,
ABRAHAM CLARK.

Pennsylvania.

ROBERT MORRIS,
BENJAMIN RUSH,
BENJAMIN FRANKLIN,
JOHN MORTON,
GEORGE CLYMER,
JAMES SMITH,
GEORGE TAYLOR,
JAMES WILSON,
GEORGE ROSS.

Connecticut.

ROGER SHERMAN,
SAMUEL HUNTINGTON,
WILLIAM WILLIAMS,
OLIVER WOLCOTT.

Delaware.

CÆSAR RODNEY,
GEORGE READ,
THOMAS MCKEAN.

Maryland.

SAMUEL CHASE,
WILLIAM PACA,
THOMAS STONE,
CHARLES CARROLL, of Carrollton.

Virginia.

GEORGE WYTHE,
RICHARD HENRY LEE,

THOMAS JEFFERSON,
BENJAMIN HARRISON,
THOMAS NELSON, JR.,
FRANCIS LIGHTFOOT LEE,
CARTER BRAXTON.

North Carolina.

WILLIAM HOOPER,
JOSEPH HEWES,
JOHN PENN.

South Carolina.

EDWARD RUTLEDGE,
THOMAS HEYWARD, JR.,
THOMAS LYNCH, JR.,
ARTHUR MIDDLETON.

Georgia.

BUTTON GWINNETT,
LYMAN HALL,
GEORGE WALTON.

APPENDIX B.

THE CONSTITUTION OF THE UNITED STATES.

We, the people of the United States, in order to form a more perfect union, establish justice, insure domestic tranquillity, provide for the common defense, promote the general welfare, and secure the blessings of liberty to ourselves and our posterity, do ordain and establish this Constitution for the United States of America.

ARTICLE I.

SECTION 1.   All legislative powers herein granted shall be vested in a Congress of the United States, which shall consist of a Senate and House of Representatives.

SEC. 2.   The House of Representatives shall be composed of members chosen every second year by the people of the several States, and the electors in each State shall have the qualifications requisite for electors of the most numerous branch of the State Legislature.

No person shall be a representative who shall not have attained to the age of twenty-five years, and been seven years a citizen of the United States, and who shall not, when elected, be an inhabitant of that State in which he shall be chosen.

Representatives and direct taxes shall be apportioned among the several States which may be included within this Union, according to their respective numbers, which shall be determined by adding to the whole number of free persons, including those bound to service for a term of years, and excluding Indians not taxed, three-fifths of all other persons.   The actual enumeration shall be made within three years after the first meeting of the Congress of the United States, and within every subsequent term of ten years, in such manner as they shall by law direct.   The number of representatives shall not exceed one for every thirty thousand, but each State shall have at least one representative; and until such enumeration shall be made, the State of New Hampshire shall be entitled to choose three; Massachusetts, eight; Rhode Island and Providence Plantations, one; Connecticut, five; New York, six; New Jersey, four; Pennsylvania, eight; Delaware, one; Maryland, six; Virginia, ten; North Carolina, five; South Carolina, five; and Georgia, three.

When vacancies happen in the representation from any State, the executive authority thereof shall issue writs of election to fill such vacancies.

The House of Representatives shall choose their Speaker and other officers, and shall have the sole power of impeachment.

SEC. 3.   The Senate of the United States shall be composed of two senators from each State, chosen by the Legislature thereof, for six years; and each senator shall have one vote.

Immediately after they shall be assembled in consequence of the first election, they shall be divided as equally as may be into three classes. The seats of the senators of the first class shall be vacated at the expiration of the second year; of the second class, at the expiration of the fourth year; and of the third class, at the expiration of the sixth year, so that one-third may be chosen every second year; and if vacancies happen by resignation, or otherwise, during the recess of the Legislature of any State, the executive thereof may make temporary appointments until the next meeting of the Legislature, which shall then fill such vacancies.

No person shall be a senator who shall not have attained to the age of thirty years, and been nine years a citizen of the United States, and who shall not, when elected, be an inhabitant of that State for which he shall be chosen.

The Vice President of the United States shall be president of the Senate, but shall have no vote, unless they be equally divided.

The Senate shall choose their other officers, and also a president *pro tempore*, in the absence of the Vice President, or when he shall exercise the office of President of the United States.

The Senate shall have the sole power to try all impeachments. When sitting for that purpose, they shall be on oath or affirmation. When the President of the United States is tried, the Chief Justice shall preside. And no person shall be convicted without the concurrence of two-thirds of the members present.

Judgment in cases of impeachment shall not extend further than to removal from office, and disqualification to hold and enjoy any office of honor, trust, or profit under the United States; but the party convicted shall nevertheless be liable and subject to indictment, trial, judgment, and punishment, according to law.

SEC. 4. The times, places, and manner of holding elections for senators and representatives shall be prescribed in each State by the Legislature thereof; but the Congress may at any time, by law, make or alter such regulations, except as to the places of choosing senators.

The Congress shall assemble at least once in every year, and such meeting shall be on the first Monday in December, unless they shall, by law, appoint a different day.

SEC. 5. Each house shall be the judge of the elections, returns, and qualifications of its own members, and a majority of each shall constitute a quorum to do business; but a smaller number may adjourn from day to day, and be authorized to compel the attendance of absent members, in such manner and under such penalties as each house may provide.

Each house may determine the rules of its proceedings, punish its members for disorderly behavior, and, with the concurrence of two-thirds, expel a member.

Each house shall keep a journal of its proceedings, and from time to time publish the same, excepting such parts as may in their judgment require secrecy; and the yeas and nays of the members of either house on any question shall, at the desire of one-fifth of those present, be entered on the journal.

Neither house, during the session of Congress, shall, without the consent of the other, adjourn for more than three days, nor to any other place than that in which the two houses shall be sitting.

SEC. 6. The senators and representatives shall receive a compensation for their services, to be ascertained by law, and paid out of the treasury of the United States. They shall in all cases, except treason, felony, and breach of the peace, be privileged from arrest during their attendance at the session of their respective houses, and in going to and returning from the same; and for any speech or debate in either house they shall not be questioned in any other place.

No senator or representative shall, during the time for which he was elected, be appointed to any civil office under the authority of the United States, which shall have been created, or the emoluments whereof shall have been increased, during such time; and no person holding any office under the United States shall be a member of either house during his continuance in office.

SEC. 7. All bills for raising revenue shall originate in the House of Representatives; but the Senate may propose or concur with amendments, as on other bills.

Every bill which shall have passed the House of Representatives and the Senate, shall, before it become a law, be presented to the President of the United States; if he approve, he shall sign it; but if not, he shall return it, with his objections, to that house in which it shall have originated, who shall enter the objections at large on their journal, and proceed to reconsider it. If after such reconsideration two-thirds of that house shall agree to pass the bill, it shall be sent, together with the objections, to the other house, by which it shall likewise be reconsidered; and if approved by two-thirds of that house, it shall become a law. But in all such cases, the votes of both houses shall be determined by yeas and nays, and the names of the persons voting for and against the bill shall be entered on the journal of each house respectively. If any bill shall not be returned by the President within ten days (Sunday excepted) after it shall have been presented to him, the same shall be a law in like manner as if he had signed it, unless the Congress by their adjournment prevent its return; in which case it shall not be a law.

Every order, resolution, or vote to which the concurrence of the Senate and the House of Representatives may be necessary (except on a question of adjournment) shall be presented to the President of the United States; and before the same shall take effect, shall be approved by him, or, being disapproved by him, shall be repassed by two-thirds of the Senate and House of Representatives, according to the rules and limitations prescribed in the case of a bill.

SEC. 8. The Congress shall have power—

To lay and collect taxes, duties, imposts, and excises, to pay the debts and provide for the common defense and general welfare of the United States; but all duties, imposts, and excises shall be uniform throughout the United States;

To borrow money on the credit of the United States;

To regulate commerce with foreign nations, and among the several States, and with the Indian tribes;

To establish a uniform rule of naturalization, and uniform laws on the subject of bankruptcies throughout the United States;

To coin money, regulate the value thereof, and of foreign coin, and fix the standard of weights and measures;

To provide for the punishment of counterfeiting the securities and current coin of the United States;

To establish post offices and post roads;

To promote the progress of science and useful arts, by securing, for limited times, to authors and inventors, the exclusive right to their respective writings and discoveries;

To constitute tribunals inferior to the Supreme Court;

To define and punish piracies and felonies committed on the high seas, and offenses against the law of nations;

To declare war, grant letters of marque and reprisal, and make rules concerning captures on land and water;

To raise and support armies, but no appropriation of money to that use shall be for a longer term than two years;

To provide and maintain a navy;

To make rules for the government and regulation of the land and naval forces;

To provide for calling forth the militia to execute the laws of the Union, suppress insurrections, and repel invasions;

To provide for organizing, arming, and disciplining the militia, and for governing such part of them as may be employed in the service of the United States, reserving to the States respectively the appointment of the officers, and the authority of training the militia according to the discipline prescribed by Congress;

To exercise exclusive legislation in all cases whatsoever over such district (not exceeding ten miles square) as may, by cession of particular States, and the acceptance of Congress, become the seat of the Government of the United States, and to exercise like authority over all places purchased by the consent of the Legislature of the State in which the same shall be, for the erection of forts, magazines, arsenals, dockyards, and other needful buildings; and—

To make all laws which shall be necessary and proper for carrying into execution the foregoing powers, and all other power vested by this Constitution in the Government of the United States, or in any department or officer thereof.

SEC. 9.   The migration or importation of such persons as any of the States now existing shall think proper to admit, shall not be prohibited by the Congress prior to the year one thousand eight hundred and eight, but a tax or duty may be imposed on such importation, not exceeding ten dollars for each person.

The privilege of the writ of *habeas corpus* shall not be suspended, unless when in cases of rebellion or invasion the public safety may require it.

No bill of attainder or *ex post facto* law shall be passed.

No capitation or other direct tax shall be laid, unless in proportion to the census or enumeration hereinbefore directed to be taken.

No tax or duty shall be laid on articles exported from any State.

No preference shall be given by any regulation of commerce or revenue to the ports of one State over those of another; nor shall vessels bound to or from one State, be obliged to enter, clear, or pay duties in another.

No money shall be drawn from the treasury, but in consequence of appropriations made by law; and a regular statement and account of the receipts and expenditures of all public money shall be published from time to time.

No title of nobility shall be granted by the United States; and no person holding any office of profit or trust under them, shall, without the consent of the Congress, accept of any present, emolument, office, or title, of any kind whatever, from any king, prince, or foreign State.

SEC. 10. No State shall enter into any treaty, alliance, or confederation; grant letters of marque and reprisal; coin money; emit bills of credit; make anything but gold and silver coin a tender in payment of debts; pass any bill of attainder, *ex post facto* law, or law impairing the obligation of contracts, or grant any title of nobility.

No State shall, without the consent of the Congress, lay any imposts or duties on imports or exports, except what may be absolutely necessary for executing its inspection laws; and the net produce of all duties and imposts laid by any State on imports or exports, shall be for the use of the treasury of the United States; and all such laws shall be subject to the revision and control of the Congress.

No State shall, without the consent of Congress, lay any duty on tonnage, keep troops or ships of war in time of peace, enter into any agreement or compact with another State, or with a foreign power, or engage in war, unless actually invaded, or in such imminent danger as will not admit of delay.

ARTICLE II.

SECTION 1. The executive power shall be vested in a President of the United States of America. He shall hold his office during the term of four years, and, together with the Vice President chosen for the same term, be elected as follows:—

Each State shall appoint, in such manner as the Legislature thereof may direct, a number of electors, equal to the whole number of senators and representatives to which the State may be entitled in the Congress; but no senator or representative, or person holding an office of trust or profit under the United States, shall be appointed an elector.

The Congress may determine the time of choosing the electors, and the day on which they shall give their votes; which day shall be the same throughout the United States.

No person, except a natural-born citizen, or a citizen of the United States at the time of the adoption of this Constitution, shall be eligible to the office of President; neither shall any person be eligible to that office who shall not have attained to the age of thirty-five years, and been fourteen years a resident within the United States.

In case of the removal of the President from office, or of his death, resignation, or inability to discharge the powers and duties of the said office, the same shall devolve on the Vice President, and the Congress may by law provide for the case of removal, death, resignation, or inability, both of the President and Vice President, declaring what officer shall then act as President, and such officer shall act accordingly, until the disability be removed, or a President shall be elected.

The President shall, at stated times, receive for his services a compensation, which shall neither be increased nor diminished during the period for which he shall have been elected, and he shall not receive within that period any other emolument from the United States, or any of them.

Before he enters on the execution of his office, he shall take the following oath or affirmation:—

"I do solemnly swear (or affirm) that I will faithfully execute the office of President of the United States, and will, to the best of my ability, preserve, protect, and defend the Constitution of the United States."

SEC. 2. The President shall be Commander in Chief of the army and navy of the United States, and of the militia of the several States, when called into the actual service of the United States; he may require the opinion, in writing, of the principal officer in each of the executive departments, upon any subject relating to the duties of their respective offices, and he shall have power to grant reprieves and pardons for offenses against the United States, except in cases of impeachment.

He shall have power, by and with the advice and consent of the Senate, to make treaties, provided two-thirds of the senators present concur; and he shall nominate, and by and with the advice and consent of the Senate, shall appoint ambassadors and other public ministers and consuls, judges of the Supreme Court, and all other officers of the United States whose appointments are not herein otherwise provided for, and which shall be established by law; but the Congress may by law vest the appointment of such inferior officers as they think proper in the President alone, in the courts of law, or in the heads of departments.

The President shall have power to fill up all vacancies that may happen during the recess of the Senate, by granting commissions, which shall expire at the end of their next session.

SEC. 3. He shall from time to time give to the Congress information of the state of the Union, and recommend to their consideration such measures as he shall judge necessary and expedient; he may, on extraordinary occasions, convene both houses, or either of them, and in case of disagreement between them, with respect to the time of adjournment, he may adjourn them to such time as he shall think proper; he shall receive ambassadors and other public ministers; he shall take care that the laws be faithfully executed, and shall commission all the officers of the United States.

SEC. 4. The President, Vice President, and all civil officers of the United States, shall be removed from office on impeachment for, and conviction of, treason, bribery, or other high crimes and misdemeanors.

ARTICLE III.

SECTION I. The judicial power of the United States shall be vested in one Supreme Court, and in such inferior courts as the Congress may from time to time ordain and establish. The judges, both of the supreme and inferior courts, shall hold their offices during good behavior, and shall, at stated times, receive for their services a compensation, which shall not be diminished during their continuance in office.

SEC. 2. The judicial power shall extend to all cases in law and equity arising under this Constitution, the laws of the United States, and treaties made, or which shall be made, under their authority; to all cases affecting ambassadors, other public ministers, and consuls; to all cases of admiralty and maritime jurisdiction; to controversies to which the United States shall be a party; to controversies between two or more States; between a State and citizens of another State;

between citizens of different States; between citizens of the same State claiming lands under grants of different States, and between a State, or the citizens thereof, and foreign States, citizens, or subjects.

In all cases affecting ambassadors, other public ministers, and consuls, and those in which a State shall be party, the Supreme Court shall have original jurisdiction. In all the other cases before mentioned, the Supreme Court shall have appellate jurisdiction, both as to law and fact, with such exceptions and under such regulations as the Congress shall make.

The trial of all crimes, except in cases of impeachment, shall be by jury; and such trial shall be held in the State where the said crime shall have been committed; but when not committed within any State, the trial shall be at such place or places as the Congress may by law have directed.

SEC. 3. Treason against the United States shall consist only in levying war against them, or in adhering to their enemies, giving them aid and comfort.

No person shall be convicted of treason unless on the testimony of two witnesses to the same overt act, or on confession in open court.

The Congress shall have power to declare the punishment of treason, but no attainder of treason shall work corruption of blood, or forfeiture except during the life of the person attainted.

ARTICLE IV.

SECTION I. Full faith and credit shall be given in each State to the public acts, records, and judicial proceedings of every other State. And the Congress may by general laws prescribe the manner in which such acts, records, and proceedings shall be proved, and the effect thereof.

SEC. 2. The citizens of each State shall be entitled to all privileges and immunities of citizens in the several States.

A person charged in any State with treason, felony, or other crime, who shall flee from justice, and be found in another State, shall on demand of the executive authority of the State from which he fled, be delivered up, to be removed to the State having jurisdiction of the crime.

No person held to service or labor in one State, under the laws thereof, escaping into another, shall, in consequence of any law or regulation therein, be discharged from such service or labor, but shall be delivered up on claim of the party to whom such service or labor may be due.

SEC. 3. New States may be admitted by the Congress into this Union; but no new State shall be formed or erected within the jurisdiction of any other State, nor any State be formed by the junction of two or more States, or parts of States, without the consent of the Legislatures of the States concerned, as well as of the Congress.

The Congress shall have power to dispose of and make all needful rules and regulations respecting the territory or other property belonging to the United States; and nothing in this Constitution shall be so construed as to prejudice any claims of the United States, or of any particular State.

SEC. 4. The United States shall guarantee to every State in this Union a republican form of government, and shall protect each of them against invasion, and, on application of the Legislature or of the executive (when the Legislature cannot be convened), against domestic violence.

ARTICLE V.

The Congress, whenever two-thirds of both houses shall deem it necessary, shall propose amendments to this Constitution, or on the application of the Legislatures of two-thirds of the several States, shall call a convention for proposing amendments, which, in either case, shall be valid, to all intents and purposes, as part of this Constitution, when ratified by the Legislatures of three-fourths of the several States, or by conventions in three-fourths thereof, as the one or the other mode of ratification may be proposed by the Congress; provided, that no amendment which may be made prior to the year one thousand eight hundred and eight shall in any manner affect the first and fourth clauses in the ninth section of the first Article, and that no State, without its consent, shall be deprived of its equal suffrage in the Senate.

ARTICLE VI.

All debts contracted and engagements entered into before the adoption of the Constitution, shall be as valid against the United States under this Constitution as under the Confederation.

This Constitution, and the laws of the United States which shall be made in pursuance thereof, and all treaties made, or which shall be made, under the authority of the United States, shall be the supreme law of the land; and the judges in every State shall be bound thereby, anything in the Constitution or laws of any State to the contrary notwithstanding.

19

The senators and representatives before mentioned, and the members of the several State Legislatures, and all executive and judicial officers, both of the United States and of the several States, shall be bound by oath or affirmation to support this Constitution; but no religious test shall ever be required as a qualification to any office or public trust under the United States.

Article VII.

The ratification of the conventions of nine States shall be sufficient for the establishment of this Constitution between the States so ratifying the same.

____

AMENDMENTS TO THE CONSTITUTION.

Article I.

Congress shall make no law respecting an establishment of religion, or prohibiting the free exercise thereof; or abridging the freedom of speech, or of the press; or the right of the people peaceably to assemble, and to petition the government for a redress of grievances.

Article II.

A well-regulated militia being necessary to the security of a free State, the right of the people to keep and bear arms shall not be infringed.

Article III.

No soldier shall, in time of peace, be quartered in any house without the consent of the owner, nor in time of war, but in a manner to be prescribed by law.

Article IV.

The right of the people to be secure in their persons, houses, papers, and effects, against unreasonable searches and seizures, shall not be violated; and no warrants shall issue but upon probable cause, supported by oath or affirmation, and particularly describing the place to be searched, and the persons or things to be seized.

Article V.

No person shall be held to answer for a capital or otherwise infamous crime, unless on a presentment or indictment of a Grand Jury, except in cases arising in the land or naval forces, or in the militia, when in actual service, in time of war and public danger; nor shall any person be subject for the same offense to be twice put in jeopardy of life or limb, nor shall be compelled in any criminal case to be a witness against himself; nor to be deprived of life, liberty, or property, without due process of law; nor shall private property be taken for public use without just compensation.

ARTICLE VI.

In all criminal prosecutions, the accused shall enjoy the right to a speedy and public trial, by an impartial jury of the State and district wherein the crime shall have been committed, which district shall have been previously ascertained by law, and to be informed of the nature and cause of the accusation; to be confronted with the witnesses against him; to have compulsory process for obtaining witnesses in his favor, and to have the assistance of counsel for his defense.

ARTICLE VII.

In suits at common law, where the value in controversy shall exceed twenty dollars, the right of trial by jury shall be preserved, and no fact tried by a jury shall be otherwise reëxamined in any court of the United States than according to the rules of the common law.

ARTICLE VIII.

Excessive bail shall not be required, nor excessive fines be imposed, nor cruel and unusual punishments inflicted.

ARTICLE IX.

The enumeration in the Constitution of certain rights shall not be construed to deny or disparage others retained by the people.

ARTICLE X.

The powers not delegated to the United States by the Constitution, nor prohibited by it to the States, are reserved to the States respectively, or to the people.

ARTICLE XI.

The judicial power of the United States shall not be construed to extend to any suit in law or equity, commenced or prosecuted against one of the United States by citizens of another State, or by citizens or subjects of any foreign State.

ARTICLE XII.

The electors shall meet in their respective States, and vote by ballot for President and Vice President, one of whom, at least, shall not be an inhabitant of the same State with themselves. They shall name in their ballots the person voted for as President, and in distinct ballots the person voted for as Vice President; and they shall make distinct lists of all persons voted for as President, and of all persons voted for as Vice President, and of the number of votes for each, which lists they shall sign and certify, and transmit, sealed, to the seat of the Government of the United States, directed to the president of the Senate. The president of the Senate shall, in the presence of the Senate and House of Representatives, open all the certificates, and the votes shall then be counted; the person having the greatest number of votes for President shall be the President, if such number be a majority of the whole number of electors appointed; and if no person have such majority, then from the persons having the highest numbers, not exceeding three, on the list of those voted for as President, the House of Representatives shall choose immediately, by ballot, the President. But in choosing the President, the votes shall be taken by States, the representation from each State having one vote; a quorum for this purpose shall consist of a member or members from two-thirds of the States, and a majority of all the States shall be necessary to a choice. And if the House of Representatives shall not choose a President, whenever the right of choice shall devolve upon them, before the fourth day of March next following, then the Vice President shall act as President, as in the case of the death or other Constitutional disability of the President. The person having the greatest number of votes as Vice President shall be the Vice President, if such number be a majority of the whole number of electors appointed; and if no person have a majority, then from the two highest numbers on the list, the Senate shall choose the Vice President; a quorum for the purpose shall consist of two-thirds of the whole number of senators, and a majority of the whole number shall be necessary to a choice. But no person constitutionally ineligible to the office of President shall be eligible to that of Vice President of the United States.

ARTICLE XIII.

SECTION I. Neither slavery nor involuntary servitude, except as a punishment for crime, whereof the party shall have been duly convicted, shall exist within the United States, or any place subject to their jurisdiction.

SEC. 2.   Congress shall have power to enforce this article by appropriate legislation.

ARTICLE XIV.

SECTION 1.   All persons born or naturalized in the United States, and subject to the jurisdiction thereof, are citizens of the United States, and of the State in which they reside.   No State shall make or enforce any law which shall abridge the privileges or immunities of citizens of the United States; nor shall any State deprive any person of life, liberty, or property without due process of law, nor deny to any person within its jurisdiction the equal protection of the laws.

SEC. 2.   Representatives shall be apportioned among the several States according to their respective numbers, counting the whole number of persons in each State, excluding Indians not taxed.   But when the right to vote at any election for the choice of electors for President and Vice President of the United States, representatives in Congress, the executive and judicial officers of a State, or the members of the Legislature thereof, is denied to any of the male inhabitants of such State being twenty-one years of age, and citizens of the United States, or in any way abridged, except for participation in rebellion or other crime, the basis of representation therein shall be reduced in the proportion which the number of such male citizens shall bear to the whole number of male citizens twenty-one years of age in such State.

SEC. 3.   No person shall be a senator or representative in Congress, or elector of President and Vice President, or hold any office, civil or military, under the United States, or under any State, who, having previously taken an oath as a member of Congress, or as an officer of the United States, or as a member of any State Legislature, or as an executive or judicial officer of any State, to support the Constitution of the United States, shall have engaged in insurrection or rebellion against the same, or given aid or comfort to the enemies thereof.   But Congress may, by a vote of two-thirds of each house, remove such disability.

SEC. 4.   The validity of the public debt of the United States authorized by law, including debts incurred by payment of pensions and bounties for services in suppressing insurrection or rebellion, shall not be questioned.   But neither the United States nor any State shall assume to pay any debt or obligation incurred in aid of insurrection or rebellion against the United States, or any claim for the loss or emancipation of any slave; but all such debts, obligations, and claims shall be held illegal and void.

SEC. 5. The Congress shall have power to enforce, by appropriate legislation, the provisions of this article.

ARTICLE XV.

SECTION 1. The right of the citizens of the United States to vote shall not be denied or abridged by the United States, or by any State, on account of race, color, or previous condition of servitude.

SEC. 2. The Congress shall have power to enforce this article by appropriate legislation.

APPENDIX C.

SUPREME COURT OF THE UNITED STATES

DRED SCOTT, *Plaintiff in Error,*
vs.
JOHN F. A. SANDFORD.

DECEMBER TERM, 1856.

THIS case was brought up, by writ of error, from the Circuit Court of the United States for the district of Missouri.

It was an action of trespass *vi et armis* instituted in the Circuit Court by Scott against Sandford.

Prior to the institution of the present suit, an action was brought by Scott for his freedom in the Circuit Court of St. Louis County (State court), where there was a verdict and judgment in his favor. On a writ of error to the Supreme Court of the State, the judgment below was reversed, and the case remanded to the Circuit Court, where it was continued to await the decision of the case now in question.

The declaration of Scott contained three counts: One, that Sandford had assaulted the plaintiff; one, that he had assaulted Harriet Scott, his wife; and one, that he had assaulted Eliza Scott and Lizzie Scott, his children.

Sandford appeared, and filed the following plea:—

DRED SCOTT
vs.   } *Plea to the jurisdiction of the court.*
JOHN F. A. SANDFORD.

APRIL TERM, 1854.

And the said John F. A. Sandford, in his own proper person, comes and says that this court ought not to have or take further cognizance of the action aforesaid, because, he says, that said cause of action, and each and every of them (if any such have accrued to the said Dred Scott), accrued to the said Dred Scott out of the jurisdiction of this court, and exclusively within the jurisdiction of the courts of the State of Missouri, for that, to wit: The said plaintiff, Dred Scott, is not a citizen of the State of Missouri, as alleged in his declaration, because he is a negro of African descent. His ancestors were of pure African blood, and were brought into this country and sold as negro slaves, and this the said Sandford is ready to verify. Wherefore he prays judgment, whether this court can or will take further cognizance of the action aforesaid.

JOHN F. A. SANDFORD.

To this plea there was a demurrer in the usual form, which was argued in April, 1854, when the court gave judgment that the demurrer should be sustained.

In May, 1854, the defendant, in pursuance of an agreement between counsel, and with the leave of the court, pleaded in bar of the action:

1. Not guilty.

2. That the plaintiff was a negro slave, the lawful property of the defendant, and, as such, the defendant gently laid his hands upon him, and thereby had only restrained him, as the defendant had a right to do.

3. That with respect to the wife and daughters of the plaintiff, in the second and third counts of the declaration mentioned, the defendant had, as to them, only acted in the same manner, and in virtue of the same legal right.

In the first of these pleas the plaintiff joined issue, and to the second and third filed replications alleging that the defendant, of his own wrong and without the cause in his second and third pleas alleged, committed the trespasses, etc.

The counsel then filed the following agreed statement of facts, viz.:

In the year 1834 the plaintiff was a negro slave belonging to Dr. Emerson, who was a surgeon in the army of the United States. In that year, 1834, said Dr. Emerson took the plaintiff from the State of Missouri to the military post at Rock Island, in the State of Illinois, and held him there as a slave until the month of April or May, 1836. At the time last mentioned said Dr. Emerson removed the plaintiff from said military post at Rock Island to the military post at Fort Snelling, situate on the west bank of the Mississippi River, in the territory known as Upper Louisiana, acquired by the United States of France, and situate north of the latitude of 36° 30′ north, and north of the State of Missouri. Said Dr. Emerson held the plaintiff in slavery at Fort Snelling from said last-mentioned date until the year 1838.

In the year 1835 Harriet, who is named in the second count of the plaintiff's declaration, was the negro slave of Major Taliaferro, who belonged to the army of the United States. In that year, 1835, said Major Taliaferro took said Harriet to said Fort Snelling, a military post, situated as hereinbefore stated, and kept her there as a slave until the year 1836, and then sold and delivered her as a slave at said Fort Snelling unto the said Dr. Emerson hereinbefore named. Said Dr. Emerson held said Harriet in slavery at said Fort Snelling until the year 1838.

In the year 1836 the plaintiff and said Harriet, at said Fort Snelling, with the consent of said Dr. Emerson, who then claimed to be their master and owner, intermarried, and took each other for husband and wife. Eliza and Lizzie, named in the third count of the plaintiff's declaration, are the fruit of that marriage. Eliza is about fourteen years old, and was born on board the steamboat *Gipsey*, north of the north line of the State of Missouri, and upon the river Mississippi. Lizzie is about seven years old, and was born in the State of Missouri, at the military post called Jefferson Barracks.

In the year 1838 said Dr. Emerson removed the plaintiff and said Harriet, and their said daughter Eliza, from said Fort Snelling to the State of Missouri, where they have ever since resided.

Before the commencement of this suit, said Dr. Emerson sold and conveyed the plaintiff, said Harriet, Eliza, and Lizzie, to the defendant, as slaves, and the defendant has ever since claimed to hold them, and each of them, as slaves.

At the times mentioned in the plaintiff's declaration, the defendant, claiming to be owner as aforesaid, laid his hands upon said plaintiff, Harriet, Eliza, and Lizzie, and imprisoned them, doing in this respect, however, no more than what he might lawfully do if they were of right his slaves at such times.

Further proof may be given on the trial for either party.

It is agreed that Dred Scott brought suit for his freedom in the Circuit Court of St. Louis County; that there was a verdict and judgment in his favor; that on a writ of error to the Supreme Court the judgment below was reversed, and the same remanded to the Circuit Court, where it has been continued to await the decision of this case.

In May, 1854, the cause went before a jury, who found the following verdict, viz.: "As to the first issue joined in this case, we of the
jury find the defendant not guilty; and as to the issue secondly above
joined, we of the jury find that, before and at the time when, etc., in
the first count mentioned, the said Dred Scott was a negro slave, the
lawful property of the defendant; and as to the issue thirdly above
joined, we, the jury, find that, before and at the time when, etc., in
the second and third counts mentioned, the said Harriet, wife of said
Dred Scott, and Eliza and Lizzie, the daughters of the said Dred
Scott, were negro slaves, the lawful property of the defendant."

Whereupon, the court gave judgment for the defendant.

After an ineffectual motion for a new trial, the plaintiff filed the
following bill of exceptions.

On the trial of this cause by the jury, the plaintiff, to maintain the
issues on his part, read to the jury the following agreed statement of
facts (see agreement above). No further testimony was given to the
jury by either party. Thereupon the plaintiff moved the court to give
to the jury the following instruction, viz.:—

"That, upon the facts agreed to by the parties, they ought to find
for the plaintiff. The court refused to give such instruction to the
jury, and the plaintiff, to such refusal, then and there duly excepted."

The court then gave the following instruction to the jury, on
motion of the defendant:—

" The jury are instructed that, upon the facts in this case, the law
is with the defendant." The plaintiff excepted to this instruction.

Upon these exceptions the case came up to this court.

It was argued at December term, 1855, and ordered to be reargued
at the present term.

It was now argued by *Mr. Blair* and *Mr. G. F. Curtis* for the
plaintiff in error, and by *Mr. Geyer* and *Mr. Johnson* for the defendant
in error.

The reporter regrets that want of room will not allow him to give
the arguments of counsel, but he regrets it the less because the subject is thoroughly examined in the opinion of the court, the opinions
of the concurring judges, and the opinions of the judges who dissented
from the judgment of the court.

Mr. Chief Justice Taney delivered the opinion of the court.

This case has been twice argued. After the argument at the last
term, differences of opinion were found to exist among the members
of the court; and as the questions in controversy are of the highest

importance, and the court was at that time much pressed by the ordinary business of the term, it was deemed advisable to continue the case, and direct a reargument on some of the points, in order that we might have an opportunity of giving to the whole subject a more deliberate consideration. It has accordingly been again argued by counsel, and considered by the court, and I now proceed to deliver its opinion.

There are two leading questions presented by the record:—

1. Had the Circuit Court of the United States jurisdiction to hear and determine the case between these parties? And—

2. If it had jurisdiction, is the judgment it has given erroneous or not?

The plaintiff in error, who was also the plaintiff in the court below, was, with his wife and children, held as slaves by the defendant in the State of Missouri; and he brought this action in the Circuit Court of the United States for that district, to assert the title of himself and his family to freedom.

The declaration is in the form usually adopted in that State to try questions of this description, and contains the averment necessary to give the court jurisdiction; that he and the defendant are citizens of different States; that is, that he is a citizen of Missouri, and the defendant a citizen of New York.

The defendant pleaded in abatement to the jurisdiction of the court, that the plaintiff was not a citizen of the State of Missouri, as alleged in his declaration, being a negro of African descent, whose ancestors were of pure African blood, and who were brought into this country and sold as slaves.

To this plea the plaintiff demurred, and the defendant joined in demurrer. The court overruled the plea, and gave judgment that the defendant should answer over. And he thereupon put in sundry pleas in bar, upon which issues were joined, and at the trial the verdict and judgment were in his favor. Whereupon the plaintiff brought this writ of error.

Before we speak of the pleas in bar, it will be proper to dispose of the questions which have arisen on the plea in abatement.

That plea denies the right of the plaintiff to sue in a court of the United States, for the reasons therein stated.

If the question raised by it is legally before us, and the court should be of opinion that the facts stated in it disqualify the plaintiff from becoming a citizen, in the sense in which that word is used in the Constitution of the United States, then the judgment of the Circuit Court is erroneous, and must be reversed.

It is suggested, however, that this plea is not before us, and that, as the judgment in the court below on this plea was in favor of the plaintiff, he does not seek to reverse it, or bring it before the court for revision by his writ of error; and also that the defendant waived this defense by pleading over, and thereby admitted the jurisdiction of the court.

But, in making this objection, we think the peculiar and limited jurisdiction of courts of the United States has not been averted to. This peculiar and limited jurisdiction has made it necessary in these courts to adopt different rules and principles of pleading, so far as jurisdiction is concerned, from those which regulate courts of common law in England, and in the different States of the Union which have adopted the common-law rules.

In these last-mentioned courts, where their character and rank are analogous to that of a Circuit Court of the United States; in other words, where they are what the law terms courts of general jurisdiction, they are presumed to have jurisdiction, unless the contrary appears. No averment in the pleadings of the plaintiff is necessary in order to give jurisdiction. If the defendant objects to it, he must plead it specially, and, unless the fact on which he relies is found to be true by a jury, or admitted to be true by the plaintiff, the jurisdiction cannot be disputed in an appellate court.

Now, it is not necessary to inquire whether in courts of that description a party who pleads over in bar, when a plea to the jurisdiction has been ruled against him, does or does not waive his plea; nor whether, upon a judgment in his favor on the pleas in bar, and a writ of error brought by the plaintiff, the question upon the plea in abatement would be open for revision in the appellate court. Cases that may have been decided in such courts, or rules that may have been laid down by common-law pleaders, can have no influence in the decision in this court, because, under the Constitution and laws of the United States, the rules which govern the pleadings in its courts in questions of jurisdiction stand on different principles, and are regulated by different laws.

This difference arises, as we have said, from the peculiar character of the Government of the United States; for, although it is sovereign and supreme in its appropriate sphere of action, yet it does not possess all the powers which usually belong to the sovereignty of a nation. Certain specified powers, enumerated in the Constitution, have been conferred upon it; and neither the legislative, executive, nor judicial departments of the government can lawfully exercise any authority beyond the limits marked out by the Constitution. And in regulating the judicial department, the cases in which the courts of the United States shall have jurisdiction are particularly and specifically enumerated and defined; and they are not authorized to take cognizance of any case which does not come within the description therein specified. Hence, when a plaintiff sues in a court of the United States, it is necessary that he should show in his pleading that the suit he brings is within the jurisdiction of the court, and that he is entitled to sue there. And if he omits to do this, and should, by any oversight of the Circuit Court, obtain a judgment in his favor, the judgment would be reversed in the appellate court for want of jurisdiction in the court below. The jurisdiction would not be presumed, as in the case of a common-law English or State court, unless the contrary appeared. But the record, when it comes before the appellate court, must show affirmatively that the inferior court had authority, under the Constitution, to hear and determine the case. And if the plaintiff claims a right to sue in a Circuit Court of the United States, under that provision of the Constitution which gives jurisdiction in controversies between citizens of different States, he must distinctly aver in his pleading that they are citizens of different States, and he cannot maintain his suit without showing that fact in the pleadings.

This point was decided in the case of Bingham *vs.* Cabot (in 3 Dall. 382), and ever since adhered to by the court. And in Jackson *vs.* Ashton (8 Pet. 148) it was held that the objection to which it was open could not be waived by the opposite party, because consent of parties could not give jurisdiction.

It is needless to accumulate cases on this subject. Those already referred to, and the cases of Capron *vs.* Van Noorden (in 2 Cr. 126), and Montalet *vs.* Murray (4 Cr. 46), are sufficient to show the rule of which we have spoken. The case of Capron *vs.* Van Noorden strikingly illustrates the difference between a common-law court and a court of the United States.

If, however, the fact of citizenship is averred in the declaration, and the defendant does not deny it, and put it in issue by plea in abatement, he cannot offer evidence at the trial to disprove it, and, consequently, cannot avail himself of the objection in the appellate court, unless the defect should be apparent in some other part of the record; for, if there is no plea in abatement, and the want of jurisdiction does not appear in any other part of the transcript brought up by the writ of error, the undisputed averment of citizenship in the declaration must be taken in this court to be true. In this case the citizenship is averred, but it is denied by the defendant in the manner required by the rules of pleading, and the fact upon which the denial is based is admitted by the demurrer. And, if the plea and demurrer, and judgment of the court below upon it, are before us upon this record, the question to be decided is whether the facts stated in the plea are sufficient to show that the plaintiff is not entitled to sue as a citizen in a court of the United States.

We think they are before us. The plea in abatement and the judgment of the court upon it are a part of the judicial proceedings in the Circuit Court, and are there recorded as such, and a writ of error always brings up to the Superior Court the whole record of the proceedings in the court below. And in the case of the United States *vs.* Smith (11 Wheat. 172) this court said, that the case being brought up by writ of error, the whole record was under the consideration of this court. And this being the case in the present instance, the plea in abatement is necessarily under consideration; and it becomes, therefore, our duty to decide whether the facts stated in the plea are or are not sufficient to show that the plaintiff is not entitled to sue as a citizen in a court of the United States.

This is certainly a very serious question, and one that now for the first time has been brought for decision before this court. But it is brought here by those who have a right to bring it, and it is our duty to meet it and decide it.

The question is simply this: Can a negro, whose ancestors were imported into this country, and sold as slaves, become a member of the political community formed and brought into existence by the Constitution of the United States, and as such become entitled to all the rights and privileges and immunities guaranteed by that instrument to the citizen, one of which rights is the privilege of suing in a court of the United States in the cases specified in the Constitution.

It will be observed that the plea applies to that class of persons only whose ancestors were negroes of the African race, and imported into this country, and sold and held as slaves. The only matter in issue before the court, therefore, is, whether the descendants of such slaves, when they shall be emancipated, or who are born of parents who had become free before their birth, are citizens of a State in the sense in which the word citizen is used in the Constitution of the United States. And this being the only matter in dispute on the pleadings, the court must be understood as speaking in this opinion of that class only, that is, of those persons who are the descendants of Africans who were imported into this country, and sold as slaves.

The situation of this population was altogether unlike that of the Indian race. The latter, it is true, formed no part of the colonial communities, and never amalgamated with them in social connections or in government. But although they were uncivilized, they were yet a free and independent people, associated together in nations or tribes, and governed by their own laws. Many of these political communities were situated in territories to which the white race claimed the ultimate right of dominion. But that claim was acknowledged to be subject to the right of the Indians to occupy it as long as they thought proper, and neither the English nor colonial governments claimed or exercised any dominion over the tribe or nation by whom it was occupied, nor claimed the right to the possession of the territory, until the tribe or nation consented to cede it. These Indian governments were regarded and treated as foreign governments, as much so as if an ocean had separated the red man from the white, and their freedom has constantly been acknowledged, from the time of the first emigration to the English colonies to the present day, by the different governments which succeeded each other. Treaties have been negotiated with them, and their alliance sought for in war, and the people who compose these Indian political communities have always been treated as foreigners not living under our government. It is true that the course of events has brought the Indian tribes within the limits of the United States under subjection to the white race, and it has been found necessary, for their sake as well as our own, to regard them as in a state of pupilage, and to legislate to a certain extent over them and the territory they occupy. But they may, without doubt, like the subjects of any other foreign government, be naturalized by the authority of Congress, and become citizens of a State and of the United States; and, if an individual should leave his nation or tribe, and take up his abode among the white population, he would be entitled to all the rights and privileges which would belong to an emigrant from any other foreign people.

We proceed to examine the case as presented by the pleadings.

The words "people of the United States" and "citizens" are

synonymous terms, and mean the same thing. They both describe the political body who, according to our republican institutions, form the sovereignty, and who hold the power and conduct the government through their representatives. They are what we familiarly call the "sovereign people," and every citizen is one of this people, and a constituent member of this sovereignty. The question before us is whether the class of persons described in the plea in abatement compose a portion of this people, and are constituent members of this sovereignty. We think they are not, and that they are not included, and were not intended to be included, under the word "citizens" in the Constitution, and can, therefore, claim none of the rights and privileges which that instrument provides for and secures to citizens of the United States. On the contrary, they were at that time considered as a subordinate and inferior class of beings, who had been subjugated by the dominant race, and, whether emancipated or not, yet remained subject to their authority, and had no rights or privileges but such as those who held the power and the government might choose to grant them.

It is not the province of the court to decide upon the justice or injustice, the policy or impolicy, of these laws. The decision of that question belonged to the political or law-making power, to those who formed the sovereignty and framed the Constitution. The duty of the court is to interpret the instrument they have framed, with the best lights we can obtain on the subject, and to administer it as we find it, according to its true intent and meaning when it was adopted.

In discussing this question we must not confound the rights of citizenship which a State may confer within its own limits, and the rights of citizenship as a member of the Union. It does not by any means follow because he has all the rights and privileges of a citizen of a State, that he must be a citizen of the United States. He may have all of the rights and privileges of the citizen of a State, and yet not be entitled to the rights and privileges of a citizen in any other State; for, previous to the adoption of the Constitution of the United States, every State had the undoubted right to confer on whomsoever it pleased the character of citizen, and to endow him with all its rights. But this character of course was confined to the boundaries of the State, and gave him no rights or privileges in other States beyond those secured to him by the laws of nations and the comity of States. Nor have the several States surrendered the power of conferring these rights and privileges by adopting the Constitution of the United States.

Each State may still confer them upon an alien, or anyone it thinks proper, or upon any class or description of persons, yet he would not be a citizen in the sense in which that word is used in the Constitution of the United States, nor entitled to sue as such in one of its courts, nor to the privileges and immunities of a citizen in the other States. The rights which he would acquire would be restricted to the State which gave them. The Constitution has conferred on Congress the right to establish a uniform rule of naturalization, and this right is evidently exclusive, and has always been held by this court to be so. Consequently, no State, since the adoption of the Constitution, can by naturalizing an alien invest him with the rights and privileges secured to a citizen of a State under the Federal Government, although, so far as the State alone was concerned, he would undoubtedly be entitled to the rights of a citizen, and clothed with all the rights and immunities which the Constitution and laws of the State attached to that character.

It is very clear, therefore, that no State can, by any act or law of its own passed since the adoption of the Constitution, introduce a new member into the political community created by the Constitution of the United States. It cannot make him a member of this community by making him a member of its own. And for the same reason it cannot introduce any person, or description of persons, who were not intended to be embraced in this new political family, which the Constitution brought into existence, but were intended to be excluded from it.

The question then arises whether the provisions of the Constitution, in relation to the personal rights and privileges to which the citizen of a State should be entitled, embraced the negro African race at that time in this country, or who might afterwards be imported, who had then or should afterwards be made free in any State, and to put it in the power of a single State to make him a citizen of the United States, and endue him with the full rights of citizenship in every other State without their consent. Does the Constitution of the United States act upon him whenever he shall be made free under the laws of a State, and raised there to the rank of a citizen, and immediately clothe him with all the privileges of a citizen in every other State, and in its own courts?

The court thinks the affirmative of these propositions cannot be maintained. And if it cannot, the plaintiff in error could not be a citizen of the State of Missouri within the meaning of the Constitution

20

of the United States, and, consequently, was not entitled to sue in its courts.

It is true every person, and every class and description of persons, who were at the time of the adoption of the Constitution recognized as citizens in the several States, became also citizens of this new political body, but none other. It was formed by them, and for them and their posterity, but for no one else. And the personal rights and privileges guaranteed to citizens of this new sovereignty were intended to embrace those only who were then members of the several State communities, or who should afterwards by birthright or otherwise become members, according to the provisions of the Constitution and the principles on which it was founded. It was the union of those who were at that time members of distinct and separate political communities into one political family, whose power, for certain specified purposes, was to extend over the whole territory of the United States. And it gave to each citizen rights and privileges outside of his State which he did not before possess, and placed him in every other State upon a perfect equality with its own citizens as to rights of person and rights of property. It made him a citizen of the United States.

It becomes necessary, therefore, to determine who were citizens of the several States when the Constitution was adopted. And in order to do this, we must recur to the governments and institutions of the thirteen colonies when they separated from Great Britain and formed new sovereignties, and took their places in the family of independent nations. We must inquire who, at that time, were recognized as the people or citizens of a State, whose rights and liberties had been outraged by the English Government, and who declared their independence and assumed the powers of government to defend their rights by force of arms.

In the opinion of the court, the legislation and histories of the times, and the language used in the Declaration of Independence, show that neither the class of persons who had been imported as slaves, nor their descendants, whether they had become free or not, were then acknowledged as a part of the people, nor intended to be included in the general words used in that memorable instrument.

It is difficult at this day to realize the state of public opinion in relation to that unfortunate race which prevailed in the civilized and enlightened portions of the world at the time of the Declaration of Independence, and when the Constitution of the United States was framed and adopted. But *the public history of every European nation* displays it in a manner too plain to be mistaken.

They had for more than a century before been regarded as beings of an inferior order, and altogether unfit to associate with the white race, either in social or political relations, and so far inferior that *they had no rights which the white man was bound to respect, and that the negro might justly and lawfully be reduced to slavery for his benefit.* He was bought and sold, and treated as an ordinary article of merchandise and traffic whenever a profit could be made by it. This opinion was at that time fixed and universal in the civilized portion of the white race. It was regarded as an axiom in morals as well as in politics, which no one thought of disputing, or supposed to be open to dispute, and men in every grade and position in society daily and habitually acted upon it in their private pursuits, as well as in matters of public concern, without doubting for a moment the correctness of this opinion.

And in no nation was this opinion more firmly fixed or more uniformly acted upon than by *the English Government and English people.* They not only seized them on the coast of Africa, and sold them or held them in slavery for their own use, but they took them as ordinary articles of merchandise to every country where they could make a profit on them, and were far more extensively engaged in this commerce than any other nation in the world.

The opinion thus entertained and acted upon in England was naturally impressed upon *the colonies they founded on this side of the Atlantic.* And, accordingly, a negro of the African race was regarded by them as an article of property, and held and bought and sold as such in every one of the thirteen colonies which united in the Declaration of Independence, and afterwards formed the Constitution of the United States. The slaves were more or less numerous in the different colonies, as slave labor was found more or less profitable. But no one seems to have doubted the correctness of the prevailing opinion of the time.

The legislation of the different colonies furnishes positive and indisputable proof of this fact.

It would be tedious, in this opinion, to enumerate the various laws they passed upon this subject. It will be sufficient, as a sample of the legislation which then generally prevailed throughout the British colonies, to give the laws of two of them, one being still a large slaveholding State, and the other the first State in which slavery ceased to exist.

The province of Maryland, in 1717 (ch. 13, s. 5), passed a law declaring "that if any free negro or mulatto intermarry with any white woman, or if any white man shall intermarry with any negro or mulatto woman, such negro or mulatto shall become a slave during life, excepting mulattoes born of white women, who, for such intermarriage, shall only become servants for seven years, to be disposed of as the justices of the county court where such marriage so happens shall think fit, to be applied by them towards the support of a public school within the said county. And any white man or white woman who shall intermarry as aforesaid with any negro or mulatto, such white man or white woman shall become servants during the term of seven years, and shall be disposed of by the justices as aforesaid, and be applied to the uses aforesaid."

The other colonial law to which we refer *was passed by Massachusetts in 1705* (chap. 6). It is entitled "An act for the better preventing of a spurious and mixed issue," etc., and it provides that "if any negro or mulatto shall presume to smite or strike any person of the English or other Christian nation, such negro or mulatto shall be severely whipped, at the discretion of the justices before whom the offender shall be convicted."

And "that none of her Majesty's English or Scottish subjects, nor of any other Christian nation, within this province, shall contract matrimony with any negro or mulatto; nor shall any person duly authorized to solemnize marriage, presume to join any such in marriage, on pain of forfeiting the sum of fifty pounds, one moiety thereof to her Majesty, for and towards the support of the government within this province, and the other moiety to him or them that shall inform and sue for the same in any of her Majesty's courts of record within the province, by bill, plaint, or information."

We give both of these laws in the words used by the respective legislative bodies, because *the language* in which they are framed, *as well as the provisions contained in them, show, too plainly to be misunderstood*, the degraded condition of this unhappy race. *They were still in force when the Revolution began, and are a faithful index to the state of feeling towards the class of persons of whom they speak, and of the position they occupied throughout the thirteen colonies, in the eyes and thoughts of the men who framed the Declaration of Independence and established the State constitutions and governments.* They show that a perpetual and impassable barrier was intended to be erected between the white race and the one which they had reduced to slavery, and governed as subjects with absolute and despotic power, and which they then looked upon as so far below them in the scale of created beings that intermarriages between white persons and negroes or mulattoes were regarded as unnatural and immoral, and punished as crimes, not only in the parties, but in the persons who joined them in marriage. And no distinction in this respect was made between the free negro or mulatto and the slave, but this stigma, of the deepest degradation, was fixed upon the whole race.

We refer to these historical facts for the purpose of showing the fixed opinions concerning that race upon which the statesmen of that day spoke and acted. *It is necessary to do this, in order to determine whether the general terms used in the Constitution of the United States,* as to the rights of man and the rights of the people, was intended to include them, or to give to them or their posterity the benefit of any of its provisions.

The language of *the Declaration of Independence is equally conclusive.* It begins by declaring that "when in the course of human events it becomes necessary for one people to dissolve the political bands which have connected them with another, and to assume among the powers of the earth the separate and equal station to which the laws of nature and nature's God entitle them, a decent respect for the opinions of mankind requires that they should declare the causes which impel them to the separation."

It then proceeds to say: "We hold these truths to be self-evident, that all men are created equal; that they are endowed by their Creator with certain unalienable rights; that among them is life, liberty, and the pursuit of happiness; that, to secure these rights, governments are instituted, deriving their just powers from the consent of the governed."

The general words above quoted would seem to embrace the whole human family, and, if they were used in a similar instrument at this day, would be so understood. But *it is too clear for dispute that the enslaved African race were not intended to be included, and formed no part of the people who framed and adopted this declaration,* for if the language, as understood in that day, would embrace them, the conduct of the distinguished men who framed the Declaration of Independence would have been utterly and flagrantly inconsistent with the principles they asserted; and, instead of the sympathy of mankind, to which they so confidently appealed, they would have deserved and received universal rebuke and reprobation.

Yet the men who framed this declaration were great men, high in literary acquirements, high in their sense of honor, and incapable of asserting principles inconsistent with those on which they were acting. They perfectly understood the meaning of the language they used, and how it would be understood by others; and they knew that it would not in any part of the civilized world be supposed to embrace the negro race, which, by common consent, had been excluded from civilized governments and the family of nations, and doomed to slavery. They spoke and acted according to the then established doctrines and principles, and in the ordinary language of the day, and no one misunderstood them. The unhappy black race were separated from the white by indelible marks, and laws long before established, and were never thought of or spoken of except as property, and when the claims of the owner or the profit of the trader were supposed to need protection.

This state of public opinion had undergone no change when the Constitution was adopted, as is equally evident from its provisions and language.

The brief preamble sets forth by whom it was formed, for what purposes, and for whose benefit and protection. It declares that it is formed by the *people* of the United States, that is to say, by those who were members of the different political communities in the several States, and its great object is declared to be to secure the blessings of liberty to themselves and their posterity. It speaks in general terms of the *people* of the United States, and of *citizens* of the several States, when it is providing for the exercise of the powers granted or the privileges secured to the citizen. It does not define what description of persons are intended to be included under these terms, or who shall be regarded as a citizen and one of the people. It uses them as terms so well understood that no further description or definition was necessary.

But there are two clauses in the Constitution which point directly and specifically to the negro race as a separate class of persons, and show clearly that they were not regarded as a portion of the people or citizens of the government then formed.

One of these clauses reserves to each of the thirteen States the right to import slaves until the year 1808, if it thinks proper. And the importation which it thus sanctions was unquestionably of persons of the race of which we are speaking, as the traffic in slaves in the United States had always been confined to them. And by the other provision the States pledge themselves to each other to maintain the right of property of the master, by delivering up to him any slave who may have escaped from his service, and be found within their respective territories. By the first above-mentioned clause, therefore, the right to purchase and hold this property is directly sanctioned and authorized for twenty years by the people who framed the Constitution, and by the second they pledge themselves to maintain and uphold the right of the master in the manner specified as long as the government they then formed should endure. And these two provisions show conclusively that neither the description of persons therein referred to, nor their descendants, were embraced in any of the other provisions of the Constitution, for certainly these two clauses were not intended to confer on them or their posterity the blessings of liberty, or any of the personal rights so carefully provided for the citizen.

No one of that race had ever migrated to the United States voluntarily; all of them had been brought here as articles of merchandise. The number that had been emancipated at that time were but few in comparison with those held in slavery, and they were identified in the public mind with the race to which they belonged, and regarded as a part of the slave population rather than the free. It is obvious that they were not even in the minds of the framers of the Constitution when they were conferring special rights and privileges upon the citizens of a State in every other part of the Union.

Indeed, when we look to the condition of this race in the several States at the time, it is impossible to believe that these rights and privileges were intended to be extended to them.

It is very true that in that portion of the Union where the labor of the negro race was found to be unsuited to the climate and unprofitable to the master, but few slaves were held at the time of the Declaration of Independence, and, when the Constitution was adopted, it had entirely worn out in one of them, and measures had been taken for its gradual abolition in several others. But this change had not been produced by any change of opinion in relation to this race, but because it was discovered from experience that slave labor was unsuited to the climate and productions of these States, for some of the States, where it had ceased or nearly ceased to exist, were actively engaged in the slave trade, procuring cargoes on the coast of Africa, and transporting them for sale to those parts of the Union where their labor was found to be profitable, and suited to the climate and productions. And this traffic was openly carried on, and fortunes accumulated by it, without reproach from the people of the States where they resided. And it can hardly be supposed that, in the States where it was then countenanced in its worst form, that is, in the seizure and transportation, the people could have regarded those who were emancipated as entitled to equal rights with themselves.

And we may here again refer, in support of this proposition, to the plain and unequivocal language of *the laws of the several States*, some passed after the Declaration of Independence and before the Constitution was adopted, and some since the government went into operation.

We need not refer, on this point, particularly to the laws of the present slave-holding States. Their statute books are full of provisions in relation to this class in the same spirit with the Maryland law, which we have before quoted. They have continued to treat them as an inferior class, and to subject them to strict police regulations, drawing a broad line of distinction between the citizen and the slave races, and legislating in relation to them upon the same principle which prevailed at the time of the Declaration of Independence. As relates to these States, it is too plain for argument that they have never been regarded as a part of the people or citizens of the State, nor supposed to possess any political rights which the dominant race might not withhold or grant at their pleasure. And as long ago as 1822, the Court of Appeals of Kentucky decided that free negroes and mulattoes were not citizens within the meaning of the Constitution of the United States, and the correctness of this decision is recognized and the same doctrine affirmed in 1 Meigs' Tenn. Reports 331.

And if we turn *to the legislation of the States where slavery had worn out*, or measures taken for its speedy abolition, we shall find the same opinions and principles equally fixed and equally acted upon.

Thus, Massachusetts, in 1786, passed a law similar to the colonial one of which we have spoken. The law of 1786, like the law of 1705, forbids the marriage of any white person with any negro, Indian, or mulatto, and inflicts a penalty of fifty pounds upon anyone who shall join them in marriage, and declares all such marriages absolutely null and void, and degrades thus the unhappy issue of the marriage by fixing upon it the stain of bastardy. And this mark of degradation was renewed, and again impressed upon the race, in the careful and deliberate preparation of their revised code, published in 1836. This code forbids any person from joining in marriage any white person with any Indian, negro, or mulatto, and subjects the party who shall offend in this respect to imprisonment, not exceeding six months, in the common jail, or to hard labor, and to a fine of not less than fifty nor more than two hundred dollars; and, like the law of 1786, it declares the marriage to be absolutely null and void. It will be seen that the punishment is increased by the code upon the person who shall marry them, by adding imprisonment to a pecuniary penalty.

So, too, in Connecticut. We refer more particularly to the legislation of this State, because it was not only among the first to put an end to slavery within its own territory, but was the first to fix a mark of reprobation upon the African slave trade. The law last mentioned was passed in October, 1788, about nine months after the State had ratified and adopted the present Constitution of the United States, and by that law it prohibited its own citizens, under severe penalties, from engaging in the trade, and declared all policies of insurance on the vessel or cargo made in the State to be null and void. But, up to the time of the adoption of the Constitution, there is nothing in the legislation of the State indicating any change of opinion as to the relative rights and position of the white and black races in this country, or indicating that it meant to place the latter, when free, upon a level with its citizens, and certainly nothing which would have led the slave-holding States to suppose that Connecticut designed to claim for them, under the new Constitution, the equal rights and privileges and rank of citizens in every other State.

The first step taken by Connecticut upon this subject was as early as 1774, when it passed an act forbidding the further importation of slaves into the State. But the section containing the prohibition is introduced by the following preamble:—

"And, whereas, the increase of slaves in this State is injurious to the poor, and inconvenient."

This recital would appear to have been carefully introduced, in order to prevent any misunderstanding of the motive which induced the Legislature to pass the law, and places it distinctly upon the interest and convenience of the white population, excluding the inference that it might have been intended in any degree for the benefit of the other.

And in the act of 1784, by which the issue of slaves born after the time therein mentioned were to be free at a certain age, the section is again introduced by a preamble assigning a similar motive for the act. It is in these words:—

"Whereas, sound policy requires that the abolition of slavery should be effected as soon as may be consistent with the rights of individuals, and the public safety and welfare"—showing that the right of property in the master was to be protected, and that the measure was one of policy, and to prevent the injury and inconvenience to the whites of a slave population in the State.

And still further pursuing its legislation, we find that in the same statute, passed in 1774, which prohibited the further importation of slaves into the State, there is also a provision by which any negro, Indian, or mulatto servant, who was found wandering out of the town or place to which he belonged without a written pass such as is therein described, was made liable to be seized by anyone, and taken before the next authority, to be examined and delivered up to his master, who was required to pay the charge which had accrued thereby. And a subsequent section of the same law provides that, if any free negro shall travel without such pass, and shall be stopped, seized, or taken up, he shall pay all charges arising thereby. And this law was in full operation when the Constitution of the United States was adopted, and was not repealed till 1797, so that up to that time free negroes and mulattoes were associated with servants and slaves in the police regulations established by the laws of the State.

And again, in 1833, Connecticut passed another law, which made it penal to set up or establish any school in that State for the instruction of persons of the African race not inhabitants of the State, or to instruct or teach in any such school or institution, or board or harbor for that purpose, any such person, without the previous consent in writing of the civil authority of the town in which such school or institution might be.

And it appears by the case of Crandall vs. the State, reported in 10 Conn. Rep. 340, that upon an information filed against Prudence Crandall for a violation of this law, one of the points raised in the defense was that the law was a violation of the Constitution of the United States, and that the persons instructed, although of the African race, were citizens of other States, and therefore entitled to the rights and privileges of citizens in the State of Connecticut. But Chief Justice Dagget, before whom the case was tried, held that persons of that description were not citizens of a State within the meaning of the word "citizen" in the Constitution of the United States, and were not, therefore, entitled to the privileges and immunities of citizens in other States.

The case was carried up to the Supreme Court of Errors of the State, and the question fully argued there, but the case went off upon another point, and no opinion was expressed on this question.

We have made this particular examination into the legislative and judicial action of Connecticut because, from the early hostility it displayed to the slave trade on the coast of Africa, we may expect to find the laws of that State as lenient and favorable to the subject race as those of any other State in the Union; and if we find that, at the time the Constitution was adopted, they were not even there raised to the rank of citizens, but were still held and treated as property, and the laws relating to them passed with reference altogether to the interest and convenience of the white race, we shall hardly find them elevated to a higher rank anywhere else.

A brief notice of the laws of two other States, and we shall pass on to other considerations.

By the laws of New Hampshire, collected and finally passed in 1815, no one was permitted to be enrolled in the militia of the State but free white citizens, and the same provision is found in a subsequent collection of the laws, made in 1855. Nothing could more strongly mark the entire repudiation of the African race. The alien is excluded because, being born in a foreign country, he cannot be a member of the community until he is naturalized. But why are the African race born in the State not permitted to share in one of the highest duties of the citizen? The answer is obvious,—he is not, by the institutions and laws of the State, numbered among its people. He forms no part of the sovereignty of the State, and is not, therefore, called on to uphold and defend it.

Again, in 1822, Rhode Island, in its revised code, passed a law forbidding persons who were authorized to join persons in marriage from joining in marriage any white person with any negro, Indian, or mulatto, under the penalty of two hundred dollars, and declaring all such marriages absolutely null and void, and the same law was again reënacted in its revised code of 1844; so that, down to the last-mentioned period, the strongest mark of inferiority and degradation was fastened upon the African race in that State.

It would be impossible to enumerate and compress in the space usually allotted to an opinion of a court the various laws marking the condition of this race which were passed from time to time after the Revolution, and before and since the adoption of the Constitution of the United States. In addition to those already referred to, *it is suf-*

ficient to say that Chancellor Kent, whose accuracy and research no one will question, states in the sixth edition of his Commentaries (published in 1848, 2 vol. 258, note *b*) that in no part of the country except Maine did the African race, in point of fact, participate equally with the whites in the exercise of civil and political rights.

The legislation of the States therefore shows, in a manner not to be mistaken, the inferior and subject condition of that race at the time the Constitution was adopted, and long afterwards, throughout the thirteen States by which that instrument was framed; and it is hardly consistent with the respect due to these States to suppose that they regarded at that time, as fellow-citizens and members of the sovereignty, a class of beings whom they had thus stigmatized; whom, as we are bound, out of respect to the State sovereignties, to assume they had deemed it just and necessary thus to stigmatize, and upon whom they had impressed such deep and enduring marks of inferiority and degradation; or that when they met in convention to form the Constitution, they looked upon them as a portion of their constituents, or designed to include them in the provisions so carefully inserted for the security and protection of the liberties and rights of their citizens. It cannot be supposed that they intended to secure to them rights and privileges and rank in the new political body throughout the Union, which every one of them denied within the limits of its own dominion. More especially, it cannot be believed that the large slave-holding States regarded them as included in the word "citizens," or would have consented to a Constitution which might compel them to receive them in that character from another State; for, if they were so received, and entitled to the privileges and immunities of citizens, it would exempt them from the operation of the special laws and from the police regulations which they considered to be necessary for their own safety. It would give to persons of the negro race, who were recognized as citizens in any one State of the Union, the right to enter every other State whenever they pleased, singly or in companies, without pass or passport, and without obstruction, to sojourn there as long as they pleased, to go where they pleased at every hour of the day or night without molestation, unless they committed some violation of law for which a white man would be punished; and it would give them the full liberty of speech in public and in private upon all subjects upon which its own citizens might speak; to hold public meetings upon political affairs, and to keep and carry arms wherever they went. And all of this would be done in the face of the subject race of the same color, both free and slaves, and inevitably producing discontent and insubordination among them, and endangering the peace and safety of the State.

It is impossible, it would seem, to believe that the great men of the slave-holding States, who took so large a share in framing the Constitution of the United States, and exercised so much influence in procuring its adoption, could have been so forgetful or regardless of their own safety and the safety of those who trusted and confided in them.

Besides, this want of foresight and care would have been utterly inconsistent with the caution displayed in providing for the admission of new members into this political family, for, when they gave to the citizens of each State the privileges and immunities of citizens in the several States, they at the same time took from the several States the power of naturalization, and confined that power exclusively to the federal government. No State was willing to permit another State to determine who should or should not be admitted as one of its citizens, and entitled to demand equal rights and privileges with their own people, within their own territories. The right of naturalization was, therefore, with one accord surrendered by the States, and confided to the federal government. And this power granted to Congress to establish a uniform rule of *naturalization* is, by the well-understood meaning of the word, confined to persons born in a foreign country, under a foreign government. It is not a power to raise to the rank of a citizen anyone born in the United States who, from birth or parentage, by the laws of the country, belongs to an inferior and subordinate class. And when we find the States guarding themselves from the indiscreet or improper admission by other States of emigrants from other countries, by giving the power exclusively to Congress, we cannot fail to see that they could never have left with the States a much more important power, that is, the power of transforming into citizens a numerous class of persons who in that character would be much more dangerous to the peace and safety of a large portion of the Union than the few foreigners one of the States might improperly naturalize. The Constitution, upon its adoption, obviously took from the States all power by any subsequent legislation to introduce as a citizen into the political family of the United States anyone, no matter where he was born, or what might be his character or condition, and it gave to Congress the power to confer this character upon those only who were born outside of the dominions of the United States. And no law of a State, therefore, passed since the Constitution was adopted, can give any right of citizenship outside of its own territory.

A clause similar to the one in the Constitution, in relation to the rights and immunities of citizens of one State in the other States, was contained in the Articles of Confederation. But there is a difference of language, which is worthy of note. The provision in the Articles of Confederation was "that the *free inhabitants* of each of the States, paupers, vagabonds, and fugitives from justice excepted, should be entitled to all the privileges and immunities of free citizens in the several States."

It will be observed that, under this confederation, each State had the right to decide for itself, and in its own tribunals, whom it would acknowledge as a free inhabitant of another State. The term "*free inhabitant*," in the generality of its terms, would certainly include one of the African race who had been manumitted. But no example, we think, can be found of his admission to all the privileges of citizenship in any State of the Union after these articles were formed, and while they continued in force. And, notwithstanding the generality of the words "free inhabitants," it is very clear that, according to their accepted meaning in that day, they did not include the African race, whether free or not, for the fifth section of the ninth article provides that Congress should have the power "to agree upon the number of land forces to be raised, and to make requisitions from each State for its quota in proportion to the number of *white* inhabitants in such State, which requisition should be binding."

Words could hardly have been used which more strongly mark the line of distinction between the citizen and the subject, the free and the subjugated races. The latter were not even counted when the inhabitants of a State were to be embodied in proportion to its numbers for the general defense. And it cannot for a moment be supposed that a class of persons thus separated and rejected from those who formed the sovereignty of the States were yet intended to be included under the words "free inhabitants," in the preceding article, to whom privileges and immunities were so carefully secured in every State.

But, although this clause of the Articles of Confederation is the same in principle with that inserted in the Constitution, yet the comprehensive word "*inhabitant*," which might be construed to include an emancipated slave, is omitted, and the privilege is confined to *citizens* of the State. And this alteration in words would hardly have been made unless a different meaning was intended to be conveyed, or a possible doubt removed. The just and fair inference is that, as this privilege was about to be placed under the protection of the general government, and the words expounded by its tribunals, and all power in relation to it taken from the State and its courts, it was deemed prudent to describe with precision and caution the persons to whom this high privilege was given, and the word *"citizen"* was on that account substituted for the words *"free inhabitant."* The word "citizen" excluded, and no doubt intended to exclude, foreigners who had not become citizens of some one of the States when the Constitution was adopted, and also every description of persons who were not fully recognized as citizens in the several States. This, upon any fair construction of the instruments to which we have referred, was evidently the object and purpose of this change of words.

To all this mass of proof we have still to add that Congress has repeatedly legislated upon the same construction of the Constitution that we have given. Three laws, two of which were passed almost immediately after the government went into operation, will be abundantly sufficient to show this. The first two are particularly worthy of notice, because many of the men who assisted in framing the Constitution, and took an active part in procuring its adoption, were then in the halls of legislation, and certainly understood what they meant when they used the words "people of the United States" and "citizen" in that well-considered instrument.

The first of these acts is the naturalization law, which was passed at the second session of the first Congress, March 26, 1790, and confines the right of becoming citizens "*to aliens being free white persons.*"

Now, the Constitution does not limit the power of Congress in this respect to white persons. And they may, if they think proper, authorize the naturalization of anyone, of any color, who was born under allegiance to another government. But the language of the law above quoted shows that citizenship at that time was perfectly understood to be confined to the white race, and that they alone constituted the sovereignty in the government.

Congress might, as we before said, have authorized the naturalization of Indians, because they were aliens and foreigners; but, in their then untutored and savage state, no one would have thought of admitting them as citizens in a civilized community. And, moreover, the atrocities they had but recently committed, when they were the allies of Great Britain in the Revolutionary War, were yet fresh in the recollection of the people of the United States, and they were even then guarding themselves against the threatened renewal of Indian hostilities. No one supposed then that any Indian would ask for, or was capable of enjoying, the privileges of an American citizen, and the word "white" was not used with any particular reference to them. Neither was it used with any reference to the African race imported into or born in this country, because Congress had no power to naturalize them, and, therefore, there was no necessity for using particular words to exclude them.

It would seem to have been used merely because it followed out the line of division which the Constitution has drawn between the citizen race who formed and held the government, and the African race, which they held in subjection and slavery, and governed at their own pleasure.

Another of the early laws of which we have spoken is the first militia law, which was passed in 1792, at the first session of the second Congress. The language of this law is equally plain and significant with the one just mentioned. It directs that every "free, able-bodied white male citizen" shall be enrolled in the militia. The word "white" is evidently used to exclude the African race, and the word "citizen" to exclude unnaturalized foreigners, the latter forming no part of the sovereignty, owing it no allegiance, and, therefore, under no obligation to defend it. The African race, however, born in the country did owe allegiance to the government whether they were slave or free; but it is repudiated and rejected from the duties and obligations of citizenship in marked language.

The third act to which we have alluded is even still more decisive. It was passed as late as 1813 (2 Stat. 809), and it provides "that, from and after the termination of the war in which the United States are now engaged with Great Britain, it shall not be lawful to employ on board of any public or private vessels of the United States any person or persons except citizens of the United States, *or* persons of color, natives of the United States.

Here the line of distinction is drawn in express words. Persons of color, in the judgment of Congress, were not included in the word "citizens," and they are described as another and different class of persons, and authorized to be employed if born in the United States.

And even as late as 1820 (chap. 104, sec. 8), in the charter to the city of Washington the corporation is authorized "to restrain and prohibit the nightly and other disorderly meetings of slaves, free negroes, and mulattoes," thus associating them together in its legislation, and, after prescribing the punishment that may be inflicted on the slaves, proceeds in the following words: "And to punish such free negroes and mulattoes by penalties not exceeding twenty dollars for any one offense; and, in case of the inability of any such free negro or mulatto to pay any such penalty and cost thereon, to cause him or her to be confined to labor for any time not exceeding six calendar months." And in a subsequent part of the same section the act authorizes the corporation "to prescribe the terms and conditions upon which free negroes and mulattoes may reside in the city."

This law, like the laws of the States, shows that this class of persons were governed by special legislation directed expressly to them, and always connected with provisions for the government of slaves, and not with those for the government of free white citizens. And after such a uniform course of legislation as we have stated, by the colonies, by the States, and by Congress, running through a period of more than a century, it would seem that to call persons thus marked and stigmatized, "citizens" of the United States, "fellow-citizens," a constituent part of the sovereignty, would be an abuse of terms, and not calculated to exalt the character of an American citizen in the eyes of other nations.

The conduct of the Executive Department of the government has been in perfect harmony upon this subject with this course of legislation. The question was brought officially before the late William Wirt, when he was the Attorney General of the United States, in 1821, and he decided that the words "citizens of the United States" were used in the acts of Congress in the same sense as in the Constitution, and that free persons of color were not citizens within the meaning of the Constitution and laws, and this opinion has been confirmed by that of the late Attorney General, Caleb Cushing, in a recent case, and acted upon by the Secretary of State, who refused to grant passports to them as "citizens of the United States."

But it is said that a person may be a citizen, and entitled to that character, although he does not possess all the rights which may belong to other citizens; as, for example, the right to vote or to hold particular offices, and that yet, when he goes into another State, he is entitled to be recognized there as a citizen, although the State may measure his rights by the rights which it allows to persons of a like

21

character or class resident in the State, and refuse to him the full rights of citizenship. This argument overlooks the language of the provision in the Constitution of which we are speaking.

Undoubtedly, a person may be a citizen, that is, a member of the community who form the sovereignty, although he exercises no share of the political power, and is incapacitated from holding particular offices. Women and minors, who form a part of the political family, cannot vote; and, when a proper qualification is required to vote or hold a particular office, those who have not the necessary qualification cannot vote or hold the office, yet they are citizens.

So, too, a person may be entitled to vote by the law of the State who is not a citizen even of the State itself. And in some of the States of the Union foreigners not naturalized are allowed to vote. And the State may give the right to free negroes and mulattoes, but that does not make them citizens of the State, and still less of the United States. And the provision in the Constitution giving privileges and immunities in other States does not apply to them.

Neither does it apply to a person who, being the citizen of a State, migrates to another State, for then he becomes subject to the laws of the State in which he lives, and he is no longer a citizen of the State from which he removed. And the State in which he resides may then unquestionably determine his *status* or condition, and place him among the class of persons who are not recognized as citizens, but belong to an inferior and subject race, and may deny him the privileges and immunities enjoyed by its citizens.

But so far as mere rights of person are concerned, the provision in question is confined to citizens of a State who are temporarily in another State without taking up their residence there. It gives them no political rights in the State as to voting or holding office, or in any other respect, for a citizen of one State has no right to participate in the government of another. But if he ranks as a citizen in the State to which he belongs, within the meaning of the Constitution of the United States, then, whenever he goes into another State, the Constitution clothes him, as to the rights of person, with all the privileges and immunities which belong to citizens of the State. And if persons of the African race are citizens of a State, and of the United States, they would be entitled to all of these privileges and immunities in every State, and the State could not restrict them, for they would hold these privileges and immunities under the paramount authority of the Federal Government, and its courts would be bound to maintain and enforce them, the Constitution and laws of the State to the contrary notwithstanding. And if the States could limit or restrict them, or place the party in an inferior grade, this clause of the Constitution would be unmeaning, and could have no operation, and would give no rights to the citizen when in another State. He would have none but what the State itself chose to allow him. This is evidently not the construction or meaning of the clause in question. It guarantees rights to the citizen, and the State cannot withhold them. And these rights are of a character, and would lead to consequences, which make it absolutely certain that the African race were not included under the name of citizens of a State, and were not in the contemplation of the framers of the Constitution when these privileges and immunities were provided for the protection of the citizen in other States.

The case of Legrand *vs.* Darnall (2 Peters. 664) has been referred to for the purpose of showing that this court has decided that the descendant of a slave may sue as a citizen in a court of the United States; but the case itself shows that the question did not arise and could not have arisen in the case.

It appears from the report that Darnall was born in Maryland, and was the son of a white man by one of his slaves, and his father executed certain instruments to manumit him, and devised to him some landed property in the State. This property Darnall afterwards sold to Legrand, the appellant, who gave his notes for the purchase money. But becoming afterwards apprehensive that the appellee had not been emancipated according to the laws of Maryland, he refused to pay the notes until he could be better satisfied as to Darnall's right to convey. Darnall, in the meantime, had taken up his residence in Pennsylvania, and brought suit on the notes, and recovered judgment in the Circuit Court for the district of Maryland.

The whole proceeding, as appears by the report, was an amicable one, Legrand being perfectly willing to pay the money if he could obtain a title, and Darnall not wishing him to pay unless he could make him a good one. In point of fact, the whole proceeding was under the direction of the counsel, who argued the case for the appellee, who was the mutual friend of the parties, and confided in by both of them, and whose only object was to have the rights of both parties established by judicial decision in the most speedy and least expensive manner.

Legrand, therefore, raised no objection to the jurisdiction of the court in the suit at law, because he was himself anxious to obtain the judgment of the court upon his title. Consequently, there was nothing in the record before the court to show that Darnall was of African descent, and the usual judgment and award of execution was entered. And Legrand thereupon filed his bill on the equity side of the Circuit Court, stating that Darnall was born a slave, and had not been legally emancipated, and could not, therefore, take the land devised to him, nor make Legrand a good title, and praying an injunction to restrain Darnall from proceeding to execution on the judgment, which was granted. Darnall answered, averring in his answer that he was a free man, and capable of conveying a good title. Testimony was taken on this point, and at the hearing the Circuit Court was of opinion that Darnall was a free man and his title good, and dissolved the injunction and dismissed the bill, and that decree was affirmed here upon the appeal of Legrand.

Now, it is difficult to imagine how any question about the citizenship of Darnall, or his right to sue in that character, can be supposed to have arisen or been decided in that case. The fact that he was of African descent was first brought before the court upon the bill in equity. The suit at law had then passed into judgment and award of execution, and the Circuit Court, as a court of law, had no longer any authority over it. It was a valid and legal judgment, which the court that rendered it had not the power to reverse or set aside. And unless it had jurisdiction as a court of equity to restrain him from using its process as a court of law, Darnall, if he thought proper, would have been at liberty to proceed on his judgment, and compel the payment of the money, although the allegations in the bill were true, and he was incapable of making a title. No other court could have enjoined him, for certainly no State equity court could interfere in that way with the judgment of a Circuit Court of the United States.

But the Circuit Court as a court of equity certainly had equity jurisdiction over its own judgment as a court of law, without regard to the character of the parties, and had not only the right, but it was its duty, no matter who were the parties in the judgment, to prevent them from proceeding to enforce it by execution, if the court was satisfied that the money was not justly and equitably due. The ability of Darnall to convey did not depend upon his citizenship, but upon his title to freedom. And if he was free, he could hold and convey property, by the laws of Maryland, although he was not a citizen, but if he was by law still a slave, he could not. It was, therefore, the duty of the court, sitting as a court of equity in the latter case, to prevent him from using its process, as a court of common law, to compel the payment of the purchase money when it was evident that the purchaser must lose the land. But if he was free, and could make a title, it was equally the duty of the court not to suffer Legrand to keep the land, and refuse the payment of the money, upon the ground that Darnall was incapable of suing or being sued as a citizen in a court of the United States. The character or citizenship of the parties had no connection with the question of jurisdiction, and the matter in dispute had no relation to the citizenship of Darnall. Nor is such a question alluded to in the opinion of the court.

Besides, we are by no means prepared to say that there are not many cases, civil as well as criminal, in which a Circuit Court of the United States may exercise jurisdiction, although one of the African race is a party; that broad question is not before the court. The question with which we are now dealing is whether a person of the African race can be a citizen of the United States, and become thereby entitled to a special privilege, by virtue of his title to that character, and which, under the Constitution, no one but a citizen can claim. It is manifest that the case of Legrand and Darnall has no bearing on that question, and can have no application to the case now before the court.

This case, however, strikingly illustrates the consequences that would follow the construction of the Constitution which would give the power contended for to a State. It would in effect give it also to an individual; for, if the father of young Darnall had manumitted him in his lifetime, and sent him to reside in a State which recognized him as a citizen, he might have visited and sojourned in Maryland when he pleased, and as long as he pleased, as a citizen of the United States, and the State officers and tribunals would be compelled, by the paramount authority of the Constitution, to receive him and treat him as one of its citizens, exempt from the laws and police of the State in relation to a person of that description, and allow him to enjoy all the rights and privileges of citizenship, without respect to the laws of Maryland, although such laws were deemed by it absolutely essential to its own safety.

The only two provisions which point to them and include them treat them as property, and make it the duty of the government to protect it. No other power, in relation to this race, is to be found in the Constitution, and, as it is a government of special delegated

powers, no authority beyond these two provisions can be constitutionally exercised. The government of the United States had no
right to interfere for any other purpose but that of protecting the
rights of the owner, leaving it altogether with the several States to
deal with this race, whether emancipated or not, as each State may
think justice, humanity, and the interests and safety of society require.
The States evidently intended to reserve this power exclusively to
themselves.

No one, we presume, supposes that any change in public opinion
or feeling in relation to this unfortunate race, in the civilized nations
of Europe or in this country, should induce the court to give to the
words of the Constitution a more liberal construction in their favor
than they were intended to bear when the instrument was framed and
adopted. Such an argument would be altogether inadmissible in
any tribunal called on to interpret it. If any of its provisions are
deemed unjust, there is a mode prescribed in the instrument itself by
which it may be amended; but, while it remains unaltered, it must be
construed now as it was understood at the time of its adoption. It is
not only the same in words, but the same in meaning, and delegates
the same powers to the government, and reserves and secures the
same rights and privileges to the citizen; and, as long as it continues
to exist in its present form, it speaks not only in the same words, but
with the same meaning and intent with which it spoke when it came
from the hands of its framers, and was voted on and adopted by the
people of the United States. Any other rule of construction would
abrogate the judicial character of this court, and make it the mere
reflex of the popular opinion or passion of the day. This court was
not created by the Constitution for such purposes. Higher and graver
trusts have been confided to it, and it must not falter in the path of
duty.

What the construction was at that time we think can hardly admit
of doubt. We have the language of the Declaration of Independence
and of the Articles of Confederation, in addition to the plain-words
of the Constitution itself; we have the legislation of the different
States before, about the time, and since the Constitution was adopted;
we have the legislation of Congress from the time of its adoption to a
recent period; and we have the constant and uniform action of the
Executive Department, all concurring together, and leading to the
same result. And if anything in relation to the construction of the
Constitution can be regarded as settled, it is that which we now give
to the word "citizen" and the word "people."

And upon a full and careful consideration of the subject, the court is of opinion that, upon the facts stated in the plea in abatement, Dred Scott was not a citizen of Missouri within the meaning of the Constitution of the United States, and not entitled as such to sue in its courts, and, consequently, that the Circuit Court had no jurisdiction of the case, and that the judgment on the plea in abatement is erroneous.

We are aware that doubts are entertained by some of the members of the court whether the plea in abatement is legally before the court upon this writ of error; but, if that plea is regarded as waived, or out of the case upon any other ground, yet the question as to the jurisdiction of the Circuit Court is presented on the face of the bill of exception itself, taken by the plaintiff at the trial; for he admits that he and his wife were born slaves, but endeavors to make out his title to freedom and citizenship by showing that they were taken by their owner to certain places, hereinafter mentioned, where slavery could not by law exist, and that they thereby became free, and upon their return to Missouri became citizens of that State.

Now, if the removal of which he speaks did not give them their freedom, then by his own admission he is still a slave; and, whatever opinions may be entertained in favor of the citizenship of a free person of the African race, no one supposes that a slave is a citizen of the State or of the United States. If, therefore, the acts done by his owner did not make them free persons, he is still a slave, and certainly incapable of suing in the character of a citizen.

The principle of law is too well settled to be disputed that a court can give no judgment for either party where it has no jurisdiction; and if, upon the showing of Scott himself, it appeared that he was still a slave, the case ought to have been dismissed, and the judgment against him and in favor of the defendant for costs is, like that on the plea in abatement, erroneous, and the suit ought to have been dismissed by the Circuit Court for want of jurisdiction in that court.

But, before we proceed to examine this part of the case, it may be proper to notice an objection taken to the judicial authority of this court to decide it; and it has been said that, as this court has decided against the jurisdiction of the Circuit Court on the plea in abatement, it has no right to examine any question presented by the exception, and that anything it may say upon that part of the case will be extra-judicial, and mere *obiter dicta*.

This is a manifest mistake. There can be no doubt as to the

jurisdiction of this court to revise the judgment of a Circuit Court, and to reverse it for any error apparent on the record, whether it be the error of giving judgment in a case over which it had no jurisdiction, or any other material error, and this, too, whether there is a plea in abatement or not.

The objection appears to have arisen from confounding writs of error to a State court with writs of error to a Circuit Court of the United States. Undoubtedly, upon a writ of error to a State court, unless the record shows a case that gives jurisdiction, the case must be dismissed for want of jurisdiction in *this court*. And if it is dismissed on that ground, we have no right to examine and decide upon any question presented by the bill of exceptions, or any other part of the record. But writs of error to a State court and to a Circuit Court of the United States are regulated by different laws, and stand upon entirely different principles. And in a writ of error to a Circuit Court of the United States, the whole record is before this court for examination and decision, and, if the sum in controversy is large enough to give jurisdiction, it is not only the right but it is the judicial duty of the court to examine the whole case as presented by the record; and, if it appears upon its face that any material error or errors have been committed by the court below, it is the duty of this court to reverse the judgment, and remand the case. And certainly an error in passing a judgment upon the merits in favor of either party, in a case which it was not authorized to try, and over which it had no jurisdiction, is as grave an error as a court can commit.

The plea in abatement is not a plea to the jurisdiction of this court, but to the jurisdiction of the Circuit Court. And it appears by the record before us that the Circuit Court committed an error in deciding that it had jurisdiction upon the facts in the case admitted by the pleadings. It is the duty of the appellate tribunal to correct this error, but that could not be done by dismissing the case for want of jurisdiction here, for that would leave the erroneous judgment in full force, and the injured party without remedy. And the appellate court, therefore, exercises the power for which alone appellate courts are constituted, by reversing the judgment of the court below for this error. It exercises its proper and appropriate jurisdiction over the judgment and proceedings of the Circuit Court, as they appear upon the record brought up by the writ of error.

The correction of one error in the court below does not deprive the appellate court of the power of examining further into the record, and correcting any other material errors which may have been committed by the inferior court. There is certainly no rule of law, nor any practice, nor any decision of a court, which even questions this power in the appellate tribunal. On the contrary, it is the daily practice of this court, and of all appellate courts where they reverse the judgment of an inferior court for error, to correct by its opinions whatever errors may appear on the record material to the case, and they have always held it to be their duty to do so where the silence of the court might lead to misconstruction or future controversy, and the point has been relied on by either side, and argued before the court.

In the case before us we have already decided that the Circuit Court erred in deciding that it had jurisdiction upon the facts admitted by the pleadings. And it appears that, in the further progress of the case, it acted upon the erroneous principle it had decided on the pleadings, and gave judgment for the defendant where, upon the facts admitted in the exception, it had no jurisdiction.

We are at a loss to understand upon what principle of law, applicable to appellate jurisdiction, it can be supposed that this court has not judicial authority to correct the last-mentioned error, because they had before corrected the former; or by what process of reasoning it can be made out that the error of an inferior court, in actually pronouncing judgment for one of the parties in a case in which it had no jurisdiction, cannot be looked into or corrected by this court, because we have decided a similar question presented in the pleadings. The last point is distinctly presented by the facts contained in the plaintiff's own bill of exceptions, which he himself brings here by this writ of error. It was the point which chiefly occupied the attention of the counsel on both sides in the argument, and the judgment which this court must render upon both errors is precisely the same. It must, in each of them, exercise jurisdiction over the judgment, and reverse it for the errors committed by the court below, and issue a mandate to the Circuit Court to conform its judgment to the opinion pronounced by this court, by dismissing the case for want of jurisdiction in the Circuit Court. This is the constant and invariable practice of this court, where it reverses a judgment for want of jurisdiction in the Circuit Court.

It can scarcely be necessary to pursue such a question further. The want of jurisdiction in the court below may appear on the record without any plea in abatement. This is familiarly the case where a court of chancery has exercised jurisdiction in a case where the plaintiff had a plain and adequate remedy at law, and it so appears by the transcript when brought here by appeal; so also, where it appears that a court of admiralty has exercised jurisdiction in a case belonging exclusively to a court of common law. In these cases there is no plea in abatement. And for the same reason, and upon the same principles, where the defect of jurisdiction is patent on the record, this court is bound to reverse the judgment, although the defendant has not pleaded in abatement to the jurisdiction of the inferior court.

The cases of Jackson *vs.* Ashton and of Capron *vs.* Van Noorden, to which we have referred in a previous part of this opinion, are directly in point. In the last-mentioned case, Capron brought an action against Van Noorden in a Circuit Court of the United States without showing, by the usual averments of citizenship, that the court had jurisdiction. There was no plea in abatement put in, and the parties went to trial upon the merits. The court gave judgment in favor of the defendant with costs. The plaintiff thereupon brought his writ of error, and this court reversed the judgment given in favor of the defendant, and remanded the case, with directions to dismiss it, because it did not appear by the transcript that the Circuit Court had jurisdiction.

The case before us still more strongly imposes upon this court the duty of examining whether the court below has not committed an error in taking jurisdiction and giving a judgment for costs in favor of the defendant; for in Capron *vs.* Van Noorden the judgment was reversed, because it did *not appear* that the parties were citizens of different States. They might or might not be. But in this case it *does appear* that the plaintiff was born a slave; and, if the facts upon which he relies have not made him free, then it appears affirmatively on the record that he is not a citizen, and, consequently, his suit against Sandford was not a suit between citizens of different States, and the court had no authority to pass any judgment between the parties. The suit ought, in this view of it, to have been dismissed by the Circuit Court, and its judgment in favor of Sandford is erroneous, and must be reversed.

It is true that the result either way, by dismissal or by a judgment for the defendant, makes very little, if any, difference in a pecuniary or personal point of view to either party. But the fact that the result would be very nearly the same to the parties in either form of judgment, would not justify this court in sanctioning an error in the judgment which is patent on the record, and which, if sanctioned, might be drawn into precedent, and lead to serious mischief and injustice in some future suit. We proceed, therefore, to inquire whether the facts relied on by the plaintiff entitled him to his freedom.

The case, as he himself states it, on the record brought here by his writ of error, is this:—

The plaintiff was a negro slave, belonging to Dr. Emerson, who was a surgeon in the army of the United States. In the year 1834 he took the plaintiff from the State of Missouri to the military post at Rock Island, in the State of Illinois, and held him there as a slave until the month of April or May, 1836. At the time last mentioned, said Dr. Emerson removed the plaintiff from said military post at Rock Island to the military post at Fort Snelling, situate on the west bank of the Mississippi River, in the territory known as Upper Louisiana, acquired by the United States of France, and situate north of the latitude of 36° 30′ north, and north of the State of Missouri. Said Dr. Emerson held the plaintiff in slavery at said Fort Snelling from said last-mentioned date until the year 1838.

In the year 1835 Harriet, who is named in the second count of the plaintiff's declaration, was the negro slave of Major Taliaferro, who belonged to the army of the United States. In that year, 1835, said Major Taliaferro took said Harriet to said Fort Snelling, a military post, situated as hereinbefore stated, and kept her there as a slave until the year 1836, and then sold and delivered her as a slave, at said Fort Snelling, unto the said Dr. Emerson hereinbefore named. Said Dr. Emerson held said Harriet in slavery at said Fort Snelling until the year 1838.

In the year 1836 the plaintiff and Harriet intermarried, at Fort Snelling, with the consent of Dr. Emerson, who then claimed to be their master and owner. Eliza and Lizzie, named in the third count of the plaintiff's declaration, are the fruit of that marriage. Eliza is about fourteen years old, and was born on board the steamboat *Gipsey*, north of the north line of the State of Missouri, and upon the river Mississippi. Lizzie is about seven years old, and was born in the State of Missouri, at the military post called Jefferson Barracks.

In the year 1838 said Dr. Emerson removed the plaintiff and said Harriet and their said daughter Eliza from said Fort Snelling to the State of Missouri, where they have ever since resided.

Before the commencement of this suit said Dr. Emerson sold and conveyed the plaintiff, and Harriet, Eliza, and Lizzie, to the defendant, as slaves, and the defendant has ever since claimed to hold them and each of them as slaves.

In considering this part of the controversy, two questions arise: (1) Was he, together with his family, free in Missouri by reason of the stay in the territory of the United States, hereinbefore mentioned? and (2) if they were not, is Scott himself free by reason of his removal to Rock Island, in the State of Illinois, as stated in the above admissions?

We proceed to examine the first question.

The act of Congress, upon which the plaintiff relies, declares that slavery and involuntary servitude, except as a punishment for crime, shall be forever prohibited in all that part of the territory ceded by France under the name of Louisiana, which lies north of 36° 30′ north latitude, and not included within the limits of Missouri. And the difficulty which meets us at the threshold of this part of the inquiry is whether Congress was authorized to pass this law under any of the powers granted to it by the Constitution; for, if the authority is not given by that instrument, it is the duty of this court to declare it void and inoperative, and incapable of conferring freedom upon anyone who is held as a slave under the laws of any one of the States.

The counsel for the plaintiff has laid much stress upon that article in the Constitution which confers on Congress the power "to dispose of and make all needful rules and regulations respecting the territory or other property belonging to the United States," but, in the judgment of the court, that provision has no bearing on the present controversy, and the power there given, whatever it may be, is confined, and was intended to be confined, to the territory which at that time belonged to, or was claimed by, the United States, and was within their boundaries as settled by the treaty with Great Britain, and can have no influence upon a territory afterwards acquired from a foreign government. It was a special provision for a known and particular territory, and to meet a present emergency, and nothing more.

A brief summary of the history of the times, as well as the careful and measured terms in which the article is framed, will show the correctness of this proposition.

It will be remembered that, from the commencement of the Revolutionary War, serious difficulties existed between the States in relation to the disposition of large and unsettled territories which were included in the chartered limits of some of the States. And some of the other States, and more especially Maryland, which had no unsettled lands, insisted that as the unoccupied lands, if wrested from Great Britain, would owe their preservation to the common purse and the common sword, the money arising from them ought to be applied in just proportion among the several States to pay the expenses of the war, and ought not to be appropriated to the use of the State in whose chartered limits they might happen to lie, to the exclusion of the other States, by whose combined efforts and common expense the territory was defended and preserved against the claim of the British Government.

These difficulties caused much uneasiness during the war, while the issue was in some degree doubtful, and the future boundaries of the United States yet to be defined by treaty, if we achieved our independence.

The majority of the Congress of the Confederation obviously concurred in opinion with the State of Maryland, and desired to obtain from the States which claimed it a cession of this territory, in order that Congress might raise money on this security to carry on the war. This appears by the resolution passed on the 6th of September, 1780, strongly urging the States to cede these lands to the United States, both for the sake of peace and union among themselves, and to maintain the public credit, and this was followed by the resolution of October 10, 1780, by which Congress pledged itself that, if the lands were ceded, as recommended by the resolution above mentioned, they should be disposed of for the common benefit of the United States, and be settled and formed into distinct republican States, which should become members of the Federal Union, and have the same rights of sovereignty and freedom and independence as other States.

But these difficulties became much more serious after peace took place, and the boundaries of the United States were established. Every State, at that time, felt severely the pressure of its war debt; but in Virginia, and some other States, there were large territories of unsettled lands, the sale of which would enable them to discharge their obligations without much inconvenience, while other States, which had no such resource, saw before them many years of heavy and burdensome taxation, and the latter insisted, for the reasons before stated, that these unsettled lands should be treated as the common property of the States, and the proceeds applied to their common benefit.

The letters from the statesmen of that day will show how much this controversy occupied their thoughts, and the dangers that were apprehended from it. It was the disturbing element of the time, and fears were entertained that it might dissolve the Confederation by which the States were then united.

These fears and dangers were, however, at once removed when the State of Virginia, in 1784, voluntarily ceded to the United States the immense tract of country lying northwest of the river Ohio, and which was within the acknowledged limits of the State. The only object of the State, in making this cession, was to put an end to the threatening and exciting controversy, and to enable the Congress of that time to dispose of the lands, and appropriate the proceeds as a common fund for the common benefit of the States. It was not ceded because it was inconvenient to the State to hold and govern it, nor from any expectation that it could be better or more conveniently governed by the United States.

The example of Virginia was soon afterwards followed by other States, and, at the time of the adoption of the Constitution, all of the States similarly situated had ceded their unappropriated lands, except North Carolina and Georgia. The main object for which these cessions were desired and made was on account of their money value, and to put an end to a dangerous controversy as to who was justly entitled to the proceeds when the lands should be sold. It is necessary to bring this part of the history of these cessions thus distinctly into view, because it will enable us the better to comprehend the phraseology of the article in the Constitution so often referred to in the argument.

Undoubtedly the powers of sovereignty and the eminent domain were ceded with the land. This was essential, in order to make it effectual and to accomplish its objects. But it must be remembered that, at that time, there was no government of the United States in existence with enumerated and limited powers. What was then called the United States were thirteen separate, sovereign, independent States, which had entered into a league or confederation for their mutual protection and advantage, and the Congress of the United States was composed of the representatives of these separate sovereignties, meeting together, as equals, to discuss and decide on certain measures which the States, by the Articles of Confederation, had agreed to submit to their decision. But this Confederation had none of the attributes of sovereignty in legislative, executive, or judicial power. It was little more than a congress of ambassadors, authorized to represent separate nations in matters in which they had a common concern.

It was this Congress that accepted the cession from Virginia. They had no power to accept it under the Articles of Confederation. But they had an undoubted right, as independent sovereignties, to accept any cession of territory for their common benefit, which all of them assented to; and it is equally clear that, as their common property, and having no superior to control them, they had the right to exercise absolute dominion over it, subject only to the restrictions which Virginia had imposed in her act of cession. There was, as we have said, no government of the United States then in existence with special enumerated and limited powers. The territory belonged to sovereignties who, subject to the limitations above mentioned, had a right to establish any form of government they pleased, by compact or treaty among themselves, and to regulate rights of person and rights of property in the territory, as they might deem proper. It was by a Congress, representing the authority of these several and separate sovereignties, and acting under their authority and command (but not from any authority derived from the Articles of Confederation), that the instrument usually called the ordinance of 1787 was adopted, regulating in much detail the principles and the laws by which this territory should be governed; and, among other provisions, slavery is prohibited in it. We do not question the power of the States, by agreement among themselves, to pass this ordinance, nor its obligatory force in the territory, while the confederation or league of the States in their separate sovereign character continued to exist.

This was the state of things when the Constitution of the United States was formed. The territory ceded by Virginia belonged to the several confederated States as common property, and they had united in establishing in it a system of government and jurisprudence, in order to prepare it for admission as States, according to the terms of the cession. They were about to dissolve this federative Union, and to surrender a portion of their independent sovereignty to a new government, which, for certain purposes, would make the people of the several States one people, and which was to be supreme and controlling within its sphere of action throughout the United States; but this government was to be carefully limited in its powers, and to exercise no authority beyond those expressly granted by the Constitution, or necessarily to be implied from the language of the instrument and the objects it was intended to accomplish; and, as this league of States would, upon the adoption of the new government, cease to have any power over the territory, and the ordinance they had agreed upon be incapable of execution, and a mere nullity, it was obvious that some provision was necessary to give the new government sufficient power to enable it to carry into effect the objects for which it was ceded, and the compacts and agreements which the States had made with each other in the exercise of their powers of sovereignty. It was necessary that the lands should be sold to pay the war debt; that a government and system of jurisprudence should be maintained in it, to protect the citizens of the United States who should migrate to the territory, in their rights of person and of property. It was also necessary that the new government about to be adopted should be authorized to maintain the claim of the United States to the unappropriated lands in North Carolina and Georgia, which had not then been ceded, but the cession of which was confidently anticipated upon some terms that would be arranged between the general government and these two States. And, moreover, there were many articles of value besides this property in land, such as arms, military stores, munitions, and ships of war, which were the common property of the States when acting in their independent characters as confederates, which neither the new government nor anyone else would have a right to take possession of or control without authority from them; and it was to place these things under the guardianship and protection of the new government, and to clothe it with the necessary powers, that the clause was inserted in the Constitution which gives Congress the power "to dispose of and make all needful rules and regulations respecting the territory or other property belonging to the United States." It was intended for a specific purpose, to provide for the things we have mentioned. It was to transfer to the new government the property then held in common by the States, and to give to that government power to apply it to the objects for which it had been destined by mutual agreement among the States before their league was dissolved. It applied only to the property which the States held in common at that time, and had no reference whatever to any territory or other property which the new sovereignty might afterwards itself acquire.

The language used in the clause, the arrangement and combination of the powers, and the somewhat unusual phraseology it uses, when it speaks of the political power to be exercised in the government of the territory, all indicate the design and meaning of the clause to be such as we have mentioned. It does not speak of *any* territory, nor of *territories*, but uses language which, according to its legitimate meaning, points to a particular thing. The power is given in relation only to *the* territory of the United States, that is, to a territory then in existence, and then known or claimed as the territory of the United States. It begins its enumeration of powers by that of disposing, in other words, making sale of the lands, or raising money from them, which, as we have already said, was the main object of the cession, and which is accordingly the first thing provided for in the article. It then gives the power which was necessarily associated with the disposition and sale of the lands, that is, the power of making needful rules and regulations respecting the territory. And whatever construction may now be given to these words, everyone, we think, must admit that they are not the words usually employed by statesmen in giving supreme power of legislation. They are certainly very unlike the words used in the power granted to legislate over territory which the new government might afterwards itself obtain by cession from a State, either for its seat of government, or for forts, magazines, arsenals, dock yards, and other needful buildings.

And the same power of making needful rules respecting the territory is, in precisely the same language, applied to the *other* property belonging to the United States, associating the power over the territory in this respect with the power over movable or personal property, that is, the ships, arms, and munitions of war, which then belonged in common to the State sovereignties. And it will hardly be said that this power, in relation to the last-mentioned objects, was deemed necessary to be thus specially given to the new government, in order to authorize it to make needful rules and regulations respecting the ships it might itself build, or arms and munitions of war it might itself manufacture or provide for the public service.

No one, it is believed, would think a moment of deriving the power of Congress to make needful rules and regulations in relation to property of this kind from this clause of the Constitution. Nor can it, upon any fair construction, be applied to any property but that which the new government was about to receive from the confederated States. And if this be true as to this property, it must be equally true and limited as to the territory which is so carefully and precisely coupled with it, and, like it, referred to as property in the

22

power granted. The concluding words of the clause appear to render this construction irresistible; for, after the provisions we have mentioned, it proceeds to say "that nothing in the Constitution shall be so construed as to prejudice any claims of the United States, or of any particular State."

Now, as we have before said, all of the States, except North Carolina and Georgia, had made the cession before the Constitution was adopted, according to the resolution of Congress of October 10, 1780. The claims of other States that the unappropriated lands in these two States should be applied to the common benefit, in like manner, was still insisted on, but refused by the States. And this member of the clause in question evidently applies to them, and can apply to nothing else. It was to exclude the conclusion that either party, by adopting the Constitution, would surrender what they deemed their rights. And when the latter provision relates so obviously to the unappropriated lands not yet ceded by the States, and the first clause makes provision for those then actually ceded, it is impossible, by any just rule of construction, to make the first provision general, and extend to all territories which the federal government might in any way afterwards acquire, when the latter is plainly and unequivocally confined to a particular territory, which was a part of the same controversy, and involved in the same dispute, and depended upon the same principles. The union of the two provisions in the same clause shows that they were kindred subjects, and that the whole clause is local, and relates only to lands within the limits of the United States which had been or then were claimed by a State, and that no other territory was in the mind of the framers of the Constitution, or intended to be embraced in it. Upon any other construction it would be impossible to account for the insertion of the last provision in the place where it is found, or to comprehend why, or for what object, it was associated with the previous provision.

This view of the subject is confirmed by the manner in which the present government of the United States dealt with the subject as soon as it came into existence. It must be borne in mind that the same States that formed the Confederation also formed and adopted the new government, to which so large a portion of their former sovereign powers were surrendered. It must also be borne in mind that all of these same States which had then ratified the new Constitution were represented in the Congress which passed the first law for the government of this territory; and many of the members of that legislative body had been deputies from the States under the Confederation, had united in adopting the ordinance of 1787, and assisted in forming the new government under which they were then acting, and whose powers they were then exercising. And it is obvious from the law they passed to carry into effect the principles and provisions of the ordinance, that they regarded it as the act of the States done in the exercise of their legitimate powers at the time. The new government took the territory as it found it, and in the condition in which it was transferred, and did not attempt to undo anything that had been done. And among the earliest laws passed under the new government is one reviving the ordinance of 1787, which had become inoperative and a nullity upon the adoption of the Constitution. This law introduces no new form or principles for its government, but recites in the preamble that it is passed in order that this ordinance may continue to have full effect, and proceeds to make only those rules and regulations which were needful to adapt it to the new government, into whose hands the power had fallen. It appears, therefore, that this Congress regarded the purposes to which the land in this territory was to be applied, and the form of government and principles of jurisprudence which were to prevail there, while it remained in the territorial state, as already determined on by the States when they had full power and right to make the decision, and that the new government, having received it in this condition, ought to carry substantially into effect the plans and principles which had been previously adopted by the States, and which no doubt the States anticipated when they surrendered their power to the new government. And if we regard this clause of the Constitution as pointing to this territory, with a territorial government already established in it, which had been ceded to the States for the purposes hereinbefore mentioned, every word in it is perfectly appropriate and easily understood, and the provisions it contains are in perfect harmony with the objects for which it was ceded, and with the condition of its government as a territory at the time. We can, then, easily account for the manner in which the first Congress legislated on the subject, and can also understand why this power over the territory was associated in the same clause with the other property of the United States, and subjected to the like power of making needful rules and regulations. But if the clause is construed in the expanded sense contended for, so as to embrace any territory acquired from a foreign nation by the present government, and to give it in such territory a despotic and unlimited power over persons and property, such as the confederated States might exercise in their common property, it would be difficult to account for the phraseology used, when compared with other grants of power, and also for its association with the other provisions in the same clause.

The Constitution has always been remarkable for the felicity of its arrangement of different subjects, and the perspicuity and appropriateness of the language it uses. But if this clause is construed to extend to territory acquired by the present government from a foreign nation, outside of the limits of any charter from the British Government to a colony, it would be difficult to say why it was deemed necessary to give the government the power to sell any vacant lands belonging to the sovereignty which might be found within it, and, if this was necessary, why the grant of this power should precede the power to legislate over it and establish a government there, and still more difficult to say why it was deemed necessary so specially and particularly to grant the power to make needful rules and regulations in relation to any personal or movable property it might acquire there, for the words "other property" necessarily, by every known rule of interpretation, must mean property of a different description from territory or land. And the difficulty would perhaps be insurmountable in endeavoring to account for the last member of the sentence, which provides that "nothing in this Constitution shall be so construed as to prejudice any claims of the United States or any particular State," or to say how any particular State could have claims in or to a territory ceded by a foreign government, or to account for associating this provision with the preceding provisions of the clause, with which it would appear to have no connection.

The words "needful rules and regulations" would seem, also, to have been cautiously used for some definite object. They are not the words usually employed by statesmen when they mean to give the powers of sovereignty, or to establish a government, or to authorize its establishment. Thus, in the law to renew and keep alive the ordinance of 1787, and to reëstablish the government, the title of the law is, "An act to provide for the government of the territory northwest of the river Ohio." And in the Constitution, when granting the power to legislate over the territory that may be selected for the seat of government independently of a State, it does not say Congress shall have power "to make all needful rules and regulations respecting the territory," but it declares that "Congress shall have power to exercise exclusive legislation in all cases whatsoever over such district (not exceeding ten miles square) as may, by cession of particular States and the acceptance of Congress, become the seat of the government of the United States."

The words "rules and regulations" are usually employed in the Constitution in speaking of some particular specified power which it means to confer on the government, and not, as we have seen, when granting general powers of legislation, as, for example, in the particular power to Congress "to make rules for the government and regulation of the land and naval forces, or the particular and specific power to regulate commerce," "to establish a uniform *rule* of naturalization," "to coin money and *regulate* the value thereof." And to construe the words of which we are speaking as a general and unlimited grant of sovereignty over territories which the government might afterwards acquire, is to use them in a sense and for a purpose for which they were not used in any other part of the instrument. But if confined to a particular territory, in which a government and laws had already been established, but which would require some alterations to adapt it to the new government, the words are peculiarly applicable and appropriate for that purpose.

The necessity of this special provision in relation to property, and the rights or property held in common by the confederated States, is illustrated by the first clause of the sixth article. This clause provides that "all debts, contracts, and engagements entered into before the adoption of this Constitution shall be as valid against the United States under this government as under the Confederation." This provision, like the one under consideration, was indispensable if the new Constitution was adopted. The new government was not a mere change in a dynasty, or in a form of government, leaving the nation or sovereignty the same, and clothed with all the rights and bound by all the obligations of the preceding one. But, when the present United States came into existence under the new government, it was a new political body, a new nation, then for the first time taking its place in the family of nations. It took nothing by succession from the Confederation. It had no right, as its successor, to any property or rights of property which it had acquired, and was not liable for any of its obligations. It was evidently viewed in this light by the framers of the Constitution. And as the several States would cease to exist in their former confederated character upon the adoption of the Constitution, and could not, in that character, again assemble together, special provisions were indispensable to transfer to the new government the property and rights which at that time they held in common, and at the same time to authorize it to lay taxes and appropriate money to pay the common debt which they had contracted, and this power could only be given to it by special provisions in the Constitution. The clause in relation to the territory and other property of the United States provided for the first, and the clause last quoted provided for the other. They have no connection with the general powers and rights of sovereignty delegated to the new government, and can neither enlarge nor diminish them. They were inserted to meet a present emergency, and not to regulate its powers as a government.

Indeed, a similar provision was deemed necessary in relation to treaties made by the Confederation, and when, in the clause next succeeding the one of which we have last spoken, it is declared that treaties shall be the supreme law of the land, care is taken to include, by express words, the treaties made by the confederated States. The language is, "And all treaties made, or which shall be made, under the authority of the United States shall be the supreme law of the land."

Whether, therefore, we take the particular clause in question by itself, or in connection with the other provisions of the Constitution, we think it clear that it applies only to the particular territory of which we have spoken, and cannot, by any just rule of interpretation, be extended to territory which the new government might afterwards obtain from a foreign nation. Consequently, the power which Congress may have lawfully exercised in this territory while it remained under a territorial government, and which may have been sanctioned by judicial decision, can furnish no justification and no argument to support a similar exercise of power over territory afterwards acquired by the federal government. We put aside, therefore, any argument drawn from precedents, showing the extent of the power which the general government exercised over slavery in this territory, as altogether inapplicable to the case before us.

But the case of the American and Ocean Insurance Companies *vs.* Canter (1 Pet. 511) has been quoted as establishing a different construction of this clause of the Constitution. There is, however, not the slightest conflict between the opinion now given and the one referred to, and it is only by taking a single sentence out of the latter and separating it from the context that even an appearance of conflict can be shown. We need not comment on such a mode of expounding an opinion of the court. Indeed, it most commonly misrepresents instead of expounding it. And this is fully exemplified in the case referred to, where, if one sentence is taken by itself, the opinion would appear to be in direct conflict with that now given; but the words which immediately follow that sentence show that the court did not mean to decide the point, but merely affirmed the power of Congress to establish a government in the territory, leaving it an open question whether that power was derived from this clause in the Constitution, or was to be necessarily inferred from a power to acquire territory by cession from a foreign government. The opinion on this part of the case is short, and we give the whole of it to show how well the selection of a single sentence is calculated to mislead.

The passage referred to is in page 542, in which the court, in speaking of the power of Congress to establish a territorial government in Florida until it should become a State, uses the following language:—

" In the meantime Florida continues to be a territory of the United States, governed by that clause of the Constitution which empowers Congress to make all needful rules and regulations respecting the territory or other property of the United States. Perhaps the power of governing a territory belonging to the United States which has not, by becoming a State, acquired the means of self-government, may result, necessarily, from the facts that it is not within the jurisdiction of any particular State, and is within the power and jurisdiction of the United States. The right to govern may be the inevitable consequence of the right to acquire territory. *Whichever may be the source from which the power is derived, the possession of it is unquestionable.*"

It is thus clear, from the whole opinion on this point, that the court did not mean to decide whether the power was derived from the clause in the Constitution or was the necessary consequence of the right to acquire. They do decide that the power in Congress is unquestionable, and in this we entirely concur, and nothing will be found in this opinion to the contrary. The power stands firmly on the latter alternative put by the court, that is, as "*the inevitable consequence of the right to acquire territory.*"

And what still more clearly demonstrates that the court did not mean to decide the question, but leave it open for future consideration, is the fact that the case was decided in the Circuit Court by Mr.

Justice Johnson, and his decision was affirmed by the Supreme Court. His opinion at the circuit is given in full in a note to the case, and in that opinion he states, in explicit terms, that the clause of the Constitution applies only to the territory then within the limits of the United States, and not to Florida, which had been acquired by cession from Spain. This part of his opinion will be found in the note in page 517 of the report. But he does not dissent from the opinion of the Supreme Court, thereby showing that, in his judgment, as well as that of the court, the case before them did not call for a decision on that particular point, and the court abstained from deciding it. And in a part of its opinion subsequent to the passage we have quoted, where the court speaks of the legislative power of Congress in Florida, they still speak with the same reserve. And in page 546, speaking of the power of Congress to authorize the territorial Legislature to establish courts there, the court say: "They are legislative courts, created in virtue of the general right of sovereignty which exists in the government, or in virtue of that clause which enables Congress to make all needful rules and regulations respecting the territory belonging to the United States."

It has been said that the construction given to this clause is new, and now for the first time brought forward. The case of which we are speaking, and which has been so much discussed, shows that the fact is otherwise. It shows that precisely the same question came before Mr. Justice Johnson at his circuit thirty years ago, was fully considered by him, and the same construction given to the clause in the Constitution which is now given by this court, and that, upon an appeal from his decision, the same question was brought before this court, but was not decided because a decision upon it was not required by the case before the court.

There is another sentence in the opinion which has been commented on which, even in a still more striking manner, shows how one may mislead or be misled by taking out a single sentence from the opinion of a court, and leaving out of view what precedes and follows. It is in page 546, near the close of the opinion, in which the court say: "In legislating for them [the territories of the United States] Congress exercises the combined powers of the general and of a State government." And it is said that, as a State may unquestionably prohibit slavery within its territory, this sentence decides in effect that Congress may do the same in a territory of the United States, exercising there the powers of a State as well as the power of the general government.

The examination of this passage in the case referred to would be more appropriate when we come to consider in another part of this opinion what power Congress can constitutionally exercise in a territory over the rights of person or rights of property of a citizen. But, as it is in the same case with the passage we have before commented on, we dispose of it now, as it will save the court from the necessity of referring again to the case. And it will be seen, upon reading the page on which this sentence is found, that it has no reference whatever to the power of Congress over rights of person or rights of property, but relates altogether to the power of establishing judicial tribunals to administer the laws constitutionally passed, and defining the jurisdiction they may exercise.

The law of Congress establishing a territorial government in Florida provided that the Legislature of the territory should have legislative powers over "all rightful objects of legislation, but no law should be valid which was inconsistent with the laws and Constitution of the United States."

Under the power thus conferred, the Legislature of Florida passed an act erecting a tribunal at Key West to decide cases of salvage. And in the case of which we are speaking, the question arose whether the territorial Legislature could be authorized by Congress to establish such a tribunal with such powers, and one of the parties, among other objections, insisted that Congress could not under the Constitution authorize the Legislature of the territory to establish such a tribunal with such powers, but that it must be established by Congress itself, and that a sale of cargo made under its order to pay salvors was void, as made without legal authority, and passed no property to the purchaser.

It is in disposing of this objection that the sentence relied on occurs, and the court begin that part of the opinion by stating with great precision the point which they are about to decide.

They say: "It has been contended that by the Constitution of the United States the judicial power of the United States extends to all cases of admiralty and maritime jurisdiction, and that the whole of the judicial power must be vested 'in one Supreme Court, and in such inferior courts as Congress shall from time to time ordain and establish.' Hence it has been argued that Congress cannot vest admiralty jurisdiction in courts created by the territorial Legislature."

And after thus clearly stating the point before them, and which they were about to decide, they proceed to show that these territorial tribunals were not constitutional courts, but merely legislative, and that Congress might, therefore, delegate the power to the territorial government to establish the court in question, and they conclude that part of the opinion in the following words: "Although admiralty jurisdiction can be exercised in the States in those courts only which are established in pursuance of the third article of the Constitution, the same limitation does not extend to the territories. In legislating for them Congress exercises the combined powers of the general and State governments."

Thus it will be seen by these quotations from the opinion that the court, after stating the question it was about to decide in a manner too plain to be misunderstood, proceeded to decide it, and announced, as the opinion of the tribunal, that in organizing the judicial department of the government in a territory of the United States, Congress does not act under, and is not restricted by, the third article in the Constitution, and is not bound in a territory to ordain and establish courts in which the judges hold their offices during good behavior, but may exercise the discretionary power which a State exercises in establishing its judicial department, and regulating the jurisdiction of its courts, and may authorize the territorial government to establish, or may itself establish, courts in which the judges hold their offices for a term of years only, and may vest in them judicial power upon subjects confided to the judiciary of the United States. And in doing this, Congress undoubtedly exercises the combined power of the general and a State government. It exercises the discretionary power of a State government in authorizing the establishment of a court in which the judges hold their appointments for a term of years only, and not during good behavior; and it exercises the power of the general government in investing that court with admiralty jurisdiction, over which the general government had exclusive jurisdiction in the territory.

No one, we presume, will question the correctness of that opinion, nor is there anything in conflict with it in the opinion now given. The point decided in the case cited has no relation to the question now before the court. That depended on the construction of the third article of the Constitution, in relation to the judiciary of the United States and the power which Congress might exercise in a territory in organizing the judicial department of the government. The case before us depends upon other and different provisions of the Constitution, altogether separate and apart from the one above mentioned. The question as to what courts Congress may ordain or establish in a territory to administer laws which the Constitution authorizes it to pass, and what laws it is or is not authorized by the Constitution to pass, are widely different—are regulated by different and separate articles of the Constitution, and stand upon different principles. And we are satisfied that no one who reads attentively the page in "Peters' Reports" to which we have referred, can suppose that the attention of the court was drawn for a moment to the question now before this court, or that it meant in that case to say that Congress had a right to prohibit a citizen of the United States from taking any property which he lawfully held into a territory of the United States.

This brings us to examine by what provision of the Constitution the present federal government, under its delegated and restricted powers, is authorized to acquire territory outside of the original limits of the United States, and what powers it may exercise therein over the person or property of a citizen of the United States, while it remains a territory, and until it shall be admitted as one of the States of the Union.

There is certainly no power given by the Constitution to the federal government to establish or maintain colonies bordering on the United States or at a distance, to be ruled and governed at its own pleasure, nor to enlarge its territorial limits in any way, except by the admission of new States. That power is plainly given; and, if a new State is admitted, it needs no further legislation by Congress, because the Constitution itself defines the relative rights and powers and duties of the State, and the citizens of the State, and the federal government. But no power is given to acquire a territory to be held and governed permanently in that character.

And, indeed, the power exercised by Congress to acquire territory and establish a government there, according to its own unlimited discretion, was viewed with great jealousy by the leading statesmen of the day. And in the *Federalist* (No. 38), written by Mr. Madison, he speaks of the acquisition of the Northwestern Territory by the confederated States, by the cession from Virginia, and the establishment of a government there, as an exercise of power not warranted by the Articles of Confederation, and dangerous to the liberties of the people, and he urges the adoption of the Constitution as a security and safeguard against such an exercise of power.

We do not mean, however, to question the power of Congress in this respect.   The power to expand the territory of the United States by the admission of new States is plainly given, and, in the construction of this power by all the departments of the government, it has been held to authorize the acquisition of territory not fit for admission at the time, but to be admitted as soon as its population and situation would entitle it to admission. It is acquired to become a State, and not to be held as a colony and governed by Congress with absolute authority; and, as the propriety of admitting a new State is committed to the sound discretion of Congress, the power to acquire territory for that purpose, to be held by the United States until it is in a suitable condition to become a State upon an equal footing with the other States, must rest upon the same discretion.   It is a question for the political department of the government, and not the judicial, and, whatever the political department of the government shall recognize as within the limits of the United States, the judicial department is also bound to recognize, and to administer in it the laws of the United States, so far as they apply, and to maintain in the territory the authority and rights of the government, and also the personal rights and rights of property of individual citizens, as secured by the Constitution.   All we mean to say on this point is that, as there is no express regulation in the Constitution defining the power which the general government may exercise over the person or property of a citizen in a territory thus acquired, the court must necessarily look to the provisions and principles of the Constitution, and its distribution of powers, for the rules and principles by which its decision must be governed.

Taking this rule to guide us, it may be safely assumed that citizens of the United States who migrate to a territory belonging to the people of the United States, cannot be ruled as mere colonists, dependent upon the will of the general government, and to be governed by any laws it may think proper to impose.   The principle upon which our governments rest, and upon which alone they continue to exist, is the union of States, sovereign and independent within their own limits in their internal and domestic concerns, and bound together as one people by a general government, possessing certain enumerated and restricted powers, delegated to it by the people of the several States, and exercising supreme authority within the scope of the powers granted to it throughout the dominion of the United States. A power, therefore, in the general government to obtain and hold colonies and dependent territories, over which they might legislate without restriction, would be inconsistent with its own existence in its present form. Whatever it acquires it acquires for the benefit of the people of the several States who created it. It is their trustee, acting for them, and charged with the duty of promoting the interests of the whole people of the Union in the exercise of the powers specifically granted.

At the time when the territory in question was obtained by cession from France, it contained no population fit to be associated together and admitted as a State, and it, therefore, was absolutely necessary to hold possession of it, as a territory belonging to the United States, until it was settled and inhabited by a civilized community capable of self-government, and in a condition to be admitted on equal terms with the other States as a member of the Union. But, as we have before said, it was acquired by the general government, as the representative and trustee of the people of the United States, and it must, therefore, be held in that character for their common and equal benefit, for it was the people of the several States, acting through their agent and representative, the federal government, who in fact acquired the territory in question, and the government holds it for their common use until it shall be associated with the other States as a member of the Union.

But, until that time arrives, it is undoubtedly necessary that some government should be established, in order to organize society, and to protect the inhabitants in their persons and property; and, as the people of the United States could act in this matter only through the government which represented them, and through which they spoke and acted when the territory was obtained, it was not only within the scope of its powers but it was its duty to pass such laws and establish such a government as would enable those by whose authority they acted to reap the advantages anticipated from its acquisition, and to gather there a population which would enable it to assume the position to which it was destined among the States of the Union. The power to acquire necessarily carries with it the power to preserve and apply to the purposes for which it was acquired. The form of government to be established necessarily rested in the discretion of Congress. It was their duty to establish the one that would be best suited for the protection and security of the citizens of the United States, and other inhabitants who might be authorized to take up their abode there, and that must always depend upon the existing condition of the territory, as to the number and character of its inhabitants, and their situation in the territory. In some cases a government, consisting of persons appointed by the federal government, would best subserve the interests of the territory when the inhabitants were few and scattered and new to one another. In other instances it would be more advisable to commit the powers of self-government to the people who had settled in the territory, as being the most competent to determine what was best for their own interests. But some form of civil authority would be absolutely necessary to organize and preserve civilized society, and prepare it to become a State, and what is the best form must always depend on the condition of the territory at the time, and the choice of the mode must depend upon the exercise of a discretionary power by Congress, acting within the scope of its constitutional authority, and not infringing upon the rights of person or rights of property of the citizen who might go there to reside, or for any other lawful purpose. It was acquired by the exercise of this discretion, and it must be held and governed in like manner until it is fitted to be a State.

But the power of Congress over the person or property of a citizen can never be a mere discretionary power under our Constitution and form of government. The powers of the government and the rights and privileges of the citizen are regulated and plainly defined by the Constitution itself. And when the territory becomes a part of the United States, the federal government enters into possession in the character impressed upon it by those who created it. It enters upon it with its powers over the citizen strictly defined, and limited by the Constitution, from which it derives its own existence, and by virtue of which alone it continues to exist and act as a government and sovereignty. It has no power of any kind beyond it, and it cannot, when it enters a territory of the United States, put off its character, and assume discretionary or despotic powers which the Constitution has denied to it. It cannot create for itself a new character separated from the citizens of the United States, and the duties it owes them under the provisions of the Constitution. The territory being a part of the United States, the government and the citizen both enter it under the authority of the Constitution, with their respective rights defined and marked out, and the federal government can exercise no power over his person or property beyond what that instrument confers, nor lawfully deny any right which it has reserved.

A reference to a few of the provisions of the Constitution will illustrate this proposition.

For example, no one, we presume, will contend that Congress can make any law in a territory respecting the establishment of religion, or the free exercise thereof, or abridging the freedom of speech or of the press, or the right of the people of the territory peaceably to assemble, and to petition the government for the redress of grievances.

Nor can Congress deny to the people the right to keep and bear arms, nor the right to trial by jury, nor compel anyone to be a witness against himself in a criminal proceeding.

These powers, and others, in relation to rights of person, which it is not necessary here to enumerate, are, in express and positive terms, denied to the general government, and the rights of private property have been guarded with equal care. Thus the rights of property are united with the rights of person, and placed on the same ground by the fifth amendment to the Constitution, which provides that no person shall be deprived of life, liberty, and property without due process of law. And an act of Congress which deprives a citizen of the United States of his liberty or property merely because he came himself or brought his property into a particular territory of the United States, and who had committed no offense against the laws, could hardly be dignified with the name of due process of law.

So, too, it will hardly be contended that Congress could by law quarter a soldier in a house in a territory without the consent of the owner in time of peace nor in time of war, but in a manner prescribed by law. Nor could they by law forfeit the property of a citizen in a territory who was convicted of treason for a longer period than the life of the person convicted, nor take private property for public use without just compensation.

The powers over person and property of which we speak are not only not granted to Congress, but are in express terms denied, and they are forbidden to exercise them. And this prohibition is not confined to the States, but the words are general, and extend to the whole territory over which the Constitution gives it power to legislate, including those portions of it remaining under territorial government, as well as that covered by States. It is a total absence of power everywhere within the dominion of the United States, and places the citizens of a territory, so far as these rights are concerned, on the same footing with citizens of the States, and guards them as firmly and plainly against any inroads which the general government might attempt under the plea of implied or incidental powers. And if Congress itself cannot do this, if it is beyond the powers conferred on the federal government, it will be admitted, we presume, that it could not authorize a territorial government to exercise them. It could confer no power on any local government, established by its authority, to violate the provisions of the Constitution.

It seems, however, to be supposed that there is a difference between property in a slave and other property, and that different rules may be applied to it in expounding the Constitution of the United States. And the laws and usages of nations, and the writings of eminent jurists upon the relation of master and slave and their mutual rights and duties, and the powers which governments may exercise over it, have been dwelt upon in the argument.

But in considering the question before us, it must be borne in mind that there is no law of nations standing between the people of the United States and their government, and interfering with their relation to each other. The powers of the government, and the rights of the citizen under it, are positive and practical regulations plainly written down. The people of the United States have delegated to it certain enumerated powers, and forbidden it to exercise others. It has no power over the person or property of a citizen but what the citizens of the United States have granted. And no laws or usages of other nations, or reasoning of statesmen or jurists upon the relations of master and slave, can enlarge the powers of the government, or take from the citizens the rights they have reserved. And if the Constitution recognizes the right of property of the master in a slave, and makes no distinction between that description of property and other property owned by a citizen, no tribunal, acting under the authority of the United States, whether it be legislative, executive, or judicial, has a right to draw such a distinction, or deny to it the benefit of the provisions and guarantees which have been provided for the protection of private property against the encroachments of the government.

Now, as we have already said in an earlier part of this opinion, upon a different point, *the right of property in a slave is distinctly and expressly affirmed in the Constitution.* The right to traffic in it, like an ordinary article of merchandise and property, was guaranteed to the citizens of the United States, in every State that might desire it, for twenty years, and the government in express terms is pledged to protect it in all future time, if the slave escapes from his owner. This is done in plain words—too plain to be misunderstood. And no word can be found in the Constitution which gives Congress a greater power over slave property, or which entitles property of that kind to less protection than property of any other description. The only power conferred is the power coupled with the duty of guarding and protecting the owner in his rights.

Upon these considerations it is the opinion of the court that the act of Congress which prohibited a citizen from holding and owning property of this kind in the territory of the United States north of the line therein mentioned, is not warranted by the Constitution, and is, therefore, void, and that neither Dred Scott himself, nor any of his family, were made free by being carried into this territory, even if they had been carried there by the owner, with the intention of becoming a permanent resident.

We have so far examined the case, as it stands under the Constitution of the United States, and the powers thereby delegated to the federal government.

But there is another point in the case which depends on State power and State law, and it is contended, on the part of the plaintiff, that he is made free by being taken to Rock Island, in the State of Illinois, independently of his residence in the territory of the United States, and, being so made free, he was not again reduced to a state of slavery by being brought back to Missouri.

Our notice of this part of the case will be very brief, for the principle on which it depends was decided in this court, upon much consideration, in the case of Strader *et al. vs.* Graham, reported in 10th Howard 82. In that case the slaves had been taken from Kentucky to Ohio, with the consent of the owner, and afterwards brought back to Kentucky. And this court held that their *status*, or condition, as free or slave, depended upon the laws of Kentucky, when they were brought back into that State, and not of Ohio, and that this court had no jurisdiction to revise the judgment of a State court upon its own laws. This was the point directly before the court, and the decision that this court had not jurisdiction turned upon it, as will be seen by the report of the case.

So in this case. As Scott was a slave when taken into the State of Illinois by his owner, and was there held as such, and brought back in that character, his *status*, as free or slave, depended on the laws of Missouri, and not of Illinois.

It has, however, been urged in the argument that by the laws of Missouri he was free on his return, and that this case, therefore, cannot be governed by the case of Strader *et al. vs.* Graham, where it appeared, by the laws of Kentucky, that the plaint.ffs continued to be slaves on their return from Ohio. But, whatever doubts or opinions may at one time have been entertained upon this subject, we are satisfied, upon a careful examination of all the cases decided in the State courts of Missouri referred to, that it is now firmly settled by the decisions of the highest court in the State that Scott and his family upon their return were not free, but were, by the laws of Missouri, the property of the defendant, and that the Circuit Court of the United States had no jurisdiction when, by the laws of the State, the plaintiff was a slave and not a citizen.

Moreover, the plaintiff, it appears, brought a similar action against the defendant in the State court of Missouri, claiming the freedom of himself and his family upon the same grounds and the same evidence upon which he relies in the case before the court. The case was carried before the Supreme Court of the State, was fully argued there, and that court decided that neither the plaintiff nor his family were entitled to freedom, and were still the slaves of the defendant, and reversed the judgment of the inferior State court, which had given a different decision. If the plaintiff supposed that this judgment of the Supreme Court of the State was erroneous, and that this court had jurisdiction to revise and reverse it, the only mode by which he could legally bring it before this court was by writ of error directed to the Supreme Court of the State, requiring it to transmit the record to this court. If this had been done, it is too plain for argument that the writ must have been dismissed for want of jurisdiction in this court. The case of Strader and others *vs.* Graham is directly in point, and, indeed, independent of any decision, the language of the 25th section of the act of 1789 is too clear and precise to admit of controversy.

But the plaintiff did not pursue the mode prescribed by law for bringing the judgment of a State court before this court for revision, but suffered the case to be remanded to the inferior State court, where it is still continued, and is, by agreement of parties, to await the judgment of this court on the point. All of this appears on the record before us, and by the printed report of the case.

And while the case is yet open and pending in the inferior State court, the plaintiff goes into the Circuit Court of the United States, upon the same case and the same evidence, and against the same party, and proceeds to judgment, and then brings here the same case from the Circuit Court, which the law would not have permitted him to bring directly from the State court. And if this court takes jurisdiction in this form, the result, so far as the rights of the respective parties are concerned, is in every respect substantially the same as if it had in open violation of law entertained jurisdiction over the judgment of the State court upon a writ of error, and revised and reversed its judgment upon the ground that its opinion upon the question of law was erroneous. It would ill become this court to sanction such an attempt to evade the law, or to exercise an appellate power in this circuitous way, which it is forbidden to exercise in the direct and regular and invariable forms of judicial proceedings.

Upon the whole, therefore, it is the judgment of this court that it appears by the record before us that the plaintiff in error is not a citizen of Missouri, in the sense in which that word is used in the Constitution, and that the Circuit Court of the United States, for that reason, had no jurisdiction in the case, and could give no judgment in it. Its judgment for the defendant must, consequently, be reversed, and a mandate issued directing the suit to be dismissed for want of jurisdiction.

EXTRACT FROM

JUSTICE McLEAN'S DISSENTING OPINION.

I will now consider the relation which the federal government bears to slavery in the States:—

Slavery is emphatically a State institution. In the ninth section of the first article of the Constitution it is provided "that the migration or importation of such persons as any of the States now existing shall think proper to admit shall not be prohibited by the Congress prior to the year 1808, but a tax or duty may be imposed on such importation, not exceeding ten dollars for each person."

In the convention it was proposed by a committee of eleven to limit the importation of slaves to the year 1800, when Mr. Pinckney moved to extend the time to the year 1808. This motion was carried, New Hampshire, Massachusetts, Connecticut, Maryland, North Carolina, South Carolina, and Georgia voting in the affirmative, and New Jersey, Pennsylvania, and Virginia in the negative. In opposition to the motion Mr. Madison said: "Twenty years will produce all the mischief that can be apprehended from the liberty to import slaves. So long a term will be more dishonorable to the American character than to say nothing about it in the Constitution."—*Madison Papers*.

The provision in regard to the slave trade shows clearly that Congress considered slavery a State institution, to be continued and regulated by its individual sovereignty, and to conciliate that interest the slave trade was continued twenty years, not as a general measure, but for the " benefit of such States as shall think proper to encourage it."

In the case of Groves *vs.* Slaughter (15 Peters 449; 14 Curtis 137) Messrs. Clay and Webster contended that, under the commercial power, Congress had a right to regulate the slave trade among the several States, but the court held that Congress had no power to interfere with slavery as it exists in the States, or to regulate what is called the slave trade among them. If this trade were subject to the commercial power, it would follow that Congress could abolish or establish slavery in every State of the Union.

The only connection which the federal government holds with slaves in a State arises from that provision of the Constitution which declares that " no person held to service or labor in one State, under the laws thereof, escaping into another, shall, in consequence of any law or regulation therein, be discharged from such service or labor, but shall be delivered up on claim of the party to whom such service or labor may be due."

This being a fundamental law of the federal government, it rests mainly for its execution, as has been held, on the judicial power of the Union, and, so far as the rendition of fugitives from labor has become a subject of judicial action, the federal obligation has been faithfully discharged.

In the formation of the Federal Constitution care was taken to confer no power on the federal government to interfere with this institution in the States. In the provision respecting the slave trade, in fixing the ratio of representation and providing for the reclamation of fugitives from labor, slaves were referred to as persons, and in no other respect are they considered in the Constitution.

We need not refer to the mercenary spirit which introduced the infamous traffic in slaves to show the degradation of negro slavery in our country. This system was imposed upon our colonial settlements by the mother country, and it is due to truth to say that the commercial colonies and States were chiefly engaged in the traffic.

But we know, as a historical fact, that James Madison, that great and good man, a leading member in the federal convention, was solicitous to guard the language of that instrument so as not to convey the idea that there could be property in man.

I prefer the lights of Madison, Hamilton, and Jay, as a means of construing the Constitution in all its bearings, rather than to look behind that period into a traffic which is now declared to be piracy, and punished with death by Christian nations. I do not like to draw the sources of our domestic relations from so dark a ground. Our independence was a great epoch in the history of freedom; and, while I admit the government was not made especially for the colored race, yet many of them were citizens of the New England States, and exercised the rights of suffrage when the Constitution was adopted, and it was not doubted by any intelligent person that its tendencies would greatly ameliorate their condition.

Many of the States, on the adoption of the Constitution, or shortly afterward, took measures to abolish slavery within their respective jurisdictions, and it is a well-known fact that a belief was cherished by the leading men, South as well as North, that the institution of slavery would gradually decline, until it would become extinct. The increased value of slave labor, in the culture of cotton and sugar, prevented the realization of this expectation. Like all other communities and States, the South were influenced by what they considered to be their own interests.

But if we are to turn our attention to the dark ages of the world, why confine our view to colored slavery? On the same principles white men were made slaves. All slavery has its origin in power, and is against right.

EXTRACT FROM

JUSTICE CURTIS'S DISSENTING OPINION.

Under the allegations contained in this plea, and admitted by the demurrer, the question is whether any person of African descent, whose ancestors were sold as slaves in the United States, can be a citizen of the United States. If any such person can be a citizen, this plaintiff has the right to the judgment of the court that he is so, for no cause is shown by the plea why he is not so, except his descent and the slavery of his ancestors.

The first section of the second article of the Constitution uses the language, "a citizen of the United States at the time of the adoption of the Constitution." One mode of approaching this question is to inquire who were citizens of the United States at the time of the adoption of the Constitution.

Citizens of the United States at the time of the adoption of the Constitution can have been no other than citizens of the United States under the Confederation. By the Articles of Confederation a government was organized, the style whereof was, "The United States of America." This government was in existence when the Constitution was framed and proposed for adoption, and was to be superseded by the new government of the United States of America, organized under the Constitution. When, therefore, the Constitution speaks of citizenship of the United States existing at the time of the adoption of the Constitution, it must necessarily refer to citizenship under the government which existed prior to and at the time of such adoption.

Without going into any question concerning the powers of the Confederation to govern the territory of the United States out of the limits of the States, and, consequently, to sustain the relation of government and citizen in respect to the inhabitants of such territory, it may safely be said that the citizens of the several States were citizens of the United States under the Confederation.

That government was simply a confederacy of the several States, possessing a few defined powers over subjects of general concern, each State retaining every power, jurisdiction, and right not expressly delegated to the United States in Congress assembled. And no power was thus delegated to the government of the Confederation, to act on any question of citizenship, or to make any rules in respect thereto. The whole matter was left to stand upon the action of the several States, and to the natural consequence of such action, that the citizens of each State should be citizens of that Confederacy into which that State had entered, the style whereof was, "The United States of America."

To determine whether any free persons descended from Africans held in slavery were citizens of the United States under the Confederation, and, consequently, at the time of the adoption of the Constitution of the United States, it is only necessary to know whether any such persons were citizens of either of the States under the Confederation at the time of the adoption of the Constitution.

Of this there can be no doubt. At the time of the ratification of the Articles of Confederation, all free native-born inhabitants of the States of New Hampshire, Massachusetts, New York, New Jersey, and North Carolina, though descended from African slaves, were not only citizens of those States, but such of them as had the other necessary qualifications possessed the franchise of electors on equal terms with other citizens.

The Supreme Court of North Carolina, in the case of the State *vs.* Manuel (4 Dev. and Bat. 20), has declared the law of that State on this subject, in terms which I believe to be as sound law in the other States I have enumerated, as it was in North Carolina.

"According to the laws of this State," says Judge Gaston, in delivering the opinion of the court, "all human beings within it who are not slaves fall within one of two classes. Whatever distinctions may have existed in the Roman laws between citizens and free inhabitants, they are unknown to our institutions. Before our Revolution all free persons born within the dominions of the king of Great Britain, whatever their color or complexion, were native-born British subjects. Those born out of his allegiance were aliens. Slavery did not exist in England, but it did in the British colonies. Slaves were not in legal parlance persons, but property. The moment the incapacity, the disqualification of slavery, was removed, they became persons, and were then either British subjects, or not British subjects, according as they were or were not born within the allegiance of the British king. Upon the Revolution no other change took place in the laws of North Carolina than was consequent on the transition from a colony dependent on a European king to a free and sovereign State. Slaves remained slaves. British subjects in North Carolina became North Carolina freemen. Foreigners, until made members of the State, remained aliens. Slaves manumitted here became freemen, and, therefore, if born within North Carolina, are citizens of North Carolina, and all free persons born within the State are born citizens of the State. The Constitution extended the elective franchise to every freeman who had arrived at the age of twenty-one, and paid a public tax, and it is a matter of universal notoriety that, under it, free persons, without regard to color, claimed and exercised the franchise until it was taken from free men of color a few years since by our amended Constitution."

In the State *vs.* Newcomb (5 Iredell's R. 253), decided in 1844, the same court referred to this case of the State *vs.* Manuel, and said: "That case underwent a very laborious investigation, both by the bar and the bench. The case was brought here by appeal, and was felt to be one of great importance in principle. It was considered with an anxiety and care worthy of the principle involved, and which give it a controlling influence and authority on all questions of a similar character."

An argument from speculative premises, however well chosen, that the then state of opinion in the commonwealth of Massachusetts was not consistent with the natural rights of people of color who were born on that soil, and that they were not, by the constitution of 1780 of that State, admitted to the condition of citizens, would be received with surprise by the people of that State who know their own political history. It is true, beyond all controversy, that persons of color descended from African slaves were by that constitution made citizens of the State, and such of them as have had the necessary qualifications have held and exercised the elective franchise as citizens from that time to the present. (See Com. *vs.* Aves, 18 Pick. R. 210.)

The constitution of New Hampshire conferred the elective franchise upon "every inhabitant of the State having the necessary qualifications," of which color or descent was not one.

The constitution of New York gave the right to vote to "every male inhabitant who shall have resided," etc., making no discrimination between free colored persons and others. (See Con. of N. Y., Art. 2, Rev. Stats. of N. Y., vol. 1, p. 126.)

That of New Jersey, to "all inhabitants of this colony, of full age, who are worth £50 proclamation money, clear estate."

New York, by its Constitution of 1820, required colored persons to have some qualifications as prerequisites for voting which white persons need not possess. And New Jersey, by its present Constitution, restricts the right to vote to white male citizens. But these changes can have no other effect upon the present inquiry except to show that, before they were made, no such restrictions existed, and colored, in common with white persons, were not only citizens of those States, but entitled to the elective franchise on the same qualifications as white persons, as they now are in New Hampshire and Massachusetts. I shall not enter into an examination of the existing opinions of that period respecting the African race, nor into any discussion concerning the meaning of those who asserted, in the Declaration of Independence, that all men are created equal; that they are endowed by their Creator with certain inalienable rights; that among these are life, liberty, and the pursuit of happiness. My own opinion is that a calm comparison of these assertions of universal abstract truths, and of their own individual opinions and acts, would not leave these men under any reproach of inconsistency; that the great truths they asserted on that solemn occasion they were ready and anxious to make effectual wherever a necessary regard to circumstances, which no statesman can disregard without producing more evil than good, would allow; and that it would not be just to them, nor true in itself, to allege that they intended to say that the Creator of all men had endowed the white race exclusively with the great natural rights which the Declaration of Independence asserts. But this is not the place to vindicate their memory. As I conceive, we should deal here, not with such disputes, if there can be a dispute concerning this subject, but with those substantial facts evinced by the written constitutions of States, and by the notorious practice under them. And they show, in a manner which no argument can obscure, that in some of the original thirteen States free colored persons, before and at the time of the formation of the Constitution, were citizens of those States.

The fourth of the fundamental articles of the Confederation was as follows: "The free inhabitants of each of these States, paupers, vagabonds, and fugitives from justice excepted, shall be entitled to all the privileges and immunities of free citizens in the several States."

The fact that free persons of color were citizens of some of the several States, and the consequence, that this fourth article of the Confederation would have the effect to confer on such persons the privileges and immunities of general citizenship, were not only known to those who framed and adopted those articles, but the evidence is decisive that the fourth article was intended to have that effect, and that more restricted language, which would have excluded such persons, was deliberately and purposely rejected.

On the 25th of June, 1778, the Articles of Confederation being under consideration by the Congress, the delegates from South Carolina moved to amend this fourth article, by inserting after the word "free," and before the word "inhabitants," the word "white," so that the privileges and immunities of general citizenship would be secured only to white persons. Two States voted for the amendment, eight States against it, and the vote of one State was divided. The language of the article stood unchanged, and both by its terms of inclusion, "free inhabitants," and the strong implication from its terms of exclusion, "paupers, vagabonds, and fugitives from justice," who alone were excepted, it is clear that under the Confederation, and at the time of the adoption of the Constitution, free colored persons of African descent might be, and, by reason of their citizenship in certain States, were entitled to the privileges and immunities of general citizenship of the United States.

Did the Constitution of the United States deprive them or their descendants of citizenship?

That Constitution was ordained and established by the people of the United States, through the action, in each State, of those persons who were qualified by its laws to act thereon, in behalf of themselves and all other citizens of that State. In some of the States, as we have seen, colored persons were among those qualified by law to act on this subject. These colored persons were not only included in the body of "the people of the United States," by whom the Constitution was ordained and established, but in at least five of the States they had the power to act, and doubtless did act, by their suffrages, upon the question of its adoption. It would be strange if we were to find in that instrument anything which deprived of their citizenship any part of the people of the United States who were among those by whom it was established.

I can find nothing in the Constitution which, *proprio vigore*, deprives of their citizenship any class of persons who were citizens of the United States at the time of its adoption, or who should be native-born citizens of any State after its adoption, nor any power enabling Congress to disfranchise persons born on the soil of any State, and entitled to citizenship of such State by its Constitution and laws. And my opinion is that, under the Constitution of the United States, every free person born on the soil of a State, who is a citizen of that State by force of its Constitution or laws, is also a citizen of the United States. . . .

It has been often asserted that the Constitution was made exclusively by and for the white race. It has already been shown that in five of the thirteen original States colored persons then possessed the elective franchise, and were among those by whom the Constitution was ordained and established. If so, it is not true, in point of fact, that the Constitution was made exclusively by the white race. And that it was made exclusively for the white race is, in my opinion, not only any assumption not warranted by anything in the Constitution, but contradicted by its opening declaration, that it was ordained and established by the people of the United States, for themselves and their posterity. And as free colored persons were then citizens of at least five States, and so in every sense part of the people of the United States, they were among those for whom and whose posterity the Constitution was ordained and established. . . .

The conclusions at which I have arrived on this part of the case are:—

First, that the free native-born citizens of each State are citizens of the United States.

Second, that as free colored persons born within some of the States are citizens of those States, such persons are also citizens of the United States.

Third, that every such citizen, residing in any State, has the right to sue, and is liable to be sued, in the federal courts as a citizen of that State in which he resides.

Fourth, that as the plea to the jurisdiction in this case shows no facts, except that the plaintiff was of African descent, and his ancestors were sold as slaves, and as these facts are not inconsistent with his citizenship of the United States, and his residence in the State of Missouri, the plea to the jurisdiction was bad, and the judgment of the Circuit Court overruling it was correct.

I dissent, therefore, from that part of the opinion of the majority of the court in which it is held that a person of African descent cannot be a citizen of the United States; and I regret I must go further, and dissent both from what I deem their assumption of authority to examine the constitutionality of the act of Congress commonly called the Missouri Compromise Act, and the grounds and conclusions announced in their opinion.

APPENDIX D.

SUPREME COURT OF THE UNITED STATES

No. 143.—October Term, 1891.

The Rector, Church Wardens, and Vestry-
men of the Church of the Holy Trinity,
Plaintiffs in Error,

vs.

The United States.

In error to the Circuit
Court of the United
States for the South-
ern District of New
York.

[February 29, 1892.]

Mr. Justice Brewer delivered the opinion of the court.

Plaintiff in error is a corporation, duly organized and incorporated as a religious society under the laws of the State of New York. E. Walpole Warren was, prior to September, 1887, an alien residing in England. In that month the plaintiff in error made a contract with him, by which he was to remove to the city of New York and enter into its service as rector and pastor; and, in pursuance of such contract, Warren did so remove and enter upon such service. It is claimed by the United States that this contract on the part of the plaintiff in error was forbidden by chapter 164, 23 Stat. 332, and an action was commenced to recover the penalty prescribed by that act. The Circuit Court held that the contract was within the prohibition of the statute, and rendered judgment accordingly (36 Fed. Rep. 303); and the single question presented for our determination is whether it erred in that conclusion.

The first section describes the act forbidden, and is in these words:—

"*Be it enacted by the Senate and House of Representatives of the United States of America in Congress assembled*, That from and after the passage of this act it shall be unlawful for any person, company, partnership, or corporation, in any manner whatsoever to repay the transportation, or in any way assist or encourage the importation or migration of any alien or aliens, any foreigner or foreigners, into the United States, its Territories, or the District of Columbia, under contract or agreement, parol or special, express or implied, made previous to the importation or migration of such alien or aliens, foreigner or foreigners, to perform labor or service of any kind in the United States, its Territories, or the District of Columbia."

It must be conceded that the act of the corporation is within the letter of this section, for the relation of rector to his church is one of service, and implies labor on the one side with compensation on the other. Not only are the general words labor and service both used, but also, as it were, to guard against any narrow interpretation and emphasize a breadth of meaning, to them is added "of any kind;" and, further, as noticed by the Circuit Judge in his opinion, the fifth section, which makes specific exceptions, among them professional actors, artists, lecturers, singers, and domestic servants, strengthens the idea that every kind of labor and service was intended to be reached by the first section. While there is great force to this reasoning, we cannot think Congress intended to denounce with penalties a transaction like that in the present case. It is a familiar rule that a thing may be within the letter of the statute and yet not within the statute, because not within the spirit, nor within the intention of its makers. This has been often asserted, and the reports are full of cases illustrating its application. This is not the substitution of the will of the judge for that of the legislator, for frequently words of general meaning are used in a statute, words broad enough to include an act in question, and yet a consideration of the whole legislation, or of the circumstances surrounding its enactment, or of the absurd results which follow from giving such broad meaning to the words, makes it unreasonable to believe that the legislator intended to include the particular act. As said in Plowden, 205: "From which cases, it appears that the sages of the law heretofore have construed statutes quite contrary to the letter in some appearance, and those statutes which comprehend all things in the letter they have expounded to extend to but some things, and those which generally prohibit all people from doing such an act, they have interpreted to permit some people to do it, and those which include every person in the letter, they have adjudged to reach to some persons only, which expositions have always been founded upon the intent of the Legislature, which they have collected sometimes by considering the cause and necessity of making the act, sometimes by comparing one part of the act with another, and sometimes by foreign circumstances."

In Pier Co. *vs.* Hannam (3 B. & Ald. 266), C. J. Abbott quotes from Lord Coke as follows: "Acts of Parliament are to be so construed as no man that is innocent or free from injury or wrong be, by a literal construction, punished or endangered." In the case of the State *vs.* Clark (5 Dutcher 96, 99), it appeared that an act had been passed making it a misdemeanor to willfully break down a fence in the possession of another person. Clark was indicted under that statute. The defense was that the act of breaking down the fence, though willful, was in the exercise of a legal right to go upon his own lands. The trial court rejected the testimony offered to sustain the defense, and the Supreme Court held that this ruling was error. In its opinion the court used this language: "The act of 1855, in terms, makes the willful opening, breaking down, or injuring of any fences belonging to or in possession of any other person a misdemeanor. In what sense is the term willful used? In common parlance, willful is used in the sense of intentional, as distinguished from accidental or involuntary. Whatever one does intentionally he does willfully. Is it used in that sense in this act? Did the Legislature intend to make the intentional opening of a fence for the purpose of going upon the land of another, indictable if done by permission or for a lawful purpose? . . . We cannot suppose such to have been the actual intent. To adopt such a construction would put a stop to the ordinary business of life. The language of the act, if construed literally, evidently leads to an absurd result. If a literal construction of the words of a statute be absurd, the act must be so construed as to avoid the absurdity. The court must restrain the words. The object designed to be reached by the act must limit and control the literal import of the terms and phrases employed." In United States *vs.* Kirby (7 Wall. 482, 486), the defendants were indicted for the violation of an act of Congress, providing "that if any person shall knowingly and willfully obstruct or retard the passage of the mail, or of any driver or carrier, or of any horse or carriage carrying the same, he shall, upon conviction, for every such offense pay a fine not exceeding $100." The specific charge was that the defendants knowingly and willfully retarded the passage of one Farris, a carrier of the mail, while engaged in the performance of his duty, and also in like manner retarded the steamboat *General Buell*, at that time engaged in carrying the mail. To this indictment the defendants pleaded specially that Farris had been indicted for murder by a court of competent authority in Kentucky; that a bench warrant had been issued and placed in the hands of the defendant Kirby, the sheriff of the county, commanding him to arrest Farris and bring him before the court to answer to the indictment; and that in obedience to this warrant, he and the other defendants, as his posse, entered upon the steamboat *General Buell* and arrested Farris, and used only such force as was necessary to accomplish that arrest. The question as to the sufficiency of this plea was certified to this court, and it was held that the arrest of Farris upon the warrant from the State court was not an obstruction of the mail, or the retarding of the passage of a carrier of the mail, within the meaning of the act. In its opinion the court says: "All laws should receive a sensible construction. General terms should be so limited in their application as not to lead to injustice, oppression, or an absurd consequence. It will always, therefore, be presumed that the Legislature intended exceptions to its language which would avoid results of this character. The reason of the law in such cases should prevail over its letter. The common sense of man approves the judgment mentioned by Puffendorf, that the Bolognian law which enacted 'that whoever drew blood in the streets should be punished with the utmost severity,' did not extend to the surgeon who opened the vein of a person that fell down in the street in a fit. The same common sense accepts the ruling, cited by Plowden, that the statue of 1st Edward II, which enacts that a prisoner who breaks prison shall be guilty of felony, does not extend to a prisoner who breaks out when the prison is on fire, 'for he is not to be hanged because he would not stay to be burnt.' And we think a like common sense will sanction the ruling we make, that the act of Congress which punishes the obstruction or retarding of the passage of the mail, or of its carrier, does not apply to a case of temporary detention of the mail caused by the arrest of the carrier upon an indictment for murder." The following cases may also be cited: Henry *vs.* Tilson (17 Vt. 479); Ryegate *vs.* Wardsboro (30 Vt. 746); Ex parte Ellis (11 Cal. 220); Ingraham *vs.* Speed (30 Miss. 410); Jackson *vs.* Collins (3 Cowen 89); People *vs.* Insurance Company (15 Johns 358); Burch *vs.* Newbury (10 N. Y. 374); People ex rel. *vs.* Comrs., etc. (95 N. Y. 554, 558); People ex rel. *vs.* Lacombe (99 N. Y. 43, 49); Canal Co. *vs.* Railroad Co. (4 Gill & Johnson, 152); Osgood *vs.* Breed (12 Mass. 525, 530); Wilbur *vs.* Crane (13 Pick. 284); Oates *vs.* National Bank (100 U. S. 239).

Among other things which may be considered in determining the intent of the Legislature is the title of the act. We do not mean that it may be used to add or to take from the body of the statute (Hadden *vs.* The Collector, 5 Wall. 107), but it may help to interpret its meaning. In the case of United States *vs.* Fisher (2 Cranch. 358, 386), Chief Justice Marshall said: "On the influence which the title ought to have in construing the enacting clauses much has been said; and yet it is not easy to discern the point of difference between the opposing counsel in this respect. Neither party contends that the title of an act can control plain words in the body of the statute; and neither denies that, taken with other parts, it may assist in removing ambiguities. *Where the intent is plain, nothing is left to construction. Where the mind labors to discover the design of the Legislature, it seizes everything from which aid can be derived;* and in such case the title claims a degree of notice, and will have its due share of consideration;" and in the case of United States *vs.* Palmer (3 Wheaton 610, 631), the same judge applied the doctrine in this way: "The words of the section are in terms of unlimited extent. The words 'any person or persons' are broad enough to comprehend every human being. But general words must not only be limited to cases within the jurisdiction of the State, but also to those objects to which the Legislature intended to apply them. Did the Legislature intend to apply these words to the subjects of a foreign power, who in a foreign ship may commit murder or robbery on the high seas? The title of an act cannot control its words, but may furnish some aid in showing what was in the mind of the Legislature. The title of this act is, 'An act for the punishment of certain crimes against the United States.' It would seem that offenses against the United States, not offenses against the human race, were the crimes which the Legislature intended by this law to punish."

It will be seen that words as general as those used in the first section of this act were by that decision limited, and the intent of Congress with respect to the act was gathered partially, at least, from its title. Now, the title of this act is, "An act to prohibit the importation and migration of foreigners and aliens under contract or agreement to perform labor in the United States, its Territories, and the District of Columbia." Obviously the thought expressed in this reaches only to the work of the manual laborer, as distinguished from that of the professional man. No one reading such a title would suppose that Congress had in its mind any purpose of staying the coming into this country of ministers of the gospel, or, indeed, of any class whose toil is that of the brain. The common understanding of the terms labor and laborers does not include preaching and preachers; and it is to be assumed that words and phrases are used in their ordinary meaning. So whatever of light is thrown upon the statute by the language of the title, indicates an exclusion from its penal provisions of all contracts for the employment of ministers, rectors, and pastors.

Again, another guide to the meaning of a statute is found in the evil which it is designed to remedy; and for this the court properly looks at contemporaneous events, the situation as it existed, and as it was pressed upon the attention of the legislative body. (United States *vs*. Railroad Company, 91 U. S. 72, 79.) The situation which called for this statute was briefly but fully stated by Mr. Justice Brown, when, as district judge, he decided the case of United States *vs*. Craig (28 Fed. Rep. 795, 798): "The motives and history of the act are matters of common knowledge. It has become the practice for large capitalists in this country to contract with their agents abroad for the shipment of great numbers of an ignorant and servile class of foreign laborers, under contracts, by which the employer agreed, upon the one hand, to prepay their passage, while, upon the other hand, the laborers agreed to work after their arrival for a certain time at a low rate of wages. The effect of this was to break down the labor market, and to reduce other laborers engaged in like occupations to the level of the assisted immigrant. The evil finally became so flagrant that an appeal was made to Congress for relief by the passage of the act in question, the design of which was to raise the standard of foreign immigrants, and to discountenance the migration of those who had not sufficient means in their own hands, or those of their friends, to pay their passage."

It appears, also, from the petitions, and in the testimony presented before the committees of Congress, that it was this cheap, unskilled labor which was making the trouble, and the influx of which Congress sought to prevent. It was never suggested that we had in this country a surplus of brain toilers, and, least of all, that the market for the services of Christian ministers was depressed by foreign competition. Those were matters to which the attention of Congress, or of the people, was not directed. So far, then, as the evil which was sought to be remedied interprets the statute, it also guides to an exclusion of this contract from the penalties of the act.

A singular circumstance, throwing light upon the intent of Congress, is found in this extract from the report of the Senate Committee on Education and Labor, recommending the passage of the bill: "The general facts and considerations which induce the committee to rec-

24

ommend the passage of this bill are set forth in the report of the Committee of the House. The committee report the bill back without amendment, although there are certain features thereof which might well be changed or modified, in the hope that the bill may not fail of passage during the present session. Especially would the committee have otherwise recommended amendments, substituting for the expression 'labor and service,' whenever it occurs in the body of the bill, the words 'manual labor' or 'manual service,' as sufficiently broad to accomplish the purposes of the bill, and that such amendments would remove objections which a sharp and perhaps unfriendly criticism may urge to the proposed legislation. The committee, however, believing that the bill in its present form will be construed as including only those whose labor or service is manual in character, and being very desirous that the bill become a law before the adjournment, have reported the bill without change." (6059 Congressional Record, 48th Congress.) And referring back to the report of the Committee of the House, there appears this language: "It seeks to restrain and prohibit the immigration or importation of laborers who would have never seen our shores but for the inducements and allurements of men whose only object is to obtain labor at the lowest possible rate, regardless of the social and material well-being of our own citizens, and regardless of the evil consequences which result to American laborers from such immigration. This class of immigrants care nothing about our institutions, and in many instances never even heard of them. They are men whose passage is paid by the importers; they come here under contract to labor for a certain number of years. They are ignorant of our social condition, and, that they may remain so, they are isolated and prevented from coming into contact with Americans. They are generally from the lowest social stratum, and live upon the coarsest food and in hovels of a character before unknown to American workmen. They, as a rule, do not become citizens, and are certainly not a desirable acquisition to the body politic. The inevitable tendency of their presence among us is to degrade American labor, and to reduce it to the level of the imported pauper labor." (Page 5359 Congressional Record, 48th Congress.)

We find, therefore, that the title of the act, the evil which was intended to be remedied, the circumstances surrounding the appeal to Congress, the reports of the committee of each house, all concur in affirming that the intent of Congress was simply to stay the influx of this cheap, unskilled labor.

But beyond all these matters no purpose of action against religion can be imputed to any legislation, State or national, *because this is a religious people. This is historically true. From the discovery of this continent to the present hour there is a single voice making this affirmation.* The commission to Christopher Columbus, prior to his sail westward, is from "Ferdinand and Isabella, by the grace of God, King and Queen of Castile," etc., and recites that "it is hoped that by God's assistance some of the continents and islands in the ocean will be discovered," etc. The first colonial grant, that made to Sir Walter Raleigh, in 1584, was from "Elizabeth, by the grace of God, of England, Fraunce, and Ireland, queene, defender of the faith," etc., and the grant authorizing him to enact statutes for the government of the proposed colony provided that "they be not against the true Christian faith nowe professed in the Church of England." The first charter of Virginia, granted by King James I, in 1606, after reciting the application of certain parties for a charter, commenced the grant in these words: "We, greatly commending and graciously accepting of, their Desires for the Furtherance of so noble a Work, which may, by the Providence of Almighty God, hereafter tend to the Glory of his Divine Majesty, in propagating of Christian religion to such People, as yet live in Darkness and miserable Ignorance of the true Knowledge and Worship of God, and may in time bring the Infidels and Savages, living in those parts, to human Civility, and to a settled and quiet Government; DO, by these our Letters-Patents, graciously accept of, and agree to, their humble and well-intended Desires."

Language of similar import may be found in the subsequent charters of that colony, from the same king, in 1609 and 1611; and the same is true of the various charters granted to the other colonies. *In language more or less emphatic is the establishment of the Christian religion declared to be one of the purposes of the grant.* The celebrated compact made by the Pilgrims in the *Mayflower*, 1620, recites: "Having undertaken for the Glory of God, and Advancement of the Christian Faith, and the Honour of our King and Country, a Voyage to plant the first Colony in the northern Parts of Virginia; Do by these Presents, solemnly and mutually, in the Presence of God and one another, covenant and combine ourselves together into a civil Body Politick, for our better Ordering and Preservation, and Furtherance of the Ends aforesaid."

The fundamental orders of Connecticut, under which a provisional government was instituted in 1638-1639, commence with this declaration: "Forasmuch as it hath pleased the Almighty God by the wise disposition of his diuyne pruidence so to Order and dispose of things that we the Inhabitants and Residents of Windsor, Hartford, and Wethersfield are now cohabiting, and dwelling in and vppon the River of Conectecotte and the Lands thereunto adioyneing; And well knowing where a people are gathered togather the word of God requires that to mayntayne the peace and vnion of such a people there should be an orderly and decent Gouernment established according to God, to order and dispose of the affayres of the people at all seasons as occation shall require; doe therefore assotiate and conioyne our selues to be as one Publike State or Commonwelth; and doe, for our selues and our Successors and such as shall be adioyned to vs att any tyme hereafter, enter into Combination and Confederation togather, to mayntayne and presearue the liberty and purity of the gospell of our Lord Jesus wch we now prfesse, *as also the disciplyne of the Churches, wch* according to the truth of the said gospell *is now practiced amongst vs.*"

In the charter of privileges granted by William Penn to the province of Pennsylvania, in 1701, it is recited: "Because no People can be truly happy, though under the greatest Enjoyment of Civil Liberties, if abridged of the Freedom of their Consciences, as to their Religious Profession and Worship; And Almighty God being the only Lord of Conscience, Father of Lights and Spirits; and the Author as well as Object of all divine Knowledge, Faith and Worship, who only doth enlighten the Minds, and persuade and convince the Understandings of People, I do hereby grant and declare," etc.

Coming nearer to the present time, the Declaration of Independence recognizes the presence of the divine in human affairs in these words: "We hold these truths to be self-evident, that all men are created equal, that they are endowed by their Creator with certain unalienable Rights, that among these are life, liberty, and the pursuit of happiness." "We, therefore, the Representatives of the United States of America, in General Congress assembled, appealing to the Supreme Judge of the world for the rectitude of our intentions, do, in the name and by authority of the good people of these Colonies, solemnly publish and declare," etc.; "And for the support of this Declaration, with a firm reliance on the Protection of Divine Providence, we mutually pledge to each other our lives, our fortunes, and our sacred honor."

If we examine the constitutions of the various States we find in them a constant recognition of religious obligations. Every constitution of every one of the forty-four States contains language which either directly or by clear implication recognizes a profound reverence for religion and an assumption that its influence in all human affairs is essential to the well-being of the community. This recognition may be in the preamble, such as is found in the constitution of Illinois, 1870: "We, the people of the State of Illinois, grateful to Almighty God for the civil, political, and religious liberty which he hath so long permitted us to enjoy, and looking to him for a blessing upon our endeavors to secure and transmit the same unimpaired to succeeding generations," etc.

It may be only in the familiar requisition that all officers shall take an oath closing with the declaration "so help me God." It may be in clauses like that of the constitution of Indiana, 1816, article 2, section 4: "The manner of administering an oath or affirmation shall be such as is most consistent with the conscience of the deponent, and shall be esteemed the most solemn appeal to God." Or in provisions such as are found in articles 36 and 37 of the Declaration of Rights of the Constitution of Maryland, 1867: "That, as it is the duty of every man to worship God in such manner as he thinks most acceptable to him, all persons are equally entitled to protection in their religious liberty; wherefore, no person ought, by any law, to be molested in his person or estate on account of his religious persuasion or profession, or for his religious practice, unless, under the color of religion, he shall disturb the good order, peace, or safety of the State, or shall infringe the laws of morality, or injure others in their natural, civil, or religious rights; nor ought any person to be compelled to frequent or maintain or contribute, unless on contract, to maintain any place of worship, or any ministry; nor shall any person, otherwise competent, be deemed incompetent as a witness or juror on account of his religious belief, provided he believes in the existence of God, and that, under his dispensation, such person will be held morally accountable for his acts, and be rewarded or punished therefor, either in this world or the world to come; that no religious test ought ever to be required as a qualification for any office of profit or trust in this State, other than a declaration of belief in the existence of God; nor shall the Legislature prescribe any other oath of office than the oath prescribed by this constitution." Or like that in articles 2 and 3 of part 1st of the constitution of Massachusetts, 1780:

"It is the right as well as *the duty* of all men in society, publicly and at stated seasons, to worship the Supreme Being, the great Creator and Preserver of the universe. . . . *As the happiness of a people* and the good *order and preservation of civil government* essentially depend upon *piety, religion,* and *morality,* and as these cannot be generally diffused through a community *but by the institution of the public worship of God* and *of public instructions in piety, religion,* and *morality,* therefore, to promote their happiness and to secure the good order and preservation of their government, the people of this commonwealth have a right to *invest their Legislature with power to authorize and require,* and *the Legislature shall,* from time to time, *authorize and require* the several *towns, parishes, precincts,* and other *bodies politic* or religious societies to *make suitable provisions,* at their own expense, *for the institution of the public worship of God* and *for the support and maintenance of public Protestant* teachers of piety, religion, and morality in all cases where such provision shall not be made voluntarily." Or as in sections 5 and 14 of article 7 of the constitution of Mississippi, 1832: "*No person who denies the being of a God,* or a future state of rewards and punishments, *shall hold any office in the civil department of this State.* . . . Religion, morality, and knowledge being necessary to good government, the preservation of liberty, and the happiness of mankind, schools, and the means of education, shall forever be encouraged in this State." Or by article 22 of the constitution of Delaware, 1776, which required all officers, besides an oath of allegiance, to make and subscribe the following declaration: "I, A. B., do profess faith in God the Father, and in Jesus Christ his only Son, and in the Holy Ghost, one God, blessed forevermore; and I do acknowledge the Holy Scriptures of the Old and New Testament to be given by divine inspiration."

Even the Constitution of the United States, which is supposed to have little touch upon the private life of the individual, contains in the First Amendment a declaration common to the constitutions of all the States, as follows: "Congress shall make no law respecting an establishment of religion, or prohibiting the free exercise thereof," etc. And also provides in article 1, section 7 (a provision common to many constitutions), that the Executive shall have ten days (Sundays excepted) within which to determine whether he will approve or veto a bill.

There is no dissonance in these declarations. There is a universal language pervading them all, having one meaning; they *affirm* and *reaffirm that this is a religious nation.* These are not individual sayings, declarations of private persons; they are organic utterances; *they speak the voice of the entire people.* While, because of a general recognition of this truth, the question has seldom been presented to the courts, yet we find that in Updegraph *vs.* The Commonwealth (11 Serg. & Rawle 394, 400), it was decided that "*Christianity,* general Christianity, *is, and always has been, a part of the common law of Pennsylvania;* . . . not Christianity with an established church, and tithes, and spiritual courts, but Christianity with liberty of conscience to all men." And in The People *vs.* Ruggles (8 Johns. 290, 294, 295), *Chancellor Kent,* the great commentator on American law, speaking as Chief Justice of the Supreme Court of New York, said: "The people of this State, in common with the people of this country, profess the general doctrines of Christianity as the rule of their faith and practice, and to scandalize the Author of these doctrines is not only, in a religious point of view, extremely impious, but, even in respect to the obligations due to society, is a gross violation of decency and good order. . . . The free, equal, and undisturbed enjoyment of religious opinion, whatever it may be, and free and decent discussions on any religious subject, is granted and secured; *but to revile, with malicious and blasphemous contempt, the religion professed by almost the whole community, is an abuse of that right.* Nor are we bound, by any expressions in the Constitution, as some have strangely supposed, either not to punish at all, or to punish indiscriminately, the like attacks upon the religion of *Mahomet* or of the Grand *Lama;* and for *this plain reason,* that the case assumes that we are a Christian people, and the morality of the country is deeply ingrafted upon Christianity, and not upon the doctrines or worship of those impostors." And in the famous case of Vidal *vs.* Girard's Executors (2 How. 127, 198), this court, while sustaining the will of Mr. Girard, with its provision for the creation of a college into which no minister should be permitted to enter, observed: "It is also said, and truly, that the *Christian religion* is a *part* of the common law of *Pennsylvania.*"

If we pass beyond these matters to a view of American life as expressed by its laws, its business, its customs, and its society, we find everywhere a clear recognition of the same truth. Among other matters note the following: "The form of oath universally prevailing, concluding with an appeal to the Almighty; the custom of opening sessions of all deliberative bodies and most conventions with prayer;

the prefatory words of all wills, "In the name of God, amen;" *the laws respecting the observance of the Sabbath; with the general cessation of all secular business,* and the closing of courts, legislatures, and other similar public assemblies on that day; the churches and church organizations which abound in every city, town, and hamlet; the multitude of charitable organizations existing everywhere under Christian auspices; the gigantic missionary associations, with general support, and aiming to establish Christian missions in every quarter of the globe. *These,* and many other matters which might be noticed, *add a volume of unofficial declarations* to the mass of organic utterances *that this is a Christian nation.* In the face of all these, shall it be believed that a Congress of the United States intended to make it a misdemeanor for a church of this country to contract for the services of a Christian minister residing in another nation?

Suppose in the Congress that passed this act some member had offered a bill which in terms declared that, if any Roman Catholic Church in this country should contract with Cardinal Manning to come to this country and enter into its service as pastor and priest; or any Episcopal Church should enter into a like contract with Canon Farrar; or any Baptist Church should make similar arrangements with Rev. Mr. Spurgeon; or any Jewish synagogue with some eminent rabbi, such contract should be adjudged unlawful and void, and the church making it be subject to prosecution and punishment, can it be believed that it would have received a minute of approving thought or a single vote? Yet it is contended that such was in effect the meaning of this statute. The construction invoked cannot be accepted as correct. It is a case where there was presented a definite evil, in view of which the Legislature used general terms with the purpose of reaching all phases of that evil, and thereafter, unexpectedly, it is developed that the general language thus employed is broad enough to reach cases and acts which the whole history and life of the country affirm could not have been intentionally legislated against. It is the duty of the courts, under those circumstances, to say that, however broad the language of the statute may be, the act, although within the letter, is not within the intention of the Legislature, and, therefore, cannot be within the statute.

The judgment will be reversed, and the case remanded for further proceedings in accordance with this opinion.

True copy.

Test:

Clerk Supreme Court U. S.

DECLARATION
OF
PRINCIPLES

of the

 International Religious Liberty Association

We believe in the religion taught by Jesus Christ.

We believe in temperance, and regard the liquor traffic as a curse to society.

We believe in supporting the civil government, and submitting to its authority.

We deny the right of any civil government to legislate on religious questions.

We believe it is the right, and should be the privilege, of every man to worship according to the dictates of his own conscience.

We also believe it to be our duty to use every lawful and honorable means to prevent religious legislation by the civil government; that we and our fellow-citizens may enjoy the inestimable blessings of both religious and civil liberty.

We'd love to send you a free catalogue of titles we publish or even to hear your thoughts, reactions, criticism, about things you did or didn't like about this or any other book we publish.

Just write or call us at:

TEACH Services, Inc.

254 Donovan Road
Brushton, New York 12616
800/367-1998

http://www.teachservicesinc.com